NOWHERE LIKE HOME

By Jamie Alexander

ISBN: 1481151827
ISBN-13: 978-1481151825

www.jamiealexander.org

To Hector, who will always be my favourite.

"Of course the universe is gradually slowing down and will eventually collapse inwardly on itself, according to the laws of entropy, when all its thermal and mechanical functions fail. Thus rendering all human endeavour ultimately pointless."

Bill Bailey, 2003.

PROLOGUE

It is said that you see with your mind more than with your eyes, and I'm hoping that's true because right now, what I'm seeing is twisted beyond recognition—explicit images, clips from recent experience bursting through the walls of what my senses are trying to tell me is real. I'm teetering on the insomniac's event horizon; awake, functioning, but at least half of my brain is dreaming. The only thing keeping me upright is the spice from the curry and the cramping of my stomach.

The group of people in front of me are talking about travel. Of course they are; that's what travellers talk about when they meet other travellers. It's what everyone has in common, sometimes the only thing. Where they've been, what they've done. How Thailand isn't what it used to be. How they swear this one time in Bangkok, they saw some guy take home a local girl with massive hands and an Adam's apple pointier than Kilimanjaro. How they swear that guy definitely wasn't them. Under different circumstances, I'd pull up a chair, introduce myself. But the way I smell right now, simply moving closer would be tactless.

I don't know if it is the tiredness, but my mind is tricking me, warping the boundaries of the physical, blending it with hints of the fantastic. I can almost see their voices floating, undulating through the warm night air, swirling and bouncing around the lamps that hang from posts on the edge of the rooftop, echoing down to the street below where a few men lie groaning amongst the debris of addiction: spoons, lighters, syringes. One end of a belt tied above their bicep and the other gripped between their teeth in a grim smile.

I look across to the group. A guy with dreadlocks tuts, lights up a joint, takes a few puffs, and carries on staring deeply into a label he's peeled from a bottle as though it contains the secret to getting laid. "Seeing this place, it's got to broaden your mind," he says in response to something that has been long lost in the thick haze of extreme fatigue.

The smoke hangs in the silhouette of the lightbulbs, giving the group an ethereal glow, and I think back to what I've seen since I last slept: the blur from an open train doorway, the clattering carriages, the cyclic chants of the chai wallah. And after that, the smell—the visceral, sickly aroma that catches in your throat and almost makes you feel like you're breathing burnt tomato soup—drifting across a river. Evening sunlight glinting on the edges of tiny vortices created by paddles moving through water. Black objects, bloated and rotund, effortlessly bobbing by as I plunge headfirst through the murky river, trying to get rid of that feeling.

That feeling, the feeling you get when you've seen a whole night and day pass from the window of a train or bus in heat that would make a sauna feel like Glasgow. That grungy stickiness of your body, the greasiness of your hair, the smell of your hands; metallic, from spending twenty-four hours leaning against the railings and rusty bars that stop thieves reaching through windows. That claustrophobia, trapped in your own prison of dirt and grime and stink and sweat—having that feeling washed away is worth almost anything.

There's the area where families cremate their deceased by the riverbank, the loud *pop* that sounds out above the noise of mournful wails. "Sometimes the head get too hot," laughs the boatman, as part of a blackened torso rolls out of the flames, caught in the flash of a grinning tourist's camera. Then there are the alleys that lead towards the rickshaw rank. Food vendors hovering like mystics over greasy snacks frying in large gas-heated vats of oil, the light from the flames illuminating their faces and the close walls around them in a soft orange-blue. The rush of wind as the rickshaw weaves through the Indian night towards yet another train that will eventually land me here on the roof with these guys and their half-understood conversation.

"I've seen so much in the last year, if my mind got any broader, it would explode," says a girl, and I might be the only one to see her prediction become reality. There's something faintly odd about this, something worrying, but it takes me a while to place exactly what it is.

The guy with dreadlocks says, "Travel for long enough and nothing seems so new anymore. Everything becomes recognisable."

Nothing seems so new anymore…

I look at the journal on the table in front of me, pick it up, start thumbing through the pages of jumbled, scruffy handwriting. Squiggles and smudges transform into images and memories and then, for a brief moment, I am chasing hunters through the jungles of Kalimantan, drinking tea and sharing biscuits with militants in Palestine. The writing blurs, and then I am desperately bailing a sinking boat in the Philippines, dodging hippy volunteer types in the deserts of Jordan; with Chris, cooking chicken-flavoured Maggi Noodles for separatists in New Guinea. More pages flick past, and I'm fighting blizzards, watching my blood pool on a coastal track, being chased by an angry mob in the Himalaya…and as the pages turn blank, a question flashes up in my head—an important question, one that I probably should have asked myself a long time ago. Certainly it's one that will stop this life in its tracks if only I can remember it long enough.

I take one final burning spoonful of curry and start writing: *Sumrubish Guesthouse, Calcutta. 29 April…*

ONE

Culture Shock

Presented out of context, this story would probably make me look like either a misguided fanatic, or a monumental badass. In reality, I'm neither. Actually, let me clarify: I might be a bit of a badass, but probably not quite up there with Liam Neeson.

I'd say it was Kalimantan that started this whole thing off, or maybe it really was that rainy night in Bangkok. But I've got to be honest, I can't begin this story at the beginning, because I don't know when that was. And even if I did, I wouldn't be equipped to tell anyone about it. To tell the truth, if my life so far has taught me one lesson, it's that I probably can't talk with authority about anything, save to say this story—the one you are reading—is not just a story about me.

Therefore, instead of some kind of pretence at authority, let me set the context with the imaginary tale of a young boy. Please don't take it too seriously or think it is true or anything—after all, it is just a tale.

Once upon a time, there was a magical island kingdom of rolling hills and beautiful pastures, filled with cows and postmen and gnomes. It was a place where the insignificant was treasured; where the weather rarely achieved much more than drizzle and even a circle of stones in a field was considered impressive enough to be a treasured national monument. Everything was pleasant, innocent. Everything was sweet. But then the eighties happened, and a few years later, so too did a tiny blonde kid with a set of unintentionally amusing facial expressions.

Karl Marx had once described religion as the opium of the masses, but where this kid was born, that was no longer true. Whatever he could want, it was all right there: a life full of sensations and experience, all from the comfort of his settee. You see, by the time this boy was born, technology was doing a much better job than God at keeping people in their place. Or opium for that matter.

As his chubby features became ever so slightly more angular and his hair turned strawberry blonde, technology evolved with him. Things had just moved beyond Pac-Man when he started to walk. At twelve, this little boy was driving Formula One cars in the Monaco Grand Prix. By fifteen, he was using highly detailed weaponry to blow limbs off futuristic alien invaders, aided by thermal imaging sights and heartbeat sensors. Live that life long enough, and you too would start to develop the symptoms of his generation—the fractured attention span, the waist-high boredom threshold.

Throughout his teen years, the boy shot and hacked and punched his way through thousands of mortal enemies. Some of them even killed him a few times. But at no point did he ever feel any pain. The boy smashed a hundred windows, murdered a thousand bystanders, blew up a million cars, but never were there any repercussions.

Do they really say kids grow up fast these days?

When he eventually flopped out of the fun side of puberty, the scrawny adult was entering a world of internet-based socialising, reality TV, trashy celebrity magazines and a limitless supply of other people's experiences and imaginations from which to build a meaningful existence. Each and every one of them, a copy of a copy. DVDs, CDs, MP3s, books, movies; you name it, someone had thought of it and stuck it in binary. Even the international news reports, flashing images back from war zones in lands far, far away, seemed to be at least one too many mirrors from where he was standing to be real.

But there was something missing from all this, and many people knew it. It was something that lengths of code and high-powered processors could never fully replicate. It was hidden somewhere maybe. Trapped behind a papier-mâché wall of risk assessments by an army of nasal Health and Safety elves. Suffocating underneath a guaranteed splinter-free floorboard or a hypoallergenic carpet, trying to poke its ugly head out and breathe.

The young lad began to look for it, like plenty of other people of his generation. Each of them in their own ways, trying to search this thing out. Find it, or recreate it themselves. With drink, cars, drugs, video games, whatever. But nobody really knew why it had been hidden away in the first place, or even how to find it.

Nobody really knew what *it* was.

That tiny void in their otherwise pristine lives, and nobody knew how best to fill it.

Like I said, that was just a daft tale. But it felt true enough and before I knew it, eighteen years had gone by and the only useful thing I had really learnt in life was to be critical, of everything, and I latched onto that little chestnut like a greedy squirrel.

So far I was the result of a fairly normal life. No big disasters, no great upsets, no major issues. I had a stable nuclear family—nothing to talk about in a society obsessed with the entertainment value of breakup drama. I had been to a nice enough school and had some great friends, and now I was at a good university. It didn't feel like any big achievement to be honest, just jumping through hoops because it was the done thing. Perhaps the greatest upset I had experienced was when I lost my Batman toy after it was dropped in a river when I was five. There you have it: my sob story. Until then, I thought superheroes always lived happily ever after.

But by the time I was nearing the end of my first year of adulthood, something about that life unsettled me. Maybe it was something a friend or a careers advisor said; perhaps I'd heard too many stories about people's Gap Years and I wanted some of that shit for myself. Adventurous or naïve, I had no idea, but that became my decision: before I succumbed to what I saw as the inevitable career-chase, I would find out the other side of the story. I wasn't just going to travel, I was going to go somewhere I could search out the fabled Tree of Knowledge, pick the fruit myself. Take a risk and eat it. Wash it down with a nice cool glass of Wisdom Cider.

* * *

As the Cessna bumped and glided over the vast tropical rain forests of East Kalimantan, Indonesian Borneo, my anticipation started to rise like the mountainous jungle beneath me. It didn't take long for me to wonder what exactly had possessed me to fly into one of the most remote parts of South East Asia, completely on my own.

My first year of university had just ended and in all honesty, it had been a brilliant year. I'd lived a life that many British students could empathise with—more time spent becoming familiar with the gender-specific elements of human anatomy and the longer-term effects of maintaining alcohol in the bloodstream than any academic curriculum. The only scholarly article I could possibly write would more than likely be titled, *Discourse or Intercourse: the conflicting priorities of the modern student.* By that stage, I had even been on a few trips—to Morocco, Fiji and Bali—and had one or two tales to boot, but nothing I'd done yet had really pushed me out of my comfort zone. I'd travelled, but now I wanted to experience something different, away from the transvestites and temples and guidebook-recommended backpacker-friendly hostels. I wanted somewhere that would change me, educate me. Open my eyes to new way of thinking. And this patch of rainforest was where I thought that would happen.

A few thousand feet below the Cessna's wings, the jungle spread out like a carpet of moss, and as the land grew and creased itself into hills, the vast logging camps near the coast became smaller and less frequent, shrinking until all that was left were little brown scars in the undulating sea of green.

I pointed to one of the scars.

"So these must be tiny villages, right?" I said over the plane's radio intercom to Dave, the American pilot of the missionary aircraft we were in. He was one of the few Westerners I'd seen since I arrived in Kalimantan two weeks earlier and he had recommended the village I was visiting as one of the most remote in Borneo.

"That? No, it's a landslide," my headset crackled. "Lightning hits the bigger trees and they fall and wipe everything else out on the way down. No one lives out here anymore; this is clouded-leopard country."

"Oh."

A cool wind blasted in from the inch-open window to my right, gusting onto my face and through our seats into the small cargo bay behind. "The people where we're going are friendly, but they aren't really used to visitors," Dave said. Laughing over the intercom, he continued. "It's definitely a turning point; sixty years ago these guys were fighting the Japanese with blowpipes and machetes and now they're getting their first tourist!" He looked across, taking his eyes from the instrument panel briefly. "I think you're in for quite an adventure."

I nodded slightly, swallowed, doing my best to disguise the unease I felt in my throat and stomach. *That's exactly why I'm here,* I tried to tell myself. *For an adventure.*

We passed over a wide plateau of rivers and hanging mist. The occasional tree poked its head above the canopy—a bonsai in a sea of broccoli. In the far distance, a small trail of smoke rose from beyond the undulating horizon and floated into the sky, where water vapour attached itself to the carbon particles to form a lanky cumulus cloud. Then, over the next group of mountains, a clearing emerged with a visible dirt line marking a landing strip, surrounded on one side by rice fields and small stilted huts and on all others by thick forest. "Here you are," said Dave, "this is the easternmost village of the Krayan. Just over that next ridge is Sarawak."

We descended, and with a bump we rolled along the ground, coming to a stop next to a group of children. Dave switched the ignition off and jumped out of the plane, greeting a few people in fluent Indonesian. As he unloaded his cargo of food and medical supplies in front of a bewildered audience of open-mouthed kids, Dave turned to me. "If you're not sure you want to stay, now is the time to say so. I won't be back here for a week at least."

I pulled my bag from the back of the aircraft and with that, he picked up one last parcel and gave it to a kindly looking man that had come to meet us. "This is Pastor Johan, he's the only person this far into Kalimantan who speaks English fluently."

The comforting noise of the Cessna drifted into nothing and I was left standing with the pastor on the grass and dirt landing strip listening to the sound of bees, cockerels and nervous giggles from the few children left around me.

"My name is Jamie," I said, offering my hand.

"Selamat datang Jimmy, welcome to Long Layu," Johan smiled. "The chief will be very excited to meet you."

* * *

Johan led the way past a stout-looking ox to one of the wooden stilted houses that lined the clearing. Once we reached the top of the thick length of notched tree trunk that rested against the entrance of the house, a wrinkled and heavily tattooed hand shot out of the doorway to greet me. I took it in mine and looked up.

The hand belonged to Apwi, a village elder and an exceptionally strong and athletic man, whose vigour was all the more impressive given that—as I later learnt—he was only one generation removed from the men who had fought the Japanese during World War Two. Draped over his tattooed, muscled shoulders was a Nike T-shirt.

Apwi was a close friend of the village chief, the *kepala desa*, who I met once we were inside the house. He had traditional tattoos and, like Apwi, his muscles looked to be carved out of wood. The interior of the house was lined with functional items; ladles, pans and tools hung from the walls, a machete and what looked like a shotgun rested by the doorway. We sat and chatted over a meal of rice, chicken and jackfruit.

The chief spoke and Johan translated. "We have waited for many years for tourists." To emphasise the point, Apwi darted across the room and rooted out a guestbook, dusted it off and handed it to me. "Please write your name and where you are from here," the chief said in Indonesian, pointing to the book.

I opened the front page and it was blank. Turned the book over and flicked through. Totally blank. I tried to suppress the smile as I jotted down my name, country and passport number under my own headings.

"Tomorrow, I am going hunting with two village men," Apwi told me. "You may join us."

My bag was filled with several small parcels of rice wrapped in banana plant leaves by Johan's lovely wife and, along with Apwi and two other athletic-looking Dayak men, Fin and Lipus, both dressed in football shirts, we set off through the bright morning sunlight, leaving the pastor to preach his Sunday sermon.

At a fast pace, we trod through acres of lush rice paddies, fertile and green, with the storage huts perched at the edges of wide clearings. In the open, the air was crisp and clear, but as we stepped into the overhang of secondary jungle, the atmosphere changed, becoming heavy and damp; clammy, almost claustrophobic. Even the sounds felt closer, more confined, and a sense of trepidation rose in me again, overtaking the excitement of the evening before. We continued through thick scrub until the route of the muddy path was almost indistinguishable from the surrounding vegetation, save for the occasional slash mark on a vine or sapling made by a machete. The jungle grew taller, more imposing. Ground ferns started to fan and spread as the canopy blocked more light. Cool and sticky, the mire worsened and in the dips it was as though we were following a stagnant stream. I recall seeing reflections of the trees in the mud puddles in front of me scatter under the hunters' shoes, turning into rippling shades of black by the time I reached them.

After some time the trail gained height, contouring a steep bank. From somewhere far below came the rushing sound of a torrent of water and every now and then, I caught glimpses of brown whirlpools and eddies surging around huge boulders, but the ferns and palms restricted my view. Then the path dropped away before us. With our hands on roots and saplings, knees digging into the soil, we climbed until we reached another trail. Only a few metres along it, a tributary cut a gully through the ground, blocking our path once more. A length of bamboo from a thicket nearby had been put across to act as a bridge.

One by one, I watched as the others stepped over the bamboo tightrope. I secured my shoulder straps in the vain hope that a tighter bag would aid my balance. It didn't. Halfway across, my balance tilted and I wavered for a second. My foot edged forward, but as I put it down, I slipped. I felt my stomach tighten and for a brief moment, an irritating mental image sprung into my mind—a little red face being swept mercilessly along a brown jungle river—but Lipus's hand grasped my shoulder straps from the other side of the gully. My heart racing, I scrambled up the bank, grinning the grin of someone too embarrassed to admit they had something yellow and unintentional trickling down their leg.

The difficult march carried on, but by the time we stopped for a short break, we were in a forest of such grandeur it reminded me of a cathedral. I took off my bag and looked around, marvelling, up at the tall canopy where trees the height of skyscrapers stood over us. Take everything from an English woodland; the smells, the colours, the noise, the scale—everything apart from the badgers, and triple it all. Twice. Around my feet, termite trails carried segments of foliage along the jungle floor, giving the impression of walking leaves. Squawks and unidentifiable noises, some of which could have been created by a synthesiser, reverberated through the trees. My face and clothes were soaked in sweat and my footwear had become sodden with mud, but it didn't really matter; all around, things mated and died and consumed and grew and mated—a continuous cycle of Darwinian rivalry, always improving, always recycling. Life, on an enormous scale, was everywhere.

The hunters sat on a fallen log, lit up clove cigarettes, taking relaxed puffs every now and then, but I just stared, absorbing the surroundings. Transfixed, like a child experiencing a fairground for the first time.

Over the next few hours, I followed the hunters, clambering up and down hills, wading through rivers, stumbling over enormous root systems, barely stopping again to take in the magnificent surrounding rainforest. But sometime around early afternoon, the pace slowed. Apwi had brought along his dogs, short-eared, aggressive creatures, and they sniffed the undergrowth, looking for signs of the "babi hutan", as he called it. *The forest pig.*

Fin looked more alert, his homemade shotgun—a present from missionary pilots such as Dave—at the ready. Quietly we moved with only the light rustle of damp leaves hinting our presence in the rainforest cacophony.

As I was walking, I recall feeling something unusually solid under my foot, but it was too late and my weight had already shifted. The twig snapped, radiating a series of birdcalls from our location. I spun around as a small primate—I have no idea what kind—plopped out of some branches nearby and landed with a thump on the ground. By the time my eyes reached the noise, it had already sprinted for the next tree and was grabbing its way up into invisibility. When I turned back, there was only Lipus and two rattan sacks, lying on the ground. We started running.

The dogs had picked up a scent and shot off the path into the forest. Fin and Apwi were close behind, speeding through the undergrowth, jumping over roots, logs, and scrambling up steep, thorny banks to stay within eyesight of the scent-seeking missiles. I was too weighed down by my bag and struggled to keep up. Without warning, a shot rung out, too far ahead for me to see. A shrill squeal was silenced by another.

By the time I caught up with them, the hunters were carving the meat—snout, hooves and all—into the remaining rattan sack, so we made our way back to the path.

Eventually, the ground lowered. Saplings replaced huge trees as we neared a clear, slow-flowing stream, next to a small clearing, in the centre of which stood a makeshift wooden hut, erected on previous hunting trips. “Malam’ni, kita tidur disini.” *Tonight we sleep here*, an energetic-looking Apwi declared.

By nightfall, the meat was cooked and we all sat on little rattan mats spread across the floor of the hut to dine on a two-course boar and rice dish with the multilayered audio-track of buzzes, squawks, chirrups and croaks resonating over the continuous high-pitched whirring of the cicadas in the background. Lightning flashes momentarily silhouetted the gigantic trees around the clearing against an electric blue sky, but save for the fireflies and the orange glow of the flaming embers, everything else was dark. Following the lead of the others, I picked up a piece of pork, dipped it into a small pot of salt and scooped it into my mouth with some sticky rice. It was the tastiest thing I’d ever had.

After the meal, I felt drained; my reserves of energy had been depleted. This had to have been one of the most tiring days of my life, but by far the most exhilarating. Running through the jungle earlier, I’d felt more alive than at any other time I could remember.

I lay back on the hard wooden floor and with my broken Indonesian and a few words of English, I chatted with the hunters about life and girls and the world outside the rainforest. We spoke about how Lipus wanted to go to coastal Tarakan, the nearest city and the one that I had flown from, to train as an English teacher. He had already been there for a language course and he liked the city, but from what I had seen of him, I couldn’t imagine him living away from the forest for any significant length of time. It made me smile when I remembered the anxiety I had when we entered the jungle that morning; sitting in the clearing with the crackle and pop of the flames and the gentle flow of conversation, I couldn’t have felt more at ease.

Guided by the flashing canopy and the fairy dust of fireflies, I let my mind wander for a moment. This is what life must be about, I thought—the natural existence; hunting with friends, living in the wild, eating massive pigs. How different this was to my student life at home, yet how much more rewarding.

I hadn’t thought much about it these last few days, but as the others were drifting to sleep, I started to ponder how England had been getting along without me. I guessed they had probably put life on hold when I went away, all those lovely English people; I bet they’d simply stopped what they were doing and were now just sitting there, awaiting my return. I bet they were getting really bored by now, and the economy—it was probably in *tatters*.

* * *

I was woken early by the piercing howls of a troop of monkeys in the jungle nearby. Apwi, Lipus and Fin had already packed all the remaining meat into the rattan sacks, so I stowed my gear and picked up my bag.

My body froze.

On the ground where my rucksack was, sat the Goliath of all spiders, roughly the size of my whole face, hairline to chin, and built like a lobster. Not being the biggest fan of spiders at the best of times (in fact, at the time they ranked third on my list of all-time greatest fears, after being forced to eat anchovies and waking up with Gordon Brown on my face), it was quite a surprise to see one that would probably be in the same weight category as my dog if interspecies cage fighting were to become a global sport. The spider held my gaze for a moment, tapped a few three-dimensional legs as it sized me up, then sprinted away audibly—presumably to hunt some boar for itself.

I heard someone call my name from the other side of the clearing. Lipus walked across, telling me that he would be continuing on through the forest and I'd be welcome to come to a village in Sarawak with him. Technically, this meant crossing into Malaysia illegally, but I was fairly sure we had already done that, so I agreed and headed to the stream for a wash. Upon my return, the men were ready and waiting. I bade Fin and Apwi a temporary farewell, and with that, Lipus shot off through the forest like a dart from a blowpipe.

Looking back, that second day was the hardest. I was dehydrated and still tiring from the activities of the day before; my body simply wasn't used to the physical tempo and my memories of it are hazy. I recall plenty of uphill scrambling, climbing over the gigantic root systems of titanic trees; I remember slipping about and falling; sloshing along muddy trails that looked like they were created by an animal that only reached the height of my waist, judging by the spiky foliage that scraped at my arms and neck and face. And as my concentration grew more strained, needled ferns and biting insects sensed my weakness and were unforgiving.

At one rest stop, I recall looking down to inspect my feet, only to discover an ant the size of a baby elephant chomping away on my left shin. For some reason I thought of Yeovil, a pleasant town full of nice people near my hometown in England, as I kicked the bulbous bastard onto the jungle floor and stamped on its head repeatedly until it stopped moving. When my anger subsided, I watched in irritation as it picked itself up, did a few basic stretches, then swaggered off towards a giant leaf that had apparently now taken its fancy instead. I shouted something offensive after it, startling some of the more sensitive birds in the canopy above, and when we set off again, I recall sensing Lipus's evident pride that at least I had won the battle of the wits.

Down the far side of the ridge we walked, my head pounding from dehydration but my body drenched, and gradually the jungle thickened before giving way once more to paddy fields. A low rumble in the distance hinted at the arrival of the next rainstorm. We quickened our pace through the plantations, and just in time, we crossed a long wire bridge over a raging brown torrent and dashed into a longhouse. The rain began beating a heavy baseline on the tin roof as we entered the main room, where I promptly fell asleep on the floor.

***

"Mau makan?"

Lipus was leaning over me.

Do you want to eat?

I got up slowly and looked at the room around me. Clearly I had been too tired to notice it when I entered, but it was huge. Well, very long at least. Roughly sixty metres long to be precise.

That's probably why it is called a longhouse, I thought, cleverly.

It kept the same width of about ten metres down its length, with smaller family rooms built to the sides of the main structure. Smoke drifted into the rafters from various fireplaces, around which groups of families settled and ate. Through small gaps in the floorboards I could see chickens and pigs scuffling about the stilts that held it all up, fighting for the scraps of food and human waste that dropped down from the toilet holes in the side rooms: the most effective recycling program I'd ever seen.

My eyes settled on the group that had gathered around a steaming pot a few feet from my makeshift resting spot. They were heavily tattooed, some of them, and wore few clothes, in contrast to Lipus's gang and their football shirts. They beckoned me over and Lipus ladled out a dollop of meat stew from the pot, pouring it onto a plate of rice for me.

I took the plate gratefully.

The taste was lovely, but after my first few crunching bites I noticed that the meat was incredibly bony. Pulling out a chunk of what looked like spinal cord from my mouth, I asked what it was.

Lipus pointed to a carcass that hung from the wall nearby, presumably the tasty animal's slightly more fortunate—but still ultimately unlucky—cousin or uncle. It looked like quite a lot like a skunk, but in the dark longhouse, I couldn't be sure. Does Borneo even have skunks? Something told me they hadn't imported one for this meal, so I settled for a cautious "yes".

The night approached and we stayed chatting for a while under the garish white-blue light of a few low-energy bulbs strung up in the wooden slats of the longhouse roof. Now that the rain had stopped, I could hear a generator chugging outside and, taking a sneaky look out of the windows, I noticed TV satellite dishes on a few of the houses around. How strange, I thought, that the people here looked so much more traditional with their tattoos and tribal earrings and yet had more evidence of the trappings of modern life.

The next morning, I discovered what I have since assumed the principal reason behind the evident wealth of the people to be. As we were due to leave, a rotund village chief asked me to sign another visitors' guestbook. Expecting a similar deal to the one back in Layu, this time I was surprised to see the pages were full of names and countries. I had apparently only missed a group of anthropologists from Leeds University by two weeks, which I was truly gutted about.

But in a way, that made sense. They had been incredibly hospitable, and yet I thought I noticed that the people here seemed less surprised by my presence than everyone did back in Long Layu. In fact, when I thought of it, there was a slight coldness about the way they greeted me initially, compared with those from Layu, and it was only after Lipus explained where we had walked from that they seemed to open up more.

I had enjoyed my brief stay a lot, but I began wishing I was in Long Layu again. This place seemed outwardly more traditional;

much more of a stereotypical Bornean village than anywhere I'd heard about over the border, but it lacked a certain degree of authenticity that I had found among the Dayaks back in the Krayan. I guessed this was because the influence of the outside world was much stronger in Malaysian Sarawak than Indonesian Kalimantan, and the people here were wealthier, but I couldn't tell if that really was beneficial or to the villagers' detriment. I suspected that it was the latter, judging from the chubbiness of the village leader.

Then again, maybe I had just caught them on a bad day. Well, probably not the village chief—I doubt his belly fluctuated much. But the others; they were kind and welcoming and great company. I guess I just got the feeling that there was something wrong. A slight tension in the air perhaps.

* * *

As we walked back through the rice storage huts and the scrappy shrub areas of recent jungle growth, I thought I heard another thunderstorm approaching. I muttered something about it being a soggy walk home as I looked up at the sky to see where the storm would be, but Lipus pointed out that what I had actually heard was not thunder but the crashing noise made by a bulldozer as it cleared the way for a road.

I asked him what the road was for.

He replied, "We don't know. Maybe they want to make palm oil here. Maybe it is for the tourists." The distress was not obvious on his face, but I imagined it all the same. "I think the village will get more money when the road comes. It will change."

We continued walking in silence, but as the jungle enveloped us, that last sentence weighed heavily on my mind. *Change.* I got the feeling that might not be a good thing.

Once again, we traversed ridges and squelched through valleys, all the time slashing our way through the thorns and palms and vines with machetes, leaving a trail of destruction that a chemistry teacher would have been proud of. On that scale, it didn't matter—within minutes it would all grow back just as gnarly as before.

We waded more rivers, using saplings as support while we shuffled along in the water, and there was more than one occasion where we crossed ravines with nothing more than a single length of boot-width bamboo resting across the gap. Fortunately my balance was becoming more adept and I was just about able to make it across without falling. I suspected that watching me wobble over the makeshift bridges might still have elicited some giggling from Lipus, but each time I looked back at him, he would stifle his grin diplomatically. Then he'd do a back flip and moonwalk across the bamboo, juggling a few willing parakeets with one hand and shaking a bemused orangutan with the other, or something similar.

A number of times, we walked past troops of monkeys crashing about in the canopy high above our heads. When they heard the crack of twigs under our feet they would scream and shout like slags on a hen night back in the UK, leaping across the treetops to escape our hunter wrath.

The sounds of birds and insects followed us everywhere. Cicadas with their piercing whistle, hornbills with the telltale beating *whoosh* of their powerful wings; we rarely saw the culprits, but on several occasions we spotted little brown mammals scurrying hastily up trees. After a while, I even earned a bit of mutual respect with the ants, learning to sit a good distance from any long trails of insects when we rested. I knew that if I broke this sacred covenant, I would be chopped up and carried down a series of tunnels to be fed to the queen like everything else in the forest. So I stuck to my territorial boundaries. The leeches, on the other hand, were total bastards. But we kept on walking. A black snake slithered across my path and I nearly stepped on it. A river almost swept me away, but we kept on walking.

That evening, we stayed in the jungle alone and ate the remaining parcels of rice and boar. Upon finishing dinner, Lipus fished out a mobile phone from his sack and showed me a few pictures. In return, I gave him my MP3 player for a little while, letting him listen to some of my music. It appeared he didn't share the same enthusiasm for Phil Collins, so we ended up chatting some more. I knew then that I had come to really enjoy his company; he had a quiet modesty and genuine kindness that I had rarely encountered before.

Just before the last of the light faded, I went down to the river to wash. My quick bath in the clear, shockingly cold water gave me the chance to inspect my feet. One of my toenails had come off and a big purple blood blister had formed under another—this, I presumed, was from my sodden socks when they had bunched up at the end of my trainers. My soles were cracked white and wrinkly from several days' continual immersion in muddy puddles and river water, and it stung when I touched them. Lipus, whose feet were absolutely fine, wore only what looked like a pair of rubberised bowling shoes bought for apparently less than half the price of one of my ruined socks.

Further up my legs were trickles of blood; a mixture of leeches' anticoagulant and my own sweat keeping the cuts and bites from scabbing. My precautions were clearly ineffective and, thinking again of Lipus, I realised how unsuited to this part of the world I was. Being here almost felt like having to learn to walk again; as if my whole life had been a series of bad habits I needed weaning out of.

* * *

A little over one week later and it was my final morning in Long Layu. After returning from the jungle, I had spent a few days with the villagers. We replanted rice seeds in fields that had been burned to make way for the next crop cycle. We went fishing in a dugout canoe and when we caught a few, we took them back to Pastor Johan's house where we fried and ate them. I managed to pick a fish whose coniferous skeleton exacted a reasonable measure of revenge for catching it in the first place, and I didn't enjoy the meal so much as respect it. When the days were finished, mostly we washed and chatted.

One evening, the whole village turned out for a badminton tournament. The shuttlecock, rackets and net were another gift from the missionaries and were clearly much valued in the community. One after another, the villagers took turns to play, finding my attempts at running around the court and leaping heroically into the net absolutely hilarious. After a few warm-up sessions, the fisherman who took us out on his dugout came across to play on my team. Together we battled against Lipus and Fin. For a while, their muscled, agile bodies were no match for my scheming ways, and I attempted to distract them from the game with various dances and ridiculous faces—the most effective of which was not meant to be a silly face, but there we go. These were met by an uproar of laughter that allowed us a brief chance at the lead. Only after everyone calmed down did they restore the balance and win outright.

I recall part of the conversation that night.

Despite having never been much of an environmentalist, since the walk back from Malaysia it had bugged me that there was a road piercing right through the heart of an otherwise pristine rainforest. I was sitting with the hunting party as we ate another delicious dinner of rice and stew in the kitchen of Pastor Johan's stilt house and, finally seizing the opportunity, I asked them what would happen to the villages in Malaysia when they finished building the road.

"We don't know. Sometimes logging companies arrive," Lipus said. "Then the government will replace the forest with oil palms."

The others became noticeably more animated. Again, Johan and Lipus helped to fill the gaps in my translation.

"If that happens, they will not be able to live from the land anymore and they will be forced to find a new way to exist," Apwi began, looking down.

Fin, looking uncharacteristically agitated now, joined in. "Once the forest is destroyed, the logging companies move on and the men must find work. There are never enough jobs in the plantations and some have to walk to places like Brunei and work illegally there. They do not see their families for years at a time." He picked up a handful of rice and held it scooped in his hand for a moment, in the queue for his mouth. "It is a dangerous journey. Many do not come back."

How do you know all this, I asked.

"We share our hunting grounds with the people across the border; we are all part of the same community. They tell us what happens to the villages downstream from them."

"But we are lucky so far," Lipus butted in. "This side of the border, there are too many mountains for them to build a road from the coast just yet. But I think that unless we can find enough tourists, the government might not protect the forest here forever."

"Too much tourism can be a bad thing," I said, remembering how unfriendly some of the people I met in the more touristy parts of Bali and Morocco were.

"Yes, it can." A distressed look creased Apwi's old face so that his tattoos became indistinguishable from wrinkles in the lamplight. "In one village I heard about, downstream from Bario, the women put on a dance for the tourists. They have to do this every night, for different groups. The tourists come for one day at a time, take photos and leave. This, we do not want."

"Why do you want tourists then?" I asked him.

"Because we value our lands, we want the government to continue to protect them. But we only want people who are willing to see what we are really like."

A while later, the conversation quietened. After a pause in the chatter, taking a large bead necklace out of his bag, Apwi turned to me and said, "Thank you for visiting our village Jimmy." He placed the necklace in my hands. "As long as you have this, people will welcome you and feed you. You are always at home in Long Layu."

Waiting for my flight out, with the necklace resting in my bag, I couldn't help but smile as I thought of the last part of the conversation. The Cessna's engine reverberated against the lush hills surrounding the tiny village, but this time the sound was less comforting. I shook hands with Johan for what I hoped was not the last time, picked up my bag and hobbled to the waiting aircraft.

As I climbed back in the Cessna, I thought about my time in Layu, and the more I did so, the more it occurred to me how so much of what I thought I relied upon at home was completely unnecessary. All the things I had, I started to feel like they just prevented me from experiencing the feeling you get trying to live as a natural part of the animal kingdom; not ruling, not dominating, but integrating.

I closed the door and placed the headset on. The instruments on the panel in front of me jolted into life and the propellor blew a cool breeze in through the windows. I looked across at the villagers with the same Nike T-shirts I had seen the hunters wearing. I remembered the badminton, the shotguns, and Lipus's mobile phone. It was all evidence of something I couldn't quite put my finger on. What was that word?

Change?

Globalisation.

Yes, that was it.

Modernisation; development. Westernisation. Call it what you will, but could that really be a bad thing?

The familiar bumps of the landing strip and the village became tiny again, a life raft in an ocean of green. I knew this new perspective wouldn't necessarily alter how I'd behave, and I knew I was still naïve, ignorant in my state of bliss. My short stay had been fascinating—an adventure, an education. Everything I wanted it to be, in fact. But it had presented more questions than it had answered, and now I needed to find out more. The Krayan Dayaks, relatively unscathed so far, they were the first piece of a jigsaw. Now I'd have to search out the next.

What I didn't know back then was quite how bad things could get. These days, even bliss comes with a price tag.

TWO

The Enlightened Traveller

After the forest, it felt strange being in a city.

The jungle was a concrete one; the noises were not of the high-pitched whirring variety, but of car horns and motorbikes and street vendors shouting for trade. The damp foliage smell had been replaced by the contradictory odour of open sewage intermingled with smoke from a million mango-flavoured cigarettes. Even the smiles no longer seemed like those of friendliness and welcome, but hinted at opportunistic greed and mild resentment.

Welcome back, I thought to myself, as I walked through the steamy outskirts of Kuala Lumpur's Chinatown. Compare it to Jakarta and KL seems positively gleaming, but the differences between town and country were accentuated this time and I found it unpleasant.

Stepping past a grubby alley lined with huge rats fighting with cats over scraps of tat, I banged on the gate of a hostel I had stayed at before. The lock buzzed as the proprietor let me in and I walked up a barren stairway lined with peeling paint and bright "Visit Malaysia Year 2007" posters. At the first-floor reception, I checked in and caught myself staring at the few white faces that typed away at computers nearby. One girl glanced back, looked briefly at me, then returned to her email.

I decided to take a look around the dorm rooms. There were two and you had to walk through one to reach the other, but nobody seemed to mind. It was ten in the morning and in the first room, there were no windows. In the dark, I made out the shapes of a few people sleeping in their bunks. The room smelt of alcohol and I nearly tripped over a bottle of whisky as I made my way through the door and into the next room. The second room was brighter—one of the curtains was partially opened. Down the walls were cracks, where the moisture in the air made the snot-green paint crinkle and peel away. There were several beds, but it was a small space and backpacks competed for the remaining floor.

I saw a free bunk and put my bag down next to it, set about relaxing. A few quiet moments passed while I counted the seconds it took my lungs to expand and contract, feeling my heartbeat slowing steadily, until I heard a stomping sound and a loud clunk—the noise of a glass bottle being kicked over.

"Shit!" A girl hopped in, holding her toe.

I could hear people rousing through the next door—the dawn of the dead—as the girl from the internet room glanced at me again. This time I smiled.

She sat on the bunk opposite, hoisted her leg where she could see her toe, and began inspecting. I looked away, because if she didn't mean to flash her knickers at me, she'd probably be quite embarrassed by what she was doing right now. She looked at me again briefly, down at my legs, pulled a face, then back at her toe.

"You look young," she said in an American-sounding accent.

"Thanks, I moisturise," I replied, finding something interesting on the floor to look at.

It's a huge spider.

No, wait.

No it's not, it's a clump of hair.

"How old are you?" She let her leg flop back down and I looked her in the eyes.

"I just turned nineteen." She continued staring at me with a blank expression for a few moments, so I decided to elaborate. "I was eighteen before that."

"So this must be like your first time or something right?"

I felt myself blush, "I'm sorry, I'm not really like that."

"No, dickweed. I mean your first time travelling."

"Oh, right." I cleared my throat. "Well, I've been on a few trips before, but nothing fancy. It was all just follow-the-yellow-brick-road type stuff."

"What's that supposed to mean?"

"I'm not really sure. I guess I mean I felt like Daphne or Delilah or whatever the hell her name was from that crappy old story about the Australian magician."

"You mean Dorothy. From The Wizard of Oz."

"Exactly. That girl who pranced around all these places but never seemed to do anything particularly interesting."

"She killed a witch by landing on it with a house."

"Yeah, but you know what I mean. It was a dull story." I felt way out of my depth so I changed the subject. "Anyway, what about you—this your first time? Travelling, I mean."

"No! I've been travelling for years. This trip has already been for, like, ten months now." The inflection at the end of the statement made it sound like a question.

"That's a pretty long time," I said in reply, as I looked at her bag. "So why did you leave home? Did you just get really bored of America or something?"

On her bag, I saw something red. And I realised something.

I imagine most people have probably had one of those moments where they're falling over and they see the ground coming towards them in slow motion just before it smacks their head. Well, that feeling, that sense of impending doom, is what I felt when I looked at her bag and I saw a badge, because on that badge was a red maple leaf.

Her face creased up and for a split second the wrinkles reminded me of the small cracks you might see in paving when viewed from a rapidly diminishing distance.

Her cheeks flushed red.

Then she unleashed.

"You think I'm from America? I'm CANADIAN you dipshit!" She shot a look of disgust right through me. "God, I hate it when people think I'm American and judge me just because I have this accent! Can't you see my bag? You ignorant English fu-"

"Actually, I'm part Scottish," I interjected diplomatically.

"I don't care!" she shouted. "You're all the same." At one point I thought I could see steam coming out of her ears. Everybody in the adjoining room was awake now and one of them, a chunky bald fellow with a green clover on his T-shirt, waded through the hostility and lit up a spliff. He passed it to her. You could call him a superhero.

She's still ranting and huffing and puffing but that only made the effect stronger. Within seconds, she'd mellowed. Minutes, and it was like she was sipping herbal tea in a field with rabbits and flowers and shit. The job done, the bald fellow removed the remainder of the spliff and finished it off in the next room, satisfied that his good deed for the day was complete.

"Thanks!" I shouted after him.

"No problems buddy, take it easy." His voice sounded Irish, but who was I to judge?

After a short while, I stood up to make my way out of the room.

"Hey, you know, I'm sorry," Canadian said, catching me as I passed her. The vowels were prolonged slightly, sounding rather like those of a Californian dude on an excellent adventure. I didn't tell her this. She continued, "I didn't mean to snap. I just get really annoyed when people judge me because of my accent. People are like, 'That girl's American,' and I'm like, 'No way, I didn't start the Iraq war or invade Afghanistan or do any of that shit', y'know?" She leant back on her bed. "Anyway, what happened to your legs—they're *disgusting*."

"I got eaten by leeches," I said, looking at the oozing wounds that covered my ankles and calves.

Canadian paused for a moment, in deep thought. Then she said, "Dude. Those things must *suck!*" At this witty aside, she fell into fits of giggles and her legs lifted up into the air again.

That evening, after a painful shave and a stroll around the night market in Chinatown, I was sitting at a table with a new T-shirt bought for six ringgit—the Malay equivalent of roughly one British pound at the time. To my left, the Irish-sounding chap from earlier was smoking another spliff in between swigs from his beer. Ironically, I think, he introduced himself as "Paddy". I was still not sure if I believed that was his actual name—he'd probably just called himself Paddy because he knew people would call him that anyway.

Next to Paddy was a Spaniard called Pablo and his quiet girlfriend Anita. This was less stereotypical, because in honesty, I couldn't remember what they were called so I had filled in the gaps with generics. Being Spanish, I'm pretty sure they ended in "o" and "a" respectively, so I couldn't have been too far off.

My stomach felt bloated and in front of me lay three large bottles of Tiger beer, two empty and with the labels peeled off slightly, and one half-full, judging from the condensation layer. Behind those were a few more people, maybe three or four, whose names I had no hope of remembering—I was already tipsy when they came and sat down with us. They were either Australian or Scottish, but who really cares?

To my right was Angela. In her beautiful *Canadian* accent, she was ranting about when she was in Laos two months ago: "Two months ago, I'd just had enough of the tourist trail and I was like, I know what, I'll go to Laos. And when I got there, I met these Dutch guys who were like, come tubing with us! So I went tubing and it was *so* much fun and we got *crazy* drunk everyday. But then we had an argument and they went to Vietnam…"

Sometimes you really can tell the solo travellers apart, I thought, possibly a bit hypocritically.

"Yes, tubing is good!" announced Pedro or Paulo or whatever (-o) and a few people nodded in agreement.

"And anyway, so I ended up in this fishing village and I was like, the only white girl to go there that month or something *insane* like that. And I stayed in this little tiny bed in this little tiny hut and we went fishing everyday and it was *so cool*. I mean, I learnt so *much*." She flicked her hair and looked wistfully towards the sparkling office towers that dominated the view from the rooftop. "These people, they had so little, but they seemed so *content*, you know. It was almost like they didn't need cool phones to be happy. I mean, they *had* cool phones, but they didn't *need* them. And they were so strong and welcoming. I just felt *so humble* next to them."

The rest of the group nodded and agreed, but it dawned on me that this was exactly what I thought when I left Long Layu. It also dawned on me that Angela was a bit of a dick, and I couldn't count how many times I'd had friends annoy me with their talk about that kind of thing after their Gap Years. I'd always just dismissed it as flappy bullshit and now I couldn't quite believe my Genuine Travel Experience in Borneo probably just amounted to the same old cliché I'd heard a million times before—about spending a bit of time with the locals and learning all of life's lessons in one go. *I'll show them*, I thought. *Next time I'll go somewhere crazy, like Northern Wales or the Palestinian West Bank or somewhere.*

That's it, I thought, *my next trip is going to be to the Middle East!*

Only I was a bit drunk, and I *can* think when I'm drunk, and sometimes that process happens in my head, but this time it didn't.

"MY NEXT TRIP IS GOING TO BE IN THE MIDDLE EAST!" I said, a lot louder than necessary.

The group looked round, along with half of Malaysia.

"That's a feckin' war zone!" said Paddy, turning up his mouth, clearly impressed.

"You will be shot and captured and have your head chopped off by Islamic extremists on Al-Jazeera!" Anita announced with glee, speaking for the first time that evening.

"Feck!" Paddy probably agreed.

"That would be *so cool*, I wish I could go to a war zone," continued Angela, who was also impressed and evidently quite drunk. "I was in Cambodia once and I heard this loud bang and when I looked around this car was smoking out of its engine and this woman comes out of a house nearby and…"

I zoned out.

That's not actually such a bad idea, I thought. I started bouncing ideas around my head for a while until it finally clicked in place: one of these days, I'd visit the Middle East. The *actual* Middle East, the one from all those news reports. And then I'd find some other cool places like that to go. And I'd find some way to make it all fit in to a grand theory of the world. I could discover what all these conflict things were about too. Angela was right, that *would* be cool.

Come to think of it, Angela's actually pretty hot.

I glanced at her for a moment and took all the details in. Then I continued to look deeply into the label I had peeled from my bottle, contemplating what I saw. I mean, she had hair, a face, a body; loads of stuff. And eyes—she had at least two of those. She might have even had a few legs thrown into the bargain.

In fact, I was *sure* she did.

Of course! I saw them earlier! When she was on the bed! What more could a man want?

When I zoned back in, it was just me, Angela, Paddy and a whole lot more empty beer bottles on the table. Angela was still talking shit about her amazing travel experiences and Paddy still had a spliff in his mouth, but he wasn't talking very much.

When he did talk, it sounded remarkably like snorting. Doesn't that normally mean something?

Ah, that's it.

So Paddy's asleep, Angela's wide-awake and I think I'm trying to sleep with Angela, but I can't really be sure anymore. She definitely looked a lot prettier than I remembered her looking this morning. Or earlier on this evening in fact.

Funny, what time was it anyway?

It felt quite late. I looked at my watch. The hands pointed straight up, but then they started turning faster than they normally would. Angela stopped talking for a moment.

"Hey, you okay dude?" She sounded far away and my ears felt warm. I looked up and saw that Angela wasn't travelling alone after all. She was sitting with her twin sister, who looked exactly like her but *even hotter.*

They continued their story but I was too busy taking in the surroundings to listen. The glittery towers and all the bright white beams pointing up towards the orange sky; the shiny office buildings surrounding us. The spaceship-like KL tower. The occasional beeping of traffic, even now, creatively mixed into the Bob Marley on the bar's tinny sound system. It was so damn cool. Shit, even the fairy lights on the walls were moving now, or maybe they just turned on a disco ball.

Whatever, I didn't care as long as this just kept getting better and better. Cold Tiger beer, hot American twins, sexy disco lighting: you couldn't get *this* in the jungle.

Maybe modernity isn't so bad after all…

And then the disco ball started speeding up, faster and faster. It was intense and I found it hard to concentrate on one spot. The twins were looking at me now. Angela had stopped talking, she was just staring at me. *Maybe she's about to try something,* I thought, quite optimistically. *I don't blame her.*

They leant towards me and placed their hands on my knee.

Is this really happening?

I got a strange taste in my mouth; a build up of saliva or something. I closed my eyes and rubbed them, but they felt numb so I opened them again. I didn't want to miss this.

"Dude?"

The whole roof was moving now, swirling about like some kind of swirly-whirly washing machine thing. And the twins were moving closer to me, reaching out with their free hands. There was something in these hands, something white and round and large. Angela's sister held it up to my face with two right hands.

It looked like a bucket.

And she said, "Don't worry dude, we've all been there."

All of a sudden it was my turn to talk, and I had plenty to say but it didn't quite come out the same way I planned it, or the same consistency. But Angela kept holding the bucket patiently, talking about how she was sick on rice wine back in 'Nam and some dude held a bucket for her, so she was just passing the love on.

Eventually I stopped, and Angela gently wiped my mouth with a tissue. The disco ball was off now, the roof had become much more stable, and Angela was suddenly a lot kinder than I remember her being earlier.

She walked me to my bed and I promptly fell into a deep sleep.

A few days passed by and I caught a bus to an airport, flew back to Indonesia and climbed a small volcano in the Sunda Straight called Gunung Krakatao. The sulphur smell of the caldera, wind rushing through my hair from the back of a motorbike, sun descending into the perpetual tropical smog of Jakarta, then one more flight and I was back in England.

That reverse culture shock, where people find it really strange to be back in their own country; it didn't happen to me. I don't know what I expected, but when I looked out at the wet roads around London, everything felt so…everything felt so *normal.* As though England hadn't been put on hold. Almost as if I'd never been away.

Even the bloody *economy* was fine.

THREE

The International Relatist

Sitting in the campus pub nursing my pint of lager that morning, I felt like a man in control. But I knew I wasn't the same anymore; globetrotting had changed me. Not much, but enough to know that I wanted to make travel a hobby, although at the time I didn't quite realise how important this difference was. Because it *was* important.

Before, I saw travel as a kind of course in becoming a well-rounded person. Something that you do a few times until you learn all of life's lessons, then you get a job. But when I returned from Indonesia, travel had become something more than that. It had become a fascination. It was as interesting a subject as I had ever encountered and I wanted to do more.

See more.

See *everything*.

Before, I'd look at a map and there'd be a few places I wanted to visit. Maybe a friend told me there was nice wildlife on the Bingo-bongo Peninsular, or a relative brought back some lovely photos from a holiday on Sexylush Island.

And so I'd want to go *there*.

Now I'd look at a map and see a whole world to explore. I would see nearly two hundred countries and provinces staring eagerly back at me, like Russian brides in a mail-order catalogue. Like any sensible man, I wanted to go beyond the Cilla Black introductions of guidebooks and travel magazines and get to know them, face to face. See what hidden secrets I could uncover.

This change would have consequences. I knew I'd have to prioritise much more or choosing where to go next would start to make me feel like my mother if she were standing in a superstore full of pretty shoes.

I'd have to weigh up the important factors.

How much will it cost?

Is it going to be the right season?

Does it already have a McDonalds?

Fortunately, on a drunken night on a hostel rooftop in Malaysia, I had already solved the problem of where my next adventure would be. But by now, I also had an interest in how the world worked before development strolled along, and to look at that properly I would have to visit some of its more troubled regions. After my brief encounter with the people of the Krayan, I wanted to know how these parts of the world were going to change, and why. Did it benefit the locals, or was it a hindrance? Did it benefit us? I wanted to know how things progressed—whether the trappings of the Western world made people more, or less happy. From my position of relative comfort and security and wealth, I wanted to meet the people who knew what it felt like to be uncomfortable, insecure, impoverished.

I needed to find out how green my grass really was.

* * *

Tim took a thoughtful sip of his pint. "There's a name for that you know. It's called Dark Tourism." Tim's full of useful information.

"Oh yeah?"

"Yes. It's when people go to places to see other people suffering. It's associated with War Tourism, which is similar but the subject is focused more narrowly on war zones. It is described in popular media as thrill-seeking, voyeuristic and superficial."

Tim wasn't wearing a tweed jacket, but later in life he would.

"Where do they go?" I asked.

"To any active war zone, or any place where fighting is likely to break out."

"Sounds cool! And what do they do?" I asked, feeling the temptation to start taking notes.

"They masturbate furiously."

The bar had suddenly quietened, as bars do just before someone says something outrageous. I put my notepad away.

"Really? That's sick."

"No, not really. That was a joke. I don't know what they do. Probably take photographs and boast about it."

Feeling marginally relieved, but not in *that* sense, I took another sip.

"So, how was Borneo?" Tim asked.

"Great thanks mate, the place I went to was so welcoming. The village people were incredible."

"Did they sing you the YMCA?"

"What?"

"It doesn't matter. So what's next?"

"I'm going to the Middle East." Again, I would describe this as more of a blurt than a statement, but Tim seemed unfazed as ever.

"When?"

"Easter maybe."

"Why? To be a War Tourist?"

A Waurist, I thought to myself, demonstrating my spectacular wit.

"No. I am going to do some research for my course."

"What, Drama?"

"No Tim, I don't do Drama."

"Wizardry?"

"No, the other one. The one that I actually study."

"Oh, Philosophy wasn't it?"

Ha! He'd fallen right into my trap.

"No, *actually* I study International Relations." A smug grin sat on my silly red face for a while, like a stupid cherry on a pink cupcake. "I changed it earlier this morning."

"Oh, well done." Tim brushed my expression aside with a flick of his hair. "What are you going to research?" he asked.

I scratched a small cluster of bites on the back of my ankle. "Well I don't know yet, I'll find that out when I start doing the course."

"That doesn't sound convincing. How are you supposed to do any research if you don't even know what your course is?" Tim looked unperturbed.

"I am going to find out. But I am *going* and I am going to *research* stuff. I've made my decision and everything." This time I sounded much more credible. I sounded like a man in charge of his destiny. Pleased with this, I took a healthy swig of my fizzy breakfast.

Tim paused for a second, obviously thrown off his track by my definitive answer. Then he shot me a quizzical look.

"I just hope you'll remember to take enough tissues."

I drained my pint in silence. There's no convincing some people.

Back at my student house, Guy, one of my housemates and possibly the most relaxed person I'd ever met, was sitting in the kitchen with a bowl of cereal. "Hey Ginge! How's it going?" he beamed as I walked in.

"Guy, for fuck's sake, I'm really not ginger."

"Sorry man. I'm bad with colours," he laughed. "I heard you changed your course?"

"Yeah mate, I'm an International Relations student now!" Again, I said this with a large smile on my rosy face, like I'd just been offered the job of Groin-Strain Relief Specialist for the Australian Women's Volleyball Team. "Now I can learn how to Internationally Relate!"

"Sounds sweet mate. I've just bought a van!" Guy said this with a grin that would suggest the van was, in fact, the Australian Women's Volleyball Team.

"Cool, what type?"

"A blue one!" Guy now looked like a man who had put his hand in his pocket only to discover a five-pound note that *he never knew he had!* He put a spoonful of cereal in his mouth and an expression of mild confusion flashed across his features. Moments later, his eyebrows raised in realisation. "Ginge, can you pass me the milk?"

I passed him the milk, then quickly grabbed it back.

"Sorry mate, I keep forgetting. You're not ginger. I swear. *Please* pass me the milk."

Reluctantly, I handed over the carton. As I did, a sound like machine gun fire rattled through the house, building into a crescendo as the kitchen door was flung against its meagre hinges.

"Ginge, you're back!" Kate shouted as she stormed in, giving me a bear hug. The door limped shut, clearly regretting getting in Kate's way.

"Hi Kate, nice to see you."

"Oh my god, you're so skinny! And your hair, it's gone totally oran-"

"Yes, thanks Kate."

"Must have been sunny."

"Yeah, it was. Rained everyday though."

Kate was another one of my housemates. A highly motivated, efficient and pretty girl, she terrified me.

"Kate, I've got a new van!" said Guy, eagerly.

"I know Guy, you told me," said Kate, efficiently.

"It's blue!" he grinned, then curbed his enthusiasm as best he could, sensing her wrath building.

Kate turned her attention to me. "So Ginge, where have you got planned next?"

"I'm going to the Middle East," I said as a pigeon started flapping about outside, apparently trying desperately to mate with the French windows.

"Oh really? I was just talking to Timothy about that part of the world! He mentioned you might be going there," Kate said with a look of glee. The kind of glee that might have suggested she knew something I didn't want her to.

Timothy.

Tim.

That sneaky turd. I bet he'd told everybody I'm off to do sordid things and take photos of it all. I couldn't let them think that, I had to put a stop to this rumour straight away. I composed myself as best I could and, keeping my cool, I said, "I know what you're thinking, but I'm not going there for gratification of any kind."

Silence. Apart from a faint flapping noise.

I felt marginally awkward, wondering why Kate's mouth had just flopped open an inch. As was my habit when I got nervous, I kept on talking. "And anyway, I can do plenty of that here if I wanted to so I don't see why I would go all that way and…er…that would be sick."

Guy and Kate both looked at me.

Guy's mouth had stopped chomping.

Putting all the evidence together, it dawned on me that maybe I had made a minor misjudgement, so I tried to pull a disgusted face to empathise with them, to bridge the gap, socially speaking, but in hindsight it probably just looked like I'd had a bowel movement.

"Tim didn't mention that bit then?" I asked.

"No."

"Ah. Well apparently, there are some people who…um…" the sentence trailed off. "I'm just going to research stuff."

"Sounds good Ginge," Kate said.

"Sounds great," Guy concurred.

Guy took another spoonful of cereal and I heard it crunch in his mouth as he chewed. Amber, one of my other housemates, walked in from the adjacent room and looked at me sympathetically.

"Jamie, you're *so* weird," she said.

The pigeon slumped against the glass and lit up a fag.

* * *

Months passed by quickly, like canned baked beans on a factory production line. I sat through a few seminars, I took a few exams but, like the months, they just passed me by. Like clouds out of an aircraft window.

Ninety days short of a year had gone by since Indonesia and I hadn't really thought much of it recently. Surrounding me in all directions, a grid of nervous, bored, daydreaming students, all in their own little worlds like me. Fiddling with their pencils. Pushing the upside-down papers about the desk, seeing if they could somehow find a way to read the questions on the other side. Some sat with strained expressions, as though creasing their faces would help them retain all that information from the last five minutes of desperate cramming outside the hall. Others, like me, just seemed resigned to their fate.

Like all those other exams, I couldn't wait for this one to be over. Be gone, so I could get on with my life. Sat there, in the exam hall, I began to think about those last few months. Those months—the ones that had passed like lazy camels on a desert road—they hadn't been entirely devoid of interest. I took my pens from the pocket of my shorts and placed them on the desk. Then I leant back in my chair, cracked my knuckles. Took a breath and closed my eyes.

Closed my eyes, and then I am in Aleppo, one of the oldest continually inhabited cities on earth. It is March and the air still carries a chill at night. There's activity everywhere, doused in orange light from the numerous tungsten bulbs hanging from various wires. Arabic pop music blaring from tinny speakers in several stalls. Chatter, intermingled with the sound of men shouting place names.

"Manbij! Manbij! Ajbab!"

Groups of people sit in the warm light of the tea stools, sipping from small glasses and looking around at the bustle, staring silently at passers by. One or two occasionally toke from a nargileh water pipe. Every so often, the sweet scent wafts past.

Almost everything is recognisable from magazine articles and news clips. Films, books, paintings. But like visiting the set from a Hollywood blockbuster, no matter how familiar you are with the movie, it is never quite the same as seeing real thing.

People push past from the stalls to the shabby but colourful busses parked in the courtyard, a group of men wearing stylish jeans and leather jackets. Their black hair is gelled and swept back. They walk onto a bus to my left and its exhaust pipe splutters as it grinds into gear. With a mechanical roar and the repetitive blaring of the horn, it leaves the terminal in a cloud of smoke and fumes.

"Where you want to go?" A teenager in tight jeans and a chequered shirt tugs at my arm. His dark hair is spiked with precision and he holds a stack of tickets in his hand.

"Damascus," I reply, and the teen points down a wide road, visible through the gap the departing bus just left.

"Ah, Dimashq. The bus goes from different terminal. There. Follow this road."

Moments after I leave, a crowd of women in colourful hijabs descends on the poor boy and they shout at each other, gesticulating with the aggressive intensity of rappers. An exchange of paper follows and everyone walks away, seemingly satisfied with the encounter.

I take the road, following a wide pavement that lines a park on the right, filled with green trees and benches. To the left, the traffic honks and screeches slowly by—mostly yellow cabs and small white hatchbacks. Families and couples stroll lazily down the pavement, as though promenading along a waterfront. A woman in a black burka pushes a colourful pram with fluffy toys dangling from its handles. Her husband, a portly man in a white tunic and red kaffiyeh headscarf shouts into a mobile phone, his free hand flailing as though he were falling from a skyscraper.

Back at the border, entry formalities had been straightforward; our Turkish taxi driver had slipped a few hundred Syrian pounds in with our passports when we handed them across to the immigration officials. They eyed us suspiciously, stamped our visas and without breaking eye contact, handed them back to us with the money miraculously gone. Behind them, Bashar al-Assad's unsmiling stare and thin fascist moustache oversaw the process from a picture frame hanging on the wall. "Welcome to Syria," the official said; a thickly accented monotone that hinted at anything but welcome.

Back on the street, I walk past a food vendor, selling what look like small pizzas—flatbread topped with some kind of herb or other. The vendor catches me looking at his merchandise, picks it up and hands it over. "Very good," he says, patting his stomach. I reach for my pocket and he waves me away. "Welcome to Syria," the vendor says with a warm smile. I take a bite and the taste is intensely aromatic, full of flavour.

Further up the street it gets busier—more people, more vendors. The alleys branch off here and there and the ambient noise becomes one of chatter and Arabic pop again, drowning out the honking of horns. Stalls line both sides of the wide pavement now, some kind of night market concerned only with the selling and eating of flatbread-based foods. The lights are bright white, like the vendors' clothing. Clean; crisp.

It strikes me that the whole place is immaculate, a buzzing atmosphere that is very agreeable. Part of me was expecting the worst—unfriendly, hostile people as the sensationalist media would have you believe, but the number of kids running around with grins has convinced me otherwise. The shouts of "welcome" from men and children come from all over. It feels like I am a minor celebrity in a very pleasant way. All about, arms flail and voices shout harshly at each other; guttural noises projected from faces with smiling eyes. Finishing the pizza-flatbread, I move on to another vendor who fills a wrap with diced chicken and vegetables. The taste is wonderful.

And with that taste still in my mouth, I find the bus to Damascus.

I sit next to a friendly young guy who tells me he is a Syrian army soldier. We talk for a while—I do not recall what about exactly. Mostly music, girls, army life. But every now and then, I look over my shoulder to see another man who just stares. Leather jacket, dark T-shirt, jeans. Harsh-looking. Unsmiling, unwavering, he stares at me. He is close enough to hear the conversation and the look on his face suggests disapproval, but I can't work it out.

For a while, I ignore him and continue chatting.

After a few stops, the soldier smiles and says, "Excuse me, my stop," in his perfect English. He squeezes past me and walks down the dark aisle out of the bus and into the night. Out of the window, to my right, a shiny, whitewashed building with a domed roof is illuminated in green, and a golden minaret stands tall above it. Maybe a slight horizon—a star or two. The rest is too dark to see and the dim lights inside the bus reflect my face, hair and headrest in the glass. I look further right, past the headrest, checking the reflection behind me where the man still stares, passively. So I turn around as the bus lurches forward and I face him, holding his gaze.

I hold his gaze for a second. Five seconds. A minute. He looks away, out of his window, and I settle back into my seat. At the next stop, he stands up and walks past me. His leather jacket is caught on something at the bottom, holding it an inch above the belt line of his jeans. Something black and shiny, and as he walks past, he pulls his leather jacket back over the pistol that's tucked into his trousers. He looks around, back at me, and smiles.

And then he's gone, walking off the bus into the night.

Less than twelve hours in Syria and I'd already come across the mukhabarat*. And by the end of the next week, I would be blacklisted from the country. *That really wasn't bad going*, I thought, as the moderator snapped me out of my daydream.

"You may begin."

In those months, I had visited the Middle East and I knew I would return. I had done some research and presented it in my coursework. I spent a long time reading about the mechanics of the world, about the mechanics that allowed me to have the things I had, live the way I did, but I still wanted to meet people who knew the other side of the story. I was intrigued, but not for any moral reasons. The quick trip around the Middle East had fed a different fascination and one that I would explore in time to come, and the people I'd met there had given me the rather dangerous idea that perhaps the West didn't necessarily have it right. But right now, I had a different focus. And that focus was the reason why—or at least, that's how I imagined it—I had begun cultivating links with separatists in New Guinea. Why I had begun preparing myself for an investigation that could potentially land me in an Indonesian prison, or worse.

I was that desperate to see how privileged I really was.

---

* The Secret Police.

FOUR

Necessary Evils

Once the exams were over, I had a great time celebrating with my housemates. We didn't do anything exciting, just joked and chatted and drank; I was happy, in the company of some of my best friends, surrounded by familiarity and fun. I stayed on in Exeter for a while, lapping up the best of the English summer. An idyllic life: barbecues in the rain, drinking beer by the beach, cycling along the canal with Tim (whom I had graciously forgiven). Great times, but a double-edged sword in a way. Like taking a swig from a hip flask, I looked back on those weeks and it calmed my nerves somewhat. But the effect was short-lived and I started to feel uneasy again.

Uneasy, and a tad lonely.

The dim lighting, the deep grumble of the engine, the near-empty bus. I shifted about in my seat, trying to find a position that didn't hurt my coccyx so much, but to no avail. Eventually, I settled for an extreme slouch with my back arched and my feet planted on the headrest in front.

Bright lights floated by and droplets piled up on the windows. It was cold; I shivered in my T-shirt because I didn't have anything warmer to wear.

I had done the same journey that morning, but on the way back it felt different. A sense of despondency had settled in me and as much as I shifted about in my seat, I couldn't shake it. It might have been the powerful antimalarials I'd started taking earlier in the day affecting my mood, but the impressive buildings from the morning had become imposing. The streets, reflecting the red brake lights and the neon signs; familiar, but alien. The same routine in reverse; now it held a menace that was so palpable, but for no clear reason. I knew it was the same. Same, but different.

The bus swerved into the side of the street, missing a few pedestrians by centimetres, and the door opened with a hiss. Warm air wafted into the back where I was seated, but nobody got off, probably because I was the only passenger on the bus. The door slid shut and the engine roared like afterburners on a jet. Only a few seconds later, the bus veered slowly back into the stream of traffic. Pedestrians walking on the pavements either side kept up with the pace of the bus—geocentric human satellites that made their way around a highly decorated elephant, brightly coloured and led by a man dressed like Aladdin.

A building loomed up. It was so high that it was impossible to see the top from the bus. Some of the rooms were lit, forming yellow blocks in the darkness. The bus once again veered into a few pedestrians—men and women, dressed in jeans and tight T-shirts, some wearing face masks—who moved out of the way and into the roadside stalls selling cheap clothing and steam-fried grease.

I looked down at the trade on the other side of the bus window. Like I was observing an ant colony through a magnifying glass, I felt detached. Disconnected by the freezing artificial atmosphere of the bus. The constant noise of the engine, varying in volume but not in type. Clean, comfortable. Sterilised. Ordered. A roaring little bubble of safety and cool protection, ferrying Westerners between the airport and the city; cocooned from the outside, from the bustle, the chaos I didn't want to face, because I didn't feel ready. Not yet.

The door hissed, slid open, and I shouldered my bag and walked down the cold aisle. Stepped down into the smells and interactions of the street. As the warmth grabbed at my arms and legs, I strode across the road, through rain droplets lit in headlights, racing for the lobby of the tallest building in the city. Honking horns swerved past me and I made a dash for the bright revolving doors. The golden interior, twenty-one degrees Celsius, polite porters; I walked straight into the lift: floor sixty. *Bing.* Doors slid open and my flip flops padded soft on the carpet. The lock clicked graciously as I pushed my card into the slot and walked into the expansive room. Inside, the lighting was moody, almost romantic, but that didn't help matters.

I walked into the large marbled bathroom and gathered a few possessions: a toothbrush, razor, a travel towel, and placed them into my wash bag. For one last time, I stepped into the warm jet of the shower, soaking it up. Treasuring the feeling of being warmed in somewhere relatively cool. Then I wrapped a thick hotel towel around my waist and walked to the room's floor-to-ceiling window. Through it, I could see the river—a winding snake of darkness in the upside-down yellow starlight of the city. The dank orange sky lay heavy across the cityscape, a thick duvet of water vapour that seemed to reflect my mood. I stood for a while with the air-con blowing cold against my back, then went back to the bathroom and looked at myself in the mirror for a few moments, trying to preserve the moment.

My healthiness.

My cleanliness.

My comfort.

Removing the towel and throwing it into the sink basin, I put on my grubby shorts and rain-spattered T-shirt, stepped back into the bedroom and sat on the bed, sinking into the mattress.

In the past weeks, nothing had made this any easier. The post-exam merriment. The plush hotel room, which, the night before, I was sharing with my wonderful new girlfriend of just six months. Her pillow, still dented from where she had got up that morning.

I let myself flop back on the duvet, stared up at the ceiling, became lost in my own mind.

I could give this up right now and go back, I thought; a quick change of flight, and I'd be home in a matter of days. Home to enjoy my life without having to question anything. And perhaps that was what I should do. Catch it early and let go, because if there was a moment to turn back, this was it.

Ten or twenty minutes passed before I snapped out of it. I knew it was only natural to have doubts before a trip—I had them every time I went away—but this was different. For whatever reason, something was telling me this moment, this decision, could be the biggest turning point in my life. It wasn't just the study, the dangers, the excitements that would come with it, but what I might learn and the effect that knowledge could have on me. But then, I also knew the decision had already been made. So I stood up, slung the rucksack on my back, and walked out of the door. Down the lift, card in at reception, and back into the perpetual warmth. Away from the luxurious and into the sensually rich. My legs carried me a few blocks, because I knew the rickshaw drivers would overcharge anybody they saw carrying luggage out of the city's tallest and most opulent hotel.

The driver looked up and said something I failed to understand. "Khao San," I replied.

He nodded before I finished the words.

The rickshaw revved up, ramping through the gears until it reached a coasting speed, perhaps twenty miles an hour. Droplets of rain landed on my arms occasionally, despite the canvas cover over the three-wheeler, and the breeze felt cool and moist. Good cars, shiny and silver, were no match for the little rickshaw, and in no time the driver was asking for a reasonable fare for the journey, perhaps as a courtesy for not haggling initially, perhaps because he usually operated in an area where there were fewer tourists. I paid him and with a genuine smile, he scooted off.

Then I was in Khao San.

***

You might call it sensory overload.

The Road stretched away from me; a kaleidoscope of bars and guesthouses and neon, loud bass and steam-fried noodles. This was Backpacker Central. Few places on the planet harboured such a concentration of international hedonists, seeking out excess at any cost. Worryingly, while I stared, one of the first thoughts that occurred to me was that Khao San would be the perfect sight for a future terrorist attack.

Europeans and Americans outnumbered Thais considerably, but the vendors and dealers stood out from the crowds, offering lewd promises and intoxication to anybody who'd catch their eye. Nearby, a woman was selling fried locusts from a plastic bucket, doing a roaring trade to the younger, more macho backpackers, none of whom seemed to enjoy the taste, but hey, one more crazy experience for the bank, right?

I noticed that the rain had all but stopped and the air was a pleasant temperature as I hoisted my bag over one shoulder and dived into the frenzy. All around me, white faces in varying degrees of decay floated past. Old men, younger guys. Girls in their late-teens, wearing beach shorts and strappy tops, flip-flopped by. Here, age or nationality didn't matter so much as where you'd been and how long you'd been there. Each style read like a CV in the bright artificial light of Bangkok's most famous street. Pink faces, short gelled hair, Singha Beer T-shirts: holidaymakers, probably back from Phuket, Samui or Phagnan, spending their last few days living it up in the city before they had to fly back to Essex or Birmingham or wherever. Make the tan darker, the hair longer and give them a Bintang T-shirt instead, and they became round-the-world ticket holders, on their way back from Australia or New Zealand via Bali. Make the tan even darker, the hair blonder and the shorts shorter and you have an Australian.

I passed a group of tanned girls with intentionally messy hair walking out of a Boots pharmacy complaining about the small range of shampoo: post-school gap-year backpackers probably, looking for a bit of creature comfort after a few months on the road. A bitterness in their voices suggested they'd decided to travel somewhere like India together, spur of the moment in a sixth-form common room, and hadn't enjoyed the country or the company as much as they had first imagined.

I brushed past an older couple, hand in hand, with an expression on their faces that wouldn't look out of place on a king and queen gazing out across a vast army. Jaded, but warm with familiarity. Long, thin, greasy hair; exotic tattoos on wrinkled, dark skin. Clothes that somehow managed to look like they'd been washed too much and not quite enough—ragged but practical. The creased smile of the free-love generation, all the way from the hippy trail, still living the dream.

My attention didn't linger any longer than necessary. A group of skinny guys, dreadlocks, baggy singlets, sat around in a circle to my right, drinking radioactive liquid from buckets and swapping stories.

"Hey! You wan' join us man? We havin' a good time!" A young Thai guy grabbed a plastic chair and pulled it next to a few other tourists, who did indeed look like they were having a good time. Each of them had ear to ear grins on their faces. "C'mon man, I gi' you firs' bucke' ha'-pri!" he shouted.

I waved and smiled as I passed, acting the part of the deaf but friendly mute. A few paces later, a thickset Chinese-looking man grabbed my right arm and made a loud clucking noise with his tongue sucked up against the roof of his mouth.

Pause for effect.

"Ping pong show," he leered.

"Table tennis isn't really my thing mate, sorry."

Another cluck followed and he let go of my arm. His face changed when he saw my backpack, becoming the picture of innocence. "You wanna guess house?" He pointed diagonally left to a green sign, hovering over the throng of T-shirts and white faces. Then the smirk returned. "You wash show la'er, no pobrem."

I pushed through the crowds. Bass from the latest Western hit songs blasted out of loudspeakers, thumping sonic waves visibly through my T-shirt, and a crowd of blokes erupted into cheer at a pub TV—I briefly wondered which team they just saw concede a goal. Beyond the next bar, I found a stairway leading from the street up. It wasn't anything Led Zeppelin would sing about, but I followed it anyway, up to a reception advertising rooms for 150 Bhat and checked myself in.

The room was a small one. Perhaps three paces wide and five long. The plasterboard partition did not reach the ceiling and I could hear a pair of girls chatting next me. Still, I couldn't complain—it cost the same as a cup of coffee in England.

"I can't believe I got away with that."

"You were *so* lucky."

"Oh well, one more night to par-*tay!*"

A door shut and footsteps padded off down the corridor while I lay under the ceiling fan for a moment. The baseline thumped through the bed and I tried to guess the song. *Boom, boom boom-boom, boom b'boom.* Nothing came to mind, but it was apparent that nobody in this room was going to sleep until it stopped, so I headed downstairs to reception.

"No Thais allowed", the sign under the desk read. By it, two slightly plump blonde girls were standing, waiting for the receptionist to notice them. "So what happened?" I asked. They turned, looking confused. "Sorry, I'm in the room next door. I heard you got lucky," I clarified.

"Yeah she missed her flight to India today."

"Doesn't sound that lucky."

"The airline let her get another flight tomorrow for free." The taller girl looked across to the young Thai behind the counter and waved.

"Which means I can get drunk again!" The other girl said this and did a jig to mark the prospect. As she passed her key to the bored receptionist, whose eyes seemed to simmer with resentment, I noticed a small television with a Thai soap opera blaring the standard close-up of an emotional girl's face out from the corner of the brightly lit room. Around it, a few of the staff slept on couches.

"Well, have fun tonight," I said.

"You too!" they chimed.

I treaded down the stairs and back out onto the street. Bright lights and bustle overwhelmed my eyes, ears and nostrils once more so I tried to get out of the main drag, away from the garish excess for a little while, just to get my bearings. I ducked down a small alley and took a left at the t-junction, leaving the noise behind. The path was narrow, but there were plenty of nooks and back passages—enough to make it a perfect spot for a mugging.

I carried on walking until I found some wooden stools placed around a table and a small hi-fi that played reggae music, right in the alleyway. Three Westerners sat around with a few beers between them. It looked like there might be a dead-end further up, making it potentially socially awkward to squeeze past, so instead I grabbed an empty seat at the makeshift bar and a young Thai girl asked if I wanted a beer too. "Sure," I said, and she ducked into a doorway, emerging a few moments later with a perfectly cold bottle of Chang.

Being that close to the other customers, it would have been rude not to acknowledge them, so I smiled and I said, "Cool place." Not very imaginative, I know, but I didn't realise I was going to include the statement in a book at the time.

"Yeah, it's nice to get away from the road sometimes." A bald man shifted his chair to the side. "Pull up a pew mate."

"Thanks."

"Pretty full-on out there isn't it?" another guy said.

"Yeah," I replied, "But I guess that's what most people come here for. Drink a few buckets, watch some sport, have a good time."

"Screw that." The third member of the crew was seated apart from the other two. I guessed she was the solo traveller of the three, if there was one. "This place, this is like Disneyland, Asia. Every time I come back it's changed for the worse." The other two guys looked at each other, then at me, but she continued unabated. "This ain't what it used to be. Now *India*, that's still travelling."

She looked older, old enough to know how great Thailand *was*, and that's pretty damn old in traveller terms; that practically made her a *veteran*—someone to be revered in some circles. I suspected, like most of the "old hand" types I'd met in Thailand so far, she'd talk all the talk of the pioneering hippy-trail adventurers but had fallen into a puddle of drugs along the way and didn't quite crawl out in time, and as a result was now probably a few huts short of a beach resort.

"There's 7Elevens everywhere, I even saw a Tescos—I'm not shitting you." She took a gulp of Budweiser. "I don't know why travellers even bother coming here anymore. This isn't travel."

I looked at the other guys and it was obvious they were thinking the same thing but were too polite to say it. I tried to change the subject.

"What's so great about India?" I asked, sounding more confrontational than I intended.

"It's the poverty. You just can't escape it. Everywhere you go, it's there. Staring you right in the face. No matter how much money you've got, you can't get away from the beggars."

"That's a good thing?" the bald guy asked.

The lady muttered something under her breath as she shook her head and took her beer over to the proprietor's doorway, disappearing inside. We all watched for a moment, but she didn't come back out.

"There are so many battered old relics here," the bald guy said in a hushed voice. "That woman can't stop banging on about the good old days." He looked at the doorway on the narrow street, painted in fluorescent hues with the prices of all the different beers. "When the hell are these leftovers going to stop whinging and just fuck off home?"

The two guys laughed.

We chatted for a while longer; they were on their way back from the Philippines, using Bangkok as a staging post for all the cheap South East Asian airlines, just as I was: an easy place to fly in and out of. You see, if you wanted a good time, Thailand's a great place to be. But if you wanted to have an adventure away from the crowds, nowadays it's mostly just a hub.

"Now the *Philippines*, mate, *that's* what Thailand used to be." The guys nodded enthusiastically. "Great beaches, beautiful women—plenty of places to get away from the crowds…"

"Just watch out for the sex-tourists," the other interjected. *Sexists*, I thought cleverly, until I realised it was already a word.

"Yeah and the prozzies. Shit! They can get pretty full on."

We shared a few more beers and chewed the fat. Of course we all, everybody in that road, had the same reasons to be where we were. There were plenty of other parts of Bangkok away from the nutty crowds, but Khao San was still possibly the best decompression chamber in Asia. Few other parts of the world offered a Boots Pharmacy across the street from a stall selling fried locusts.

"You should have come here earlier. The guy who just left before you, he had a mental job, didn't he?"

"Yeah, his job—wait for it—was a *body* collector."

"A what?"

"He worked for the Dutch embassy or something, picking up the unclaimed bodies of all the people from the Netherlands who died in Thailand. How fucked up is that?"

"And apparently business is *good*."

* * *

By the time I walked back from my little reggae haven, Khao San had descended into a freak show. Tie-die hippies and young backpackers filled the street; the old boys, the holidaymakers, they had gone elsewhere—Patpong, Silom. Bed. What was left was the young crowd: the kids making the most of their first or last few days in Asia; the people looking for new sensations and experiences; the people willing to sell them.

Read: drunks, druggies and dealers.

A small cocktail bar had been set up in the middle of the road, consisting of plastic chairs, an awning and a selection of fairy lights. A few young guys were drinking from buckets, swaying as though on a ship, looking seasick. Doe-eyed. Dazed. Innocent and vulnerable from my standpoint of comparative sobriety. They contrasted against the tie-die crowd, jumping and skipping, waving their arms through the air as though they were not dancing to the music, but were in fact music themselves. I imagined this probably looked a lot better in their heads, as they flapped and spun about in a colourful, twirley-whirley social awareness lesson.

I peered into the pub near my guesthouse, where a few hangers-on remained from the Carlsberg-guzzling football crowd earlier. Some of them were sharing their tables and laps with Thai girls. The rest, it seemed, were sharing their faces with Thai boys. Funny how easy an Adam's Apple is to ignore when everyone else around you is doing the same thing.

As I walked towards my stairway, one of the lads stumbled past, literally and metaphorically being led astray by an aggressive but stunningly beautiful Thai. I stood and watched the Thai step into a rickshaw at the end of the street and drag the young lad in, and I felt like a bystander to a car accident in progress, helpless to stop the inevitable carnage.

Surely girls wouldn't be that aggressive?

When I woke the following morning, the street had reverted to the daily trade of cheap T-shirts, souvenirs and flip-flops. No signs of the tranced-out hippies or stoned teenagers remained and the twenty-four hour commerce resumed the next stage of its daily cycle. I scoffed a banana pancake—something I'd never eaten back in England—and checked my email in an air-conditioned internet café.

There was one message, from my buddy Chris.

12 August, 1:23am.

Got a flight (with a hideous stopover) and all ready to go, save for what is being charged. Flying into Bangkok, arriving 2035 on the 14th. Hurray for 24hr flights!

Brilliant! That'll stop me wallowing about. I replied straight away.

14 August, 7:54am.

Glad you can make it.

I'm staying on the Khao San road, up a little stairway just beyond D & D's—you'll see it. If it all goes wrong and I don't sniff you out before, go there and bang on room 302 until 303 starts shouting (they'll probably be shagging anyway so it shouldn't bother them too much). Then try reception. They are very friendly and helpful.

The day was spent finalising kit lists, packing all the unnecessary stuff away into spare bags. Only the essentials remained: hammock, machete, first aid kit.

Boxers x2.

T-shirt.

Wash kit.
Sleeping bag.
Maps, compass, water filter.
Stove. Jungle boots.
Full-strength mosquito repellent.
Blah.

The essentials, but for this trip they still weighed a tonne.

I dropped the rest of my luggage off at a self-storage facility and got on the airport shuttle bus for the third time in two days to pick up Chris. Almost miraculous that such a sense of foreboding could dissipate so quickly, I thought, but I was getting back into the swing of things. No more fancy hotels, no more lazing by the beach. No more missing lovely girlfriends. No more bloody air-con internet cafés.

It was time to go back to the jungle.

FIVE

Morning Star

"Dude, have you got his number?" Chris squinted in the hot sun, idly swatting flies from his face and neck.

"No mate. It's on the email." I looked about, thinking what to do, and accidentally caught the eye of a man nearby.

"Hello, taxi?"

"No," I replied.

"Human," Chris elaborated, and the man's face switched to confusion.

"Hang on, I'm sure I wrote it down back in Jakarta." I rummaged through my day sack, brought out my notepad and turned to the back page. There it was: our contact's number. "Yup, got it. Now we just need a phone."

"Already there." Chris whipped out a shiny black brick from his pocket. "It's a UK SIM card though, so it'll have to be a text. Can't go spending all my valuable beer tokens on sweet talk with indigenous rebels now can I?"

He passed the phone across to me and I attempted as best I could to write a legible text message in my broken Indonesian: *Saya dan teman sudah datang di Papua. Di mana bisa jumpa dengan anda?*

As far as I was aware, it told him that we had arrived in Papua and asked where we could meet him.

"Mister! You want taxi?"

"Bloody taxi drivers," I said to Chris, turning to the man. "Belum 'pak!" *Not yet.*

A few moments later, Chris's phone buzzed in my hand.

"What's it say?"

I looked at the screen, shielding it against the bright sunlight with my free hand. "It says to take a taxi to Abepura."

"How do we get to Abepura?"

"No idea, mate." I turned to the taxi driver, slightly embarrassed at my outburst a few seconds before. "Permisi 'pak, di mana Abepura?" I said, as politely as possible. *Excuse me, where's Abepura?*

"Ta' jauh. Empat-puluh menit saja."

"Berapa uang dengan taksi?" I asked. *How much is a taxi there?*

"Tiga ratus."

I turned to Chris. "It's forty minutes from here."

"And three hundred thousand rupiah." Chris pulled a face. "I heard. Guess we should try to knock it down."

We attempted to negotiate, but the driver pointed to a price list. Even when we asked several taxi drivers nearby, they all pointed to the same price list and wouldn't budge from the extortionate value written on the wall—nearly double our daily budgets for a single taxi journey.

Eventually one offered us a deal: "Dua ratus lima puluh ribu." *Two hundred and fifty thousand.* We jumped in.

Strange, the only taxis by the airport were four wheel drives, comfortable and air conditioned inside. Not exactly what you'd expect from the least developed province in Indonesia. The doors closed with a satisfying thump; the driver started the engine and it ran smoothly. First time start, no spluttering. It was the kind of car that would look posh in Bristol. Even for elsewhere in Indonesia, this would be very weird.

Out of the tinted windows, we could see the Cyclops Mountains, with one single cloud clinging like a flag to the highest peak. From the road you couldn't tell, but the jungles that covered those mountains were the thick and impenetrable kind of forest that made western New Guinea legendary among explorers. The kind that were the last refuge for uncontacted tribespeople and animal species that you couldn't yet find in any book. A flash of exhilaration darted through me.

We were here.

It had taken months of planning, talking to the right people, weeks of research, and now we were finally in what George Monbiot described as the last place in the tropics: West Papua.

Only, so far, it didn't really feel like it. Down at eye-level, the usual array of motorcycles and *bemo*[*] minibuses cluttered the tarmac and the signs of speedy overdevelopment were everywhere. Buildings, half-completed. Stone mines. Ramshackle huts followed by shiny new shopping plazas full of electronics stores and KFC. A few camouflage uniforms and red and white national flags celebrating the day Indonesia gained its independence from Dutch colonial rule just over sixty years before. It's worth noting that this wasn't the same day Papua cut ties with Amsterdam, but that wasn't a fact the Indonesian government were keen to advertise.

The taxi stopped and we got out, stood by the roadside for a moment, disoriented. At first glance, we could have been anywhere in Indonesia. The farty motorcycles and skinny, trendy pedestrians with their bike helmets in their hands walking past small *warung* eateries. Horns beeped and traffic zoomed; few things suggested that this wasn't just a generic developing-world urban scene. Above us, to the left, was a covered footbridge with red railings. Across the road and to the right, behind the storm culvert and running parallel to the traffic, there was an iron fence, painted white. A smaller road led up through the fence, off the main road, between two ornately decorated posts and a large sign that read, "Selamat Datang di Kampus Universitas Cenderawasih." On top of that sign was a bust of a bird of paradise standing next to a smaller bird. Something about the scene told me I had seen it before.

Wide dual lanes, the elaborate posts, adorned with tribal patterns. A side road, leading through the posts and up to a leafy campus. The birds, staring out over the twin lanes like vultures.

The bridge.

I shut my eyes for a moment and the street became dusty. No, not dusty, smoky. I could see it from a raised perspective, looking down into the leafy campus from the footbridge, looking along the whole street from above. On the tarmac, rocks were strewn everywhere. There were no cars, no honking of horns. Only shouting and the occasional blast of gunfire. It took me a moment, but I knew I recognised the scene—it was from a video, dated 16 March 2006, a little under two and a half years before. I had been shown it by one of the Papuan exiles back in England when I was trying to make contacts to visit the province. He shook his head as we watched.

---

[*] A bemo is a small minibus-style shared taxi that is designed to contain around eight small people, but usually carries twelve.

The video was shot by a cameraman who had been perched under the protective roof of the footbridge, with a bird's eye view of the events unfolding on the road beneath—the road Chris and I were now standing on. Fallen branches covered the wide lanes, and hoards of screaming Papuan students were throwing stones at a line of Indonesian riot police in full protective gear.

I remembered how the video went. First, things were peaceful. Noisy, but peaceful. Then, with the teargas, the shouting grew into a frenzied wailing. Screaming, yelling, mixed with police sirens. The rocks started to come down, falling like hailstones on the heavily outnumbered Indonesian forces. Soon, a tree was felled into the tight block of riot police and they were scattered, their defensive line destroyed. Now they were running towards the footbridge, fleeing back to their vehicles with the screaming Papuans chasing them.

Rocks still rained down and a few of the police stumbled as they tried to escape the protesters' rage. One, I remember, fell against the pavement, just under the footbridge, a metre in front of where we were now standing. In the video, he is kicked down, hit with sticks, then a heavy rock lands between his shoulder blades, laying him flat. He tries to protect himself as a few more rocks hit him, small, thrown from close range by the swarm of rioters that now surrounds his body. He looks to his side and one final rock lands on his head, smashing his skull into the tarmac. The small splatter of blood that had trickled onto his riot shield becomes a large pool under his face, and as the red-smeared Perspex shield is wrenched from under his body, the camera pans up to see another policeman lying flat, dressed in uniform tan and protective clothing, but his helmet has been completely wrenched off.

Through the screaming and noise, a Papuan in an orange shirt stands above the second policeman with a heavy rock raised high; moments later he slams it into the policeman's cranium. The body jerks and the rock smashes on impact, sending a spray of blood over the dusty tarmac, but after that the policeman doesn't move. People trip over him, but he just lies there, flopping about with the impact of legs and feet. Eventually, gunshots ring out and the rioters scatter. And then the video cuts out.

I remembered the statistics; four police were stoned to death and many more injured in the student protests that day. All within metres of where we now stood.

Those riots were retaliation for a history of abuse, torture and maltreatment by security forces—a tit for tat string of violence that made passions on both sides run extremely high. Standing by the road in the hot sun, everything looked normal, but underneath the cloak of regularity simmered a very real, and very brutal conflict.

* * *

After some searching, we ended up in a beautiful Christian-mission style guesthouse set in a quiet garden of fruit trees, which was enough to distract me from the obvious dangers of what we were about to get involved in. The kindly Papuan owner provided us with some tea and we lay on our beds waiting for the next call from our contact.

We heard nothing.

I drifted off and woke a few hours later.

Still nothing.

We decided to walk the streets for a few hours to see if anybody would recognise us, being some of the only white people in the whole region, and perhaps tell us where we should go and who we could talk to. But I was wary; I didn't want to ask the questions, not until we had gauged the situation. Not until we knew who was who. Our presence in Papua was not yet illegal—as soon as we met our contact, however, that would change.

As darkness fell, I became increasingly agitated. Chris checked the phone every thirty seconds, waiting for some response, but nothing came. So, brooding over what to do, we headed to a small *warung** to talk things over, to decide what would happen if we couldn't meet the resistance after all—whether we should stay in Jayapura or go somewhere else. Indeed, whether we should stay in Papua at all. The truth was, our meagre budgets hadn't quite anticipated the inflated prices of the region and here we would pay five times as much for simple commodities as we would back in Java or Sumatra. We needed those people, if only so we could get away from the expenses of living independently as tourists in Papua. How long should we wait?

Our meals arrived and we tucked in silently. My fried rice cost as much as it would in London, only it tasted worse. I ordered the cheaper vegetarian option, but found some gristle in the third

* A *warung* is a small restaurant in the same way that a shack could be described as a house.

mouthful. Pleased with this apparent freebie, I chomped on slightly less miserably.

Suddenly, Chris looked up from his plate of rice as though he'd just found the same thing. He glanced about the dingy restaurant, back towards the door to the kitchen and out to the street where the sky had turned the darkest shade of blue. Then he picked the phone out of his pocket, looked at the screen. Hesitated for a moment, staring at the display, and said, "Dude, we're a go."

I was surprised, almost shocked. "Oh yeah? You got a message? What's it say?" The excitement rose in my voice.

He looked back down again. "It says, 'I am happy you found accommodations, see you tomorrow at 6 morning, outside the front.'" Chris looked up at me and grinned. "That's a bit scary."

I smiled back.

"Mate, it's on."

We woke early the next day, but not quite early enough. As I stumbled out of the *mandi** washroom, I heard a beep from just outside the walls of the garden. *Scratch one for subtlety*, I thought, as we raced downstairs with a selection of biscuits rapidly entering our faces. We bounded across the orchard and ended up by the open gate, panting. A portly Papuan man stepped out of a four-wheel drive with tinted windows and greeted us with a smile.

"Hello!" he said as he shook both our hands, "My name is Kaka." His smile broadened. "Welcome to West Papua, Jimi and Chris. Today we have many things to see," Kaka chuckled. "But first you must tell me what are your plans for your stay, so I can arrange the permits."

He executed a quick nine-point turn in the cramped alley, before veering out onto the main road in front of a dozen small motorbikes, each one with a dozen small people riding them. Once again, it occurred to me that besides the minor details mentioned earlier, we could be any other place in the developing world and I wouldn't be able to tell. In fact, it came to my mind that we could have been drugged, shipped across to Sulawesi in our sleep and been put in similar accommodation to make us think we were still in Papua,

* Literally translating as "to wash", the *mandi* is a bath-like basin from which water is scooped and poured over the users body. Anyone who stands in this basin is a goddamned rookie and therefore punishable under Indonesian law.

perhaps as an elaborate prank by the cheeky locals, and there would have been few things to tell me otherwise. During the drive through town however, I started to pick up more as my eyes became accustomed to the idiosyncrasies of the provincial capital.

Normally, I try to make a conscious habit of *not* noticing race, occupation or gender. Difficult as this may seem, successfully doing so often means I am more likely to learn about who a person is without attaching stereotypes to them. But in Papua, the racial distinctions were impossible to ignore. Partly because they were so obvious, partly because they were the deciding factor for a few other variables.

Papua was a land of two ethnicities. Out of the tinted window, I saw straight haired people with light brown skin. Bike helmets, jeans, mobile phones—not wealth by Western standards, but certainly not living uncomfortably. A few whizzed through the chaotic tangle of vehicles on the Jayapura-Sentani road with shiny motorbikes, many wearing the camouflage green of the Indonesian army. These, clearly, must have been the transmigrant Indonesians.

Then there were the Papuans—curly haired, with darker skin and more pronounced facial features. Around me, there were few Papuans in cars or on bikes; instead, many strolled along the sides of the road in tatty shorts and baggy T-shirts, or sat by the pavement selling betel nut. There they were, the legendary tribal peoples of New Guinea. And the contrast was as clear as day: in Papua, the natives were the lower class, the underdogs in their own land.

I suspected that this realisation was the reason we kept driving up and down the Jayapura-Sentani road, and my suspicions were confirmed when we pulled into a lay-by overlooking the beautiful Lake Sentani, where a pile of smashed Bintang beer bottles sat by the lake's edge.

The engine idling, Kaka turned to us. "You see the way the Papuan is? There are no shoes on his feet. He is poor, but the Indonesian in Papua is rich," he continued, smiling. "This is why you have come I think. To show to the world the injustice of the Indonesian occupation." He looked out of the window, across the lake and chuckled some more. "You tell me what you need and I will help."

The vehicle moved on, and I felt the burden of responsibility settle on our shoulders.

***

Rewind a few hundred years, back to the time when the Dutch had control over most of the islands between Australia and Malaya. Back to the days when western New Guinea was reputed to be an inhospitable and barbaric place, whose cannibalistic inhabitants had helped earn it a fairly low ranking in the 1925 edition of the Amsterdam Post's *Top 100 Relaxing Colonial Retreats*. Fearing disease and much worse, all but a handful of the most courageous and hardy missionaries gave it a wide berth.

And yet, between the thick swampy jungles and freezing mountain passes lived hundreds of isolated tribes, surviving as they had since human history began—in total equilibrium with the environment around them. Among the first wave of human migrants from Africa tens of thousands of years ago, the peoples of western New Guinea had settled in valleys and jungles cut-off from the outside world and each other for millennia. Over two hundred separate languages had developed as each of the clans found their own ways to communicate in the widely varying habitats. And as other humans were learning the art of hurling balls of metal at each other using a mixture of sulphurous charcoal and potassium nitrate, Papuans were still chopping down trees with stone axes and surprising the occasional bird with a frog-poisoned arrow. Call it primitive, but in western New Guinea, people were just one part of the spectacularly diverse natural world.

So, while the rest of the Dutch East Indies were being carved up and pillaged by Europeans, West New Guinea* remained pristine. Wars came and went. Strange things buzzed across the heavens, cross-shaped with big red circles on the tips, and for a while, some light-coloured people ran about along a few sections of the coast, excitedly dropping things on other people and generally making a bit of a racket. Things started landing on them with deafening frequency for a while, before even lighter coloured people turned up briefly and made some more noise. After a while, both groups left, the Dutch returned, and for the most part western New Guinea was unchanged.

Unfortunately, that wasn't the case for rest of the Dutch East Indies. Java and its surrounds had long since been turned into a series of profitable plantations whose endless stream of riches flowed one

* As it was referred to under the Dutch.

way. By 1948, the natives of Java, angry and bored of being pillaged for so long, had fought and won independence for themselves and most of the rest of the archipelago. The Republic of Indonesia was born.

There was however one exception to this colonial liberation: western New Guinea. Recognising the cultural and ethnic differences between the natives of New Guinea and the Indonesians, the Dutch retained control of the territory and began a massive program of training, aimed at creating a free and independent country ruled by the curly-haired tribespeople of Papua.

By the late 1950s, these Papuans were deemed ready for the transition to independence and on 1 December 1961, the red, blue and white Morning Star was raised as the national flag of the soon-to-be nation of West Papua.

But it wasn't soon to be.

Intoxicated by victory over the Dutch and united by a shared oppression, the Republic of Indonesia began harbouring hopes of a greater empire, encompassing all the formerly colonised island nations of South East Asia. Under the militarised government of President Suharto, idealism turned to ruthless realism as the Indonesians realised the potential wealth of actualising their neo-colonialist ambitions. And so, with a little help from a few corporate-sponsored governments, the Dutch were persuaded to cede control of West Papua to the UN, who then allowed the Indonesians responsibility over the region on the basis that they would conduct a referendum in 1969, allowing the Papuans to choose whether they would remain a part of Indonesia or not. When the referendum—the "Act of Free Choice"—was held, 1,054 representatives were chosen to decide the fate of Papua.

Not one voted against Indonesian integration.

Which, to be fair, is more or less what you'd expect when you put a gun to the representative's head and dangled his screaming brother from a helicopter by the feet.

Now fast forward a half-century or so.

Papua had changed into what can only be described as the archetypal Third World cliché. The province now provided more revenue for the Indonesian government than any other, but its native people remained among the poorest in the world. The territory had been colonised by wave upon wave of economic migrants seeking better living conditions and pay, such that only half the population of

Papua in 2008 was indigenous. These natives had since been economically and socially marginalised by the entrepreneurial transmigrants; sacred landmarks were destroyed—whole mountains turned into craters for the sake of gold or copper. Vast rivers were poisoned along with the incredible ecosystems and indigenous inhabitants they once supported, simply because a US-owned mining company needed somewhere to pump its waste.

Papua was the coalface of free-market neoliberalism. The place where addiction to commodity took its toll.

In reaction to this invasion, a small army of tribal warriors armed with arrows and spears had started a rebellion from their base in the remote central highlands, and the free Papua movement, the OPM was born.* From there, the idea of independence gained momentum over the decades, giving rise to a largely pacifist civilian majority by the turn of the millennium. When President Suharto finally ceded power in 1998, ending military dictatorship in the archipelago, the OPM sensed their opportunity and became especially vocal. All across the province, Papuans raised the Morning Star, the banned flag of West Papua*, symbolically declaring independence from the government in Jakarta. But their challenges to the central authority often had bloody outcomes; estimates range from 30,000 to 200,000 Papuans dead as a result of Indonesian military and police action.

Papua was that remote, nobody knew.

In short, what Europeans did to the Indonesians, the Indonesians have done, and were still doing, to the Papuans. To paraphrase the words of Paulo Freire, the oppressed are the greatest oppressors. And if you look at Papua today, you get the colonial history of the rest of the planet in microcosm: one race of humans dominating the other in order to transform the natural world into profit. And that fact alone, more than any other, was why I was there. After Borneo, this was the next piece of the jigsaw puzzle. Seeing it first hand would tell me more about the modern world, the world I was born into, than any textbook or journal could back home.

---

* OPM stands for *Organisasi Papua Merdeka:* Papuan Independence Organisation. Although, it is as much an organisation as a mentality—almost every Papuan who supports independence will claim membership.

* "West Papua", being the name the Dutch would have given the area had it become independent in the sixties, was adopted by the resistance as the name for the province.

* * *

"The Indonesian government is occupying our country illegally. You will help us be free," Kaka chuckled as we drove down the scenic road into Jayapura once again. The bay stretched out in front of us with a multitude of commercial fishing vessels and tankers sprawled across the blue.

"We will both do our best." I tried to look as sincere as I could, but casting my eyes back towards the road, I caught a glimpse of my face in the wing mirror and realised how silly it looked—like a drama student who'd just seen a small child drop his ice cream on the floor. It may have been overacting on my part, but naïve as it would later seem, I still believed I could actually do something to help.

The car drove on, passing through the insipid, soulless streets of Jayapura, which did their utmost to distract from the stunning setting of the bay. Up a hill, I saw a man sprinting in sports kit; short hair, strong physique and a camouflage T-shirt with the word "Kopassus" on the back—the name of the Indonesian Special Forces who had been responsible for some of the most serious Human Rights violations in the province. As we neared the centre of town, we went by the West Irian Liberation Statue, a metallic bust of an Indonesian soldier throwing his chest victoriously in the air as he stood amongst the discarded beer bottles and plastic bags of a small park. Past a mural that portrayed camouflaged paratroopers pointing weapons at naked rejoicing tribals. I couldn't read it, but the title for the painting probably had the word "liberation" in it somewhere.

On a wall nearby, the word "freedom" was spray-painted in large black letters.

By the sides of the roads, we saw the generic Indo-shops, with their dark, musty interiors and dried noodle packets. On the pavement outside were Papuans selling sweet limes and mango. Then, after a few shanty buildings with corrugated roofing, Kaka turned onto a road that we hadn't been down before. "Now I will show you the transmigration camps," he said, rolling the steering wheel.

The drive took an hour and we passed four military bases. The sealed road didn't seem to have a single pothole and we passed over a sturdy-looking bridge into an area of plantations and secondary jungle. A small number of ramshackle wooden houses decomposed in the vicinity of the road; under the ragged tarpaulins we saw their Papuan occupants staring blank-faced as we passed them in dark-tinted luxury. After a while, we entered a suburb with clean, whitewashed houses spaced at regular intervals. It seemed ordered, sterilised.

"This is Arso," Kaka exclaimed, saying no more.

Last I read, Arso was the place the government put the first waves of transmigrants after they were offered their inevitable share of the wealth and prosperity of Papua. Back then, soon after Indonesia's acquisition of Papua, it was a swampland and without effective irrigation or drainage, outbreaks of cholera were as common as bouts of man-flu back home.

It seemed as though the government had managed to get its act together at some point between then and now—the place looked just like an American suburb. By Indonesian standards, that practically made it Beverly Hills. Through the windows of the houses we saw the customers of the electrical shops in town relaxing in front of TVs and nearly every house had a satellite. I was amazed; part of me felt pleased that they had come so far from those horrible early days. But I knew that not a single one of these houses would have ever housed an indigenous Papuan, and Kaka reminded us that the area we were driving through was once the ancestral hunting ground of the people in the mouldy tarpaulin huts back down the road.

This land, the land we were driving through, was their livelihood.

The car drove on, through the suburban order of Arso. "You take photos," Kaka ordered Chris with a genial smile, and Chris accepted the challenge. As he darted about in the back of the truck, snapping away like a member of the cartoon paparazzi, it occurred to me how great he'd been so far on the trip.

I'd first mentioned the prospect of a summer jaunt at a house party organised by my efficient housemate Kate. Fearing that I would be left alone in the jungle and stalked relentlessly by a team of athletic velociraptors over a matter of weeks, I'd suggested he come to Papua too. He said something along the lines of, "Yeah, wicked!" just before I ran upstairs and proposed a similar plan to my girlfriend in a more physical way. She would never have gone to Papua, but made two weeks' acclimatisation holiday in Thailand a reasonable compromise instead.

Chris seemed game that night, but people always do when they are drinking tequila, so I didn't think about again it until I bumped into him a few days later. To my amazement, he could not only remember the plan, but was still interested. Over the weeks I let him know the idea and the risks involved; never once did he voice anything other than absolute optimism. Still, I was certain he would bail on me. Not because he was that kind of guy, but because the plan was ridiculous. What kind of student would want to go halfway across the world to stir up a tribal independence movement in their summer break? It wasn't until I saw him at the airport in Bangkok, strolling through the crowds with his Bergen rucksack and his shiny new jungle boots that I grasped quite how true to his word he'd been. It was my project and the result would be my final-year thesis, but he was quite happy to be strung along for the ride.

That didn't matter now though. What mattered was that we seemed credible to Kaka. That we continued to earn his trust and learn about the politics of Papua and recognise the wider implications of that knowledge. But it was good to have Chris on board.

And so, the first day was spent exploring the area. Seeing what we saw, Kaka had very little input unless he happened to think we hadn't noticed something important. The next day, we travelled to the market in Abepura. Kaka dropped us off at a location nearby and told us to call him when we were done. As we walked through the stands, we saw only Indonesian faces selling a wide array of goods. We asked the proprietors where they were from. Sulawesi, Sumatra, Java, they replied. Flores, even Timor. But never Papua.

On the streets outside the market, the Papuan traders sat on the ground with their betel nut and sweet lime laid out on tarpaulins before them. Papuans traded with Papuans, Indonesians with Indonesians. It was clear who was getting the better deal.

On the third day, I told Kaka that I was ready to start interviewing people.

* * *

Nikson, our Papuan guardian for the last few days, had been telling me about Reggae before his phone went off. Something about a gangly Rastafarian called Lucky Dube. Apparently, his music had inspired the anti-Apartheid uprisings in South Africa, just as Bob Marley had sung about similar themes in a global context from Jamaica. Now he was having a hushed conversation in the adjacent room while I twiddled my thumbs and watched some video of the tribal dances of neighbouring Papua New Guinea—entertaining enough, I'll admit, because the participants were all semi-naked pretty women.

A few minutes later, he came back into the room and sat cross-legged on the couch, a concerned look on his face. "Kaka say you must not walking around town."

Chris was out and I was still waiting for him to return.

"Why?" I asked, aware for the first time that Chris could be in trouble. "What's the problem?"

Nikson shifted uneasily on the seat and adjusted his beanie hat, which was seated on top of his afro like a Papuan version of *Hey Arnold!* "I tell you," he said, walking into the kitchen where he rummaged around, then came back and sat still for a minute, silent. I waited for him to continue.

Kaka had moved us to a new place after the first few days of interviews as a precaution, he said, but he didn't elaborate further. It was not a guesthouse as such, more a safe house. Comfy rooms, unused mattresses, still in their original plastic seal. It had confused me at first, but at least we weren't obliterating our budgets anymore. We'd been ferried around the offices of various Papuan leaders in Jayapura for one more day, while I asked my questions and Chris noted the answers down, but his genial smile seemed less forthcoming. That night, he had dropped us off at the safe house, saying simply "Sampai jumpa".

Until we meet: it was a usual enough phrase in Indonesian, but to me it felt ominous. I had all the research I needed from the area, but we still didn't have the promised permits to travel in the highlands.

Anyway, that was the night before and after a small bout of food poisoning, I had spent the morning in bed recovering while Chris went into town to check on the progress of our *Surat Jalan*—our travel documentation. I hadn't seen him since and it was now dark outside. Save for the traffic and the occasional shouting drunkard—a common sight in Jayapura—I had heard nothing either.

Nikson shuffled some more and finally cleared his throat. "Kaka calling me to say his contact telling him police looking for you. They looking for dua mahasiswa Ingriss." *Two British students.*

I started to feel vulnerable—how did they know we were students?

"Where Chris?"

"I don't know Nikson. He left this morning."

Nikson stared at the ground in front. Then he looked up. "You going meet him?"

"He was going to come back here as soon as he finds out the deal with our permits." Nikson shot me a confused look. "He is coming back here," I said.

Nikson nodded his head in comprehension. Another silence and we both looked at the ground.

"Shit," I said.

Nikson looked up. "How long he gone?"

"Eight hours maybe. Shit, Nikson, he's got the only phone. Can you get Kaka to call him?"

Nikson shook his head. "Kaka already trying. But he being watched. He thinking they listen to his phone."

"Shit," I said again, quieter this time.

We can still blag this, I told myself as I went into the bedroom and rooted around my bag, looking for all the notes. *We can still get away with it.*

We walked outside and Nikson gave me the lighter; I watched the pages of background information and interview transcripts float up into the sky from the small fire. It didn't really matter—I had already made secure electronic copies of most of it. That done, we walked back inside.

"What Chris taking this morning?" Nikson asked me.

"Not much, nothing incriminating. Just our passport photos and some photocopies.

"Incimarating?"

"Yeah, stuff like that." I pointed outside, to the smouldering ash pile. "Illegal stuff. *Merdeka* stuff."

"Oh." Nikson looked a little relieved, but not much. "Good."

I checked through my bag again and through Chris's Bergen. "Nothing incriminating," I said again, to no one in particular.

I remembered one of the interviews; we were with Agus Aluar, the cultural representative of the Tribal People's Assembly, and an Indonesian man burst through the door. He said a few words that I could not understand, apologised, and walked back out, pretending not to notice us. Agus told us it was fine, that we shouldn't worry, but I did. We called the meeting to a close and left, but I suspected that the damage was done. That was two days ago.

"Kaka saying someone seeing you talking political leaders and telling the police," Nikson then told me. I'd guessed that, so I asked what else he heard in his conversation with Kaka. "No more. Just not going to town," he said.

I started lacing up my boots. "Send a message to Kaka. Tell him to call you if he hears anything about Chris. I'll see you later."

Nikson looked as though he was about to start speaking, but the gate creaked outside and something distracted him. We both spun to the sound of heavy booted footsteps marching down the hall.

"Fuck me!" I heard as the front door slammed back against the frame. Heavy breathing. "Fuck. Nikson, I need a beer."

"Where the hell have you been?"

"Don't ask. Just get me a beer."

Nikson came back into the room with three bottles of Bintang in a plastic bag—something we'd put in the fridge earlier to celebrate leaving Jayapura.

"Wait, nobody's following you are they?"

"No. No way. I switched bemos about six times. Even I didn't know where I was. Fuck me." He looked up, "Shit, the notes. Where are they?"

"Gone," I replied.

Chris settled into the sofa. "Good," he said, popping the bottle cap off with his knife.

"So, you gonna tell us what's going on?" I asked.

"Me? Am I gonna tell *you* what's going on? Since when were they searching for us?"

"We've only just got a call. Did Kaka send anything to you?"

"No! Nothing. My phone has been dead all afternoon. I found out from the police that they were searching for us. Well, two British guys at least. Fuck."

"What happened?"

Chris poured his beer into his mouth. Nikson and I did the same. "I went to the police station to get our travel permits sorted and they took me into this room and started asking questions."

"So?"

"Well, they wanted to know where I was from, if I was travelling with anyone, what I was doing, whether I was here for political purposes, if I knew that was illegal."

"And?" Nikson and I looked at each other, then back at Chris.

"I told them I was travelling alone. That I was here to work with a Dutch charity in Cendarwasi."

"Did they believe you?"

"About six hours later, yeah." He took another gulp and burped into his hand. "I think they were waiting for you to turn up. When you didn't they just let me go."

"Unbelievable."

"Yeah, thanks for doing that mate."

"Anytime."

"So," Chris said. "Where do we go from here?"

Nikson picked up his mobile. "You must go I think so. Tonight I get you a flights, then you go Wamena. They still thinking you here, so not looking for you there." He walked out of the room and we heard his steps crunching off as he closed the gate.

"Thanks for inviting me on this trip dude," Chris said, and I started to laugh. We sat there for a while, laughing, taking swigs of beer. An hour later, Nikson returned, and handed us each an airline ticket and placed some food on the table in front of the couch. We looked at the ticket and on the ticket it said, "Wamena."

The birthplace of the OPM.

SIX

Welcome to West Papua

Kaka arrived at the house early in the morning and wished us the best in our journey. He handed me a short list of contacts, first names only with the places to ask where to find them, and two letters written in Indonesian with the words "Surat Jalan" on the top—our permits. Shaking us by the hand, he bade us farewell and drove off just as the sun reached the tip of the Cyclops Mountains through the dawn-blue sky. Nikson revved the engine of a truck nearby; we jumped into the back of it and sat on our bags. The wind blew through our hair, cool and refreshing, on the dark empty road to the airport in Sentani.

After saying our farewells to Nikson, we checked in, walked through the dingy departure room, out onto the tarmac and up the stairs into the plane. The passengers were almost entirely Indonesian and nobody batted an eyelid as we took our seats next to the windows at the rear. But I was still on edge, even though Nikson didn't think anyone would contact the police in Wamena for a few days at least.

Engines on, and the static momentum pulled me back into my chair as we lifted off the runway. As the aircraft banked, I saw Arso and the transmigration districts with their straight roads cutting slices through the shadowy jungle, contrasting against the worm-like wiggle of brown rivers near the settlements. Moments later, all I saw was green until the clouds engulfed the aircraft. Every now and then, the mist would part to reveal a jungle that no human had ever explored, an inhospitable swampland between the Jayawijaya and the Van Rees ranges, a lost world full of pterodactyls and other crazy beasts, I imagined. And then the cloud would thicken and the view would disappear.

When it parted again, the aircraft was low enough to see pigs grazing amongst small thatched huts and little plots separated by wood-weave fences. Hectares of agricultural land spread away from the huts, with even rows of small leafy plants poking their heads through the soil. Further out, forest-cloaked mountains marked the jagged edge of the Baliem Valley. The wings wobbled with uncertainty as we touched down and a few moments later, we were in Wamena.

* * *

The first thing I noticed was that the air was cool; it had a distinctly British flavour to it and the ground was damp with drizzle. Only the banana plants gave it away as tropical. Exiting the airfield, we walked onto a road covered in cycle-rickshaws with bored-looking Papuans sitting on them. An old guy, naked except for a penis gourd, came up to us and asked if we wanted a bracelet for a few thousand rupiah. The next road along, another frail-looking tribesman walked past us, carrying a plastic bag with some vegetables in it. On the corner was the police station, but it had a queue of Papuans a hundred metres long at the entrance, so we easily avoided it.

We walked for half an hour, looking for a cheap place to stay. Eventually we found one in our price range, bartered down to 100,000 rupiah—roughly six pounds, over double the price of a decent room in Jakarta. The room was grim, windowless and with mould-stains on what may have once been white walls. They were now a kind of giardia-green and the beds looked as enticing as Slough. We made a decision to spend as little time in the place as possible.

Wamena itself was small and unremarkable; characterless houses and concrete buildings lined the wide roads—once again, generic shops selling the usual mix of packet noodles and rice, with a few empty tourist hostels and eateries. I found it strange how such a fascinating place as Papua had managed to spawn possibly the most soulless settlements I had ever come across. As with Jayapura, the streets seemed designed to sidetrack the oblivious visitor from the surrounding natural beauty. On this day, however, the weather wasn't doing the place any favours and the mountains could have been in Northern Ireland. Feeling the chill, we strolled for half an hour more in our fleeces, looking in shops and scouting eateries.

It was quiet; most people were clearly elsewhere and only a faint giggling sound seemed to be audible. With nothing of interest nearby, save for a large cow, we headed out of town and down a small dirt path lined with the wicker fences we had seen from the air. Fat, hairy domesticated pigs chomped away inside pens, near small thatched-grass huts that barely reached head height—for us, at least. We reached the end of the path, where a few trees met the Baliem River.

Here we were, surrounded by the last significant human civilisation to be discovered by the outside world and I couldn't shake the feeling of being back in the UK.

I looked about, trying to find something unfamiliar. Upstream, the tree line parted to show a craggy mountainside, cloaked in a thick grey layer of cloud. In the foreground, a hundred or so metres away, a single boatman paddled from the far side of the Baliem in a dugout canoe, his reflection perfectly visible in the calm surface of the water. There was a smell of pine mingling with the dusty whiff of compacted dirt, reminding me of English summertime forest walks, but what I noticed more was that the faint giggling noise had been increasing in volume since we stopped moving.

It didn't take long for the source to emerge.

Egged on by each other, small children crept out from behind the bushes and trees where they had been stalking us and within minutes we were surrounded by dozens of staring, giggling Papuan kids. After a few more minutes, they plucked up the courage and said, "Foto?"

As usual, Chris obliged. The older, more mature kids puffed out their chests in pride while the younger ones tried in vain to contain their excitement. The giggling continued in such a way that it could be likened to a relay—when one child stopped, another took over. Thus, they managed to maintain a continuous chuckle for hours, it seemed, until Chris showed the photo on the glowing display of his camera.

The children gathered around him, silent—for the first time ever probably—mouths open. An expression of wonder filled their eyes. But the effect was not long-lived; seconds later, the giggling erupted with a new ferocity.

It was done. We were now friends for life.

With our new status they grabbed our hands and led us to a game of volleyball in a grass field further back along the path. A net had been strung up between two branches dug into the ground and Chris decided to take a picture of it. I broke myself free from the youngsters, leaving Chris to fend for himself as a group of Papuan girls tried to pose for his camera. Just before I turned away, I could see the fear in his eyes as they swarmed in to see their image on the digital display.

Walking to a group of young lads, all Papuan, I introduced myself and they responded in Indonesian, smiling warmly. We chatted and they asked if I was a tourist. I told them that I was here for a friend.

"Who?" they asked. I mentioned the nickname of my contact. They turned and spoke amongst themselves for a few seconds, too fast for me to understand. Then they faced me again. "Welcome to West Papua," they said in turn, shaking my hand.

* * *

The sky had cleared and Wamena was a hot, dusty place as we walked with our rucksacks through the vegetable markets to the bustling taxi station, where we caught a shared lift in a *bemo* that was just leaving. Our bags were hoisted onto the roof and tied in place while Chris and I tried to squeeze our overly nourished bodies into the womb-sized passenger compartment.

The small van bounced its way along the dirt path, past local women with net bags packed with sweet potato hanging from their foreheads, and with eight of us cramped in the back I started to feel like a piece from a Boggle set each time we went over a pothole. It became quite a sociable event—I landed on my fellow passengers, as they landed on me. The thought did occur that this would have been even more enjoyable if the commuters happened to be Swedish lingerie models and the dust and flies were replaced by blackcurrant jelly, but as the wrinkled bottom of a nude tribal elder landed firmly in my lap, squashing an orange beetle, alas, I realised this was not the case.

Eventually, the vehicle halted and all the sardines crawled from the back; apparently it was the final stop. Chris and I stretched our aching bodies, removed the straps holding our bags to the roof of the vehicle, hoisted the rucksacks down and stood by the side of the road waiting for something to happen. The *bemo* picked up a few more passengers and turned around, and before we had even lost sight of the vehicle bounding along the road back towards Wamena, everybody had disappeared. All those people who had shared my lap, gone without even a word of goodbye.

I felt used.

We shouldered our rucksacks and looked about. Tall grasslands, sweet potato fields and forest enclosures stretched to the edges of the valley and a wide, shallow river flowed past us—presumably the direction our cramped compadres had taken.

Thinking logically, we decided that the river would be the best way to find somewhere to spend the night in the forests by the valley's edge. The drag against each step was insignificant and it was easy to find a stable foothold. In the open and free at last, we were beginning to enjoy ourselves. And with Chris splashing alongside, it felt like we were explorers trekking into the great unknown.

Gradually, the flow became stronger as the stream narrowed, but still we saw no sign of settlement. Either side of us, the forest thickened to impenetrable, so we continued splashing as the water reached our knees.

After some time, we stumbled across a few items of ragged clothing lying on rocks, tough and sun-dried. Spotting a small path leading from the water's edge, we walked to it and brushed through thick foliage and the webs of tiny, colourful, crab-like spiders until the trail widened into a clearing. Scorch marks on the ground implied a recent human presence and the leaves were cleared and compacted but too dry to hold any footprints. We stood still for a moment, looked ahead to see which way the path would lead. Shifting the dirt of the clearing with my feet, I turned to Chris. "Where the hell are these people?"

"Don't know dude. But they must be close," he replied, sniffing the air for effect.

The sound of a twig cracking nearby made me swing back towards the entrance of the clearing where six children stood, staring silently at us. Two of them were completely naked, the others wore either shorts or T-shirts. I smiled, but they looked away, shy.

Remembering the kids back in Wamena, I took my camera out and snapped a photo, knelt down and flashed the display in their direction. Slowly, they came forward and when they saw the screen, they started to smile. Minutes later, they were giggling and running around in child-sized circles.

We continued walking until we left the forest altogether and stepped out onto the bottom of a steep grass hill. While we climbed the slope, the two naked kids ran ahead to beat each other up in a small patch of long grass. The others joined in, and we passed them all at the halfway mark.

It was mid-afternoon by the time we reached the crest of the hill and the view across the valley was clear and bright. Not only that, but it was stunning.

Chris and I set our bags down and gazed out at the savannah-like landscape, interspersed with clusters of small thatched huts, sweet potato fields and trees. Wisps of smoke rose here and there, right up to the mountainous distance. The breeze shifted and blew cool against the sweat on our backs, so we sat for a while, letting our bodies dry. After a few minutes the kids lost interest in the fight and ran back down the hill into the forest, leaving us to observe the area in peace.

No concrete, no power lines, nothing. Just people living in agricultural harmony, as they had for millennia. I couldn't help but think how incredible it must have been to stumble across a civilisation as sizeable as this living totally independent of the outside world as Richard Archibald did when flying over the New Guinea highlands back in 1938. The remoteness of the valley kept it almost completely unexplored until the fifties, and even today the influence of the outside world remained insignificant away from Wamena—superficially, at least. So, stretching out before us was a landscape that probably hadn't changed much in ten thousand years. Which was as good an excuse as any for a biscuit.

"Pretty nice isn't it?" I said to Chris.

"Beats Wiltshire," Chris mumbled, in between bites of his digestive.

In the golden light, I sat back and absorbed the scene. Grass swaying, the breeze and its gentle *swoosh-swish*, the smell of the clean mountain air; it was truly idyllic. This, I thought, is what my personal heaven would look like. Then a fly flew straight into my ear canal, breaking the peace.

"We better get moving mate," I said to Chris, and picked up my rucksack. "We'll need to find a campsite before dark."

We walked down the hill, back into the forest, taking a smaller track to find an area to string our hammocks. We soon came across a suitable location—a group of trees far enough from the path to be discrete, but not so far that we would be disoriented in the morning—and set about clearing the ground with our machetes.

In the warmth of the early evening air and with dappled sunlight painting golden blobs on my skin, I hacked away at the foliage and vines near my selected hammock site until a safe area, free from the perils of unseen creepy-crawlies, emerged in the forest. By the time the light had dimmed through the thin canopy we had made the beginnings of a fireplace and had collected a few bits of kindling, but not much more.

As Chris prepared the pots for our noodles, I inspected the camp. Wandered about, kicked a few leaves out of the way. Other useful things like that. Then, looking further into the forest around us, I noticed a lady walking along the path from which we had separated, apparently completely oblivious to our presence nearby. I watched her stroll along for a moment and saw that we had picked our site well, for we did not want any unnecessary attention.

"Shit!" Chris shouted, just as there was a loud clash of pots behind me. The lady stopped, spun to look our way. An expression of complete surprise washed over her features—I didn't blame her, I doubt many Papuans that day thought they'd find something so handsome and talented pottering about in *their* backyard.

But we had been compromised.

With no way to hide, I smiled, waved and walked towards her. She smiled back and I saw that she was with a young boy, maybe five years old. As I neared, she hobbled about, hopping on her right foot. I shook her hand and greeted her in the local Dani language with the only phrase I knew. Luckily, she did not seem to take offence to our presence in the forest.

Glancing down, I saw that she had an infection on the big toe of her left foot, so I told her to wait, speaking in mumbled Indonesian, then dashed to the rucksack that was karabinered to the underside of my hammock and retrieved the first aid kit. Jogging back to the lady, I asked if I could help her.

She nodded and sat down.

Carefully, I washed the pus and dirt away from the lady's toenail as best I could, soaking the infection for a few minutes while the kid crashed around in the trees behind. Chris came across to lend a hand for a while, then returned to tend to the fire, leaving me a selection of useful gauzes and sterile swabs. With those, I finished off the treatment by putting some antibiotic cream on the wound and wrapping it all with a small bandage to keep more dirt out. I had no idea if the treatment would do any good without a decent course of antibiotics, but I really hoped so.

When I was done, the lady thanked me with a broad smile and a shy bow of her head, and walked on with the kid in tow, back along the forest path. I turned around to see Chris sitting next to a roaring fire.

"While you were saving the world one toenail at a time, that little kid got all this deadwood. Check this out!" He pointed to a large pile of logs, dry and brittle, that reached my thighs. "Not bad for a little nipper."

"Not bad at all," I agreed, helping myself to a bowl of Maggi Noodles mixed with tinned sardines. The taste was not quite Jamie Oliver standard, but it was a lot better than the food we had in Jayapura.

By the time we were finished eating, the only light source was the fire, which turned the leaves and trees a flickering orange around the shadow outline of our backs. Being male, Chris and I became fixated on the flames and had set about making them blaze as hot and tall as possible. Which was always great fun, while it lasted. Within the hour, however, the roaring flames had engulfed the last of the boy's deadwood. We settled back down and watched, helpless, as the fire relaxed into the gentle glow of red embers, turning the edges of the clearing back to the colour of shadows.

With no more flames to singe away the hairs on our face, I noticed that the air had cooled considerably, so I shuffled my way back to my rucksack for an extra layer. As I did, something moved a few metres from the clearing, a dark shape shifting in front of something even darker. The flames had taken my night vision and I stared into the blackness, waiting for confirmation that I wasn't just imagining it. Nothing more appeared so I put my coat on and returned to the embers.

When I sat down, Chris looked on edge.

"Don't think we're alone here dude," he said. "It's just a hunch, but something tells me we are about to be attacked by an army of midgets."

"Agreed," I said, wishing that my eyes were better at coping with the dark. We gawped at the foliage around us, knowing that if we did this long enough, even a small shrub would become a child or a monster or both. Still, I stared into the blackness, looking for shapes, searching for another movement. I focused on one dark area that hovered about five metres from where we were sitting. It appeared to be completely still and for a moment, I couldn't quite tell if it was a shadow at all. Then it climbed up a tree and smashed down a branch with a machete.

This, we both agreed, suggested it wasn't just a bush.

The deadwood landed with a thump next to my hammock and the shadow jumped down next to it. It appeared to be wearing shorts and a T-shirt, the shadow dragging this log, and when the wood was deposited into the middle of the clearing, I noticed that the machete in his hand belonged to Chris. Not one to rock the boat, observationally speaking, I said, "Chris, I think that is your machete."

Chris, not wishing to be the argumentative type that evening, said, "Yes, I think it is."

Another thump.

A naked child sprinted through the clearing and disappeared. We spun, looking behind us, to see a guy wearing jeans and a T-shirt, carrying another huge machete in his hands. I took a photo of him, hoping that it would break the ice as it did earlier on, but his expression did not change.

Chris and I quickly stood up as one more kid leapt into the clearing and began puffing long breaths of life towards the glowing embers of our failed fire. Within seconds, the logs were ablaze.

In the light it became clear that there were at least six kids and this one adult, standing menacingly with his large knife, darting around our campsite, picking up more deadwood. The kids had started to enjoy themselves; the crashing thump of brittle logs landing on foliage all over the place paid testament to this.

The older guy picked up a branch, dragged it into the flames and sat down. Still marginally bewildered, I took a seat opposite him. Initially, nobody said anything and I just watched, helpless, as the scene unfolded, but after a few minutes the fire looked like it was taking shape. I noticed that this time it was being arranged so that rather than being piled up into a pyramid as Chris and I had done, the logs were placed flat on the ground in a kind of cross. The tips of each log only met in the middle, where there was enough kindling to keep the wood burning. When the flame died out momentarily, the kids pushed the tips of the logs back into the middle and the concentration of heat would reignite the embers. It struck me as obvious but also ingenious—such an easy way of regulating a fire and maintaining fuel.

With the intentions of our guests seemingly friendly, Chris picked up the cooking pot with the leftovers of our meal inside and passed it to the guy with the machete, who thanked us with a nod of the head. Within seconds, the kids had surrounded him and were grabbing at the pot.

A commanding but gentle voice broke up the noodle-based carnage. I turned to see an older man and his wife walk into the clearing. He took the pot from the kids and returned it to Chris as his wife hobbled up, smiled and sat down with her bandaged toe tucked under her leg.

"Shall we?" Chris looked at me, holding the pot.

"Yeah, sure."

We boiled up some more noodles and the whole gathering clustered around the fire. I started to chat to them in a mixture of Indonesian and charades.

It emerged that the two men, father and son, had fled with the rest of their extended family to this remote patch of forest to escape the atrocities committed by both Papuans and Indonesians during the independence demonstrations of 2000. Surviving on sweet potatoes and whatever could be traded with those around them, they were part of a much larger community of refugees that nestled itself in the surrounding hillsides further upstream. Taking the opportunity to ask them how they saw the Indonesian presence, they told me that they had joined the OPM in order to free West Papua many years ago and were still waiting for independence to come. When they explained this, the younger guy pulled out a slingshot from his jeans and used a machete to make a quick arrow from a sapling. He stretched the slingshot back and fired the arrow at a tree nearby; it shattered on impact.

"Polisi Indonesia," he laughed, miming the arrow hitting a human target.

The noodles had cooked so Chris drained the water into the ground and passed the pot out to the family. Log tips were once again pushed into the centre of the embers and a flame appeared within a few seconds.

The family left us with one last gift: a small hut made from bent saplings woven with ivy. It took the kids minutes to erect but seemed just as effective a shelter as our hammocks, save for the occasional bug. They all walked back down the path, smiling warmly and shaking our hands gently as they passed, and we were once again alone in the forest. With the fire sorted and nothing better to occupy our time, we took turns sitting in the hut while the other tended the logs.

As we watched the coals glow red, absorbed, it occurred to me that we had just had our first encounter with people who had been actively involved in the resistance against Indonesia.

I knew it wasn't going to be the last.

***

The night was a cold one and I was restless in my hammock. The sleeping bag I had was more than adequate for the temperature, but where it was compressed underneath me, the insulation was ineffective. A gentle breeze blew and left me cold on whichever side I chose to lie. I woke early, looked at my watch: 4:52 a.m. I remember this because I wrote it down in my journal later that day.

Groaning, I swung my legs out of the hammock and climbed onto my feet. The clearing was still dark, but I could make out around twenty people standing, silently, staring at our camp. Women, children, men.

"Uh, Chris?"

Groan.

"Chris, mate, wake up."

Snort.

"Chris, you dick, wake up!"

Chris groaned a bit more, rolled around, making the whole hammock ensemble swing slightly, then let out a huge fart. A few moments passed.

"CHRIS!" I shouted.

"Wha-" he paused, "Oh for fuck's sake. Tell them to go away."

"Go away," I told the audience, then turned back to Chris. "They won't go away."

I did a small dance, more for my own amusement than anything else, and still there was no reaction.

"Mate, get up. This is getting weird."

Chris rolled out of his hammock; in his daze he seemed almost oblivious to the crowd. We both broke camp in silence, bagged up our hammocks, repacked our rucksacks and walked through the forest and away from the strange gathering.

Turns out, I had underestimated Chris again; little did I know that he had a plan for the stragglers who followed us back to the river. Judging from the surprise on their faces, they did not know this either until Chris jumped into the water stark naked.

"Bit nippy this morning isn't it?" he said as he splashed himself down. The kids laughed as though they understood the joke.

After drying and munching on the now-traditional morning biscuit, we set off north to where I had been led to believe that the heart of the resistance movement in the area was. We walked for a few miles, until the late morning heat got the better of us.

"Dude, do you have any idea where we are going?" Chris turned to me, glistening with sweat.

"Well, yeah," I responded, as a fly tried to make friends with my eyelashes. "They should be around here somewhere."

"You think if we keep walking we'll just stumble into them?"

"Something like that," I shrugged.

A couple of pigs strolled casually by.

To be honest, I half expected a naked guy with a spear to leap out of a hedge, thank me for rescuing Papua and present me with a chicken called Audrey. Given last night's events, it didn't seem out of the question.

Then I thought twice.

"I suppose it wouldn't hurt to ask someone."

Chris scratched for a while, indicating tacit agreement, and we walked on for a few hundred yards more until we saw a wooden sign with the words "Aba Netaiken Foreign Language Academy" on it. Just under the sign was a small kiosk selling orange juice.

"I think we should ask someone here."

"I think so too."

Chris stepped up the bank to the kiosk and looked back. "I think we should also ask someone here for an orange juice as well."

"I think so too."

Chris looked up to the girl staffing the kiosk. "Can I have six cartons of orange juice ple-"

"Make it seven," I interjected.

"Good idea. Store one for later." He turned to the girl. "*Seven* cartons of orange juice please."

The girl looked bewildered, so Chris picked up a carton. "Seven please. Um, bisa tujuh?"

"We only have four," she said in English, with a sympathetic expression on her face as she looked down at my glistening rosy features.

I nodded.

Chris handed the money across and threw two cartons my way. It was a kind of concentrate squash mixture, excessively sweet and more sherbet than orange but still incredibly refreshing. By the time the girl had counted the cash, the second carton slurped empty. I peered up, eyes narrowed in the sun, and cleared my throat. "We are British students and we want to learn about the situation in Papua," I said, with an unintentional colonial twang in my voice. "Is there anyone we might talk to?"

"Wait a moment," she replied.

The girl trotted up the side of a grass bank towards a large whitewashed wooden building that reminded me of the church back in Long Layu. I pondered this, trying to find some sort of meaning in the coincidence, as the girl jogged back down the hill with an older man in tow.

"Please, bring your bags, you may stay," the man waved, beaming a warm Papuan smile at us. "My name is Paul, I am the headmaster of the school. You will learn a lot about Papua here."

SEVEN

Audrey

Chris jogged back to me, breathless.

"Bloody amazing place isn't it?" he panted.

"Yup, it really is." I passed the water filter across to the two Papuan students I had been demonstrating it to and they started pumping water from a bucket. As the first squirt landed on a patch of grass nearby, they chuckled, pumped more into their hands and slurped experimentally. A ball bounced past us and another student, wearing only one football boot, kicked it back into the centre of the field where it was headed into a goal post to the sound of a two-tone cheer. The students passed the filter back to me, their curiosity satisfied, so I put it back in its little bag and glanced up once more.

From where I was sitting, it was possible to see almost all of the northern Baliem, with the smoke from evening fires drifting towards the sky. Along the far side of the valley, a dark grey cloud dragged a reluctant white curtain of rain over the unlucky easterners.

We had whiled away a few days inadvertently falling into their simple routine. The afternoons were spent chatting to the students on the grass lawns, strumming away at the guitar in between their classes, and in the evenings, we ate a simple dinner of rice and vegetables with them and listened to their hymns, sung in melodic harmonies. In the first few days, politics rarely entered conversations. Initially, I held back on the subject for fear of putting words into the students' mouths. But after a while, I started to forget all about the study. Instead, we both just absorbed the cleansing, almost monastic lifestyle of the place. Until one night, a few days after our arrival, I was reminded why I came.

I was lying in my bed, listening to the faint sounds of drums and singing as they drifted up from the valley below. My window shutters were open and I tried to see where the noise was coming from but with no electricity in the valley, the view was almost completely black—a shadowy silhouette of mountains and stars. Besides the whistling cicadas and the occasional rumble of equatorial thunder, there were few other noises to distract from the muffled musical tones.

In the darkness, I imagined the scene: elaborately dressed tribal figures dancing around a roaring fire, radiating shadows into the straw walls around them, an animal slowly turning to crisp in the flames. I held this thought for a while, picturing the feathered hats jumping in time with the drumbeat. The merriment. Dancing and feasting—not a bad way to spend an evening.

The distance muffled it slightly but the bang was loud, much louder than the singing and drums, which had now stopped. A few voices carried across, high pitched but too indistinct to make out even the mood of the interactions. I strained my ears for a while, but heard nothing else.

Eventually, I fell asleep.

Everything carried on as usual the following day, but the noise had stayed in my head as a short soundbite on repeat, struggling to stay fresh, free from confabulation. Sitting on our porch that afternoon, I mentioned it to Chris.

"Didn't hear anything dude. Maybe it was just your imagination," he replied as he flicked some grass at a passing butterfly.

"You're right, it was probably nothing. It did sound strange though. I can't think of anything around here that would create a noise that loud. Sounded like an explosion or something."

"I doubt it."

That was a day ago, and now I was sitting on the edge of the football field, having largely forgotten the blast. One of the students walked over to us. "There is a man in the village, he wants to meet you."

We walked over the lawn and back down to the road where an old man stood waiting, with his arms crossed behind his back. He smiled meekly and offered his wrinkled hand in a long gentle handshake, gesturing for us to follow him around the campus. Together we walked along the picturesque embankment to a cluster of huts just behind the football field.

The old man talked quietly to the student, pointed, drew lines on the ground around us with his hands. Folded his arms behind his back again and looked at us. The young student hesitated, choosing the right words, then translated. "There was a big gun here. The Indonesian army used it to shoot the villagers all around when they were farming. They killed thousands of Papuans from this place during the war."

The war? What war?

When did this happen, I asked. "Kapan itu terjadi?"

"Thirty years before. When Indonesia first arrive in the Baliem," the student returned the translation.

The old guy talked again, pointing to a wooden shed nearby, tilted, decaying. "When the soldiers staying here, they took local women from the village for sex, they kept them in this shed for many months each," the student explained. "One woman escaped, she was raped each day and now very old. She have many health problems. She is still alive but not here anymore."

"Where is she?" I asked.

"Tak tahu," the old guy replied—*I don't know.*

"How long was she kept here?" I asked.

"Mungkin dua bulan." *Two months*, he said. His short body was well postured, upright in his tatty clothes. Arms folded. Feet bare.

"And the gun?"

"Dua tahun." *Two years.*

He looked at the student, asked a few questions, listened. Then he spoke again, longer, and I made out the word *seratus*. When he was finished, the student turned to us. "He say there is a hill on the other side of the school, I think it is near your rooms. He says it is a mass grave for tribal leaders. He says one hundred dead there, in that mound. He wants to tell you this because his son was taken by the police two nights before. They say he is OPM, but he done nothing wrong."

"What will happen to his son?" I asked the student.

"They interrogate him and maybe tomorrow he will be released," came the reply.

"How do they interrogate people?" I asked.

"Sometimes they use sticks, or maybe a bucket of water or something. But some have been beaten to death, so the people are worried. He is a student here, he was visiting home nearby."

The old man nodded, smiled at the student, shook our hands gently and walked back down to the village. From where we stood, we could see the shadows stretching across the beautiful valley, but now it looked to me like the view from a perfect firing position.

I thought back to when I was researching the trip; I had read that the Indonesian army had used Papua as a punishment posting for soldiers who had a tendency to be disobedient or who had committed offences in different areas. Because it was so far from families and home comforts, it was considered one of the worst places to be sent in the archipelago. Perhaps it was also thought likely that somewhere so remote, these soldiers wouldn't get into any trouble. At least, any trouble that would have repercussions.

Walking back to our room, the student warned us, "Sometimes, the people makes it sound worse."

"Oh. So was he lying?" Chris asked.

"No, what he say is true. But when you are speaking to other people… Just be careful."

The student wished us farewell and we strolled across the campus back to the guest accommodation.

I'd strung my hammock up between a few trees as a place to relax in between the daily activities and the strings creaked when I put my weight on it. Chris took a seat on the porch.

"My stomach is rumbling. It must be noodle o'clock," Chris said.

"I think it's worth writing all this down before I forget," I replied, pulling my waterproof notepad from my pocket. "We can always go to dinner later."

"Go ahead dude, I'll put some on the stove anyway while you're doing your writing thing. Do you think you'll forget?"

"No, but if I pass this on, I want the details to be correct. Don't want to twist his words or anything."

"Sure." Chris lit his stove and poured some water into the pot on top. When I finished jotting down the conversation, the water was boiled and Chris asked me, "Do you reckon he was telling the truth?"

I paused, thinking. "Yes. I am pretty sure he was."

"Maybe you weren't imagining the sound after all then."

"Probably was."

"Yeah, you probably were. I was just trying to make you feel better." Chris looked over his shoulder, through the gap between our rooms. "There's a mound, just over there. Do you think that's the one he was talking about?"

I stood up and walked around the buildings. Sure enough, there was bump in the ground. Not high, but noticeable because of the depression around it. More of a linear bank really, covered in the same lawn as the rest of the campus. "Well, that's the only mound I can see."

"Big enough for a mass grave?" Chris asked, pouring a pack of noodles into the steam.

"No idea." I grabbed a fleece from my room, then sat back on my hammock. "Can't say I've seen many of those before. It could be I suppose. But a hundred bodies?"

"He seemed genuine," Chris said, spooning some noodles into my bowl.

"Yeah, he did…I think we should find out more about this."

"Time to put the word out?"

"I think so."

* * *

The next day, I met one of my contacts: a village elder, who greeted us as we finished our early breakfast on the porch. He shook our arms in the traditional way—holding the elbow—and spoke in the local Dani language.

A younger man accompanied him, presumably the designated translator, and introduced himself as Kelly. The elder motioned for us to follow him and we did, stomping behind in comparison to his soft plodding steps. We followed the road north for a while and eventually peeled off onto a narrow dirt path. It seemed like hours passed as the sun got higher in the sky and hotter on our necks, but the air was still cool. We hopped over the irrigation channels between sweet potato fields and followed the old villager's bare footprints along the dusty path until we reached a wicker fence with a wooden sty marking the edge of a small village.

As I climbed over the logs I noticed about thirty men standing to attention, spears by their sides. We neared the group and one stepped out of rank, turned to the men and shouted a command. They responded with a salute.

Then he gestured for us to come over as the men dispersed onto wooden benches in a semicircle around us, laying their spears on the ground or resting them against the huts. Chris, Kelly, the chief and I exchanged greetings with the group and sat down, facing them.

The man who shouted the orders introduced himself as the OPM commander of the region. He had bloodshot eyes and dark features, this commander, and he was wearing a jungle hat and a T-shirt with the words "Army Look Style" on a small faux-military logo above camouflaged print that read "AIR FORCE MILITARY AND CIVILIAN CREW". The absurdity did not escape me that we were meeting one of the highest ranking rebel commanders in Papua and he was wearing a top that was probably designed for a ten-year old boy's pyjama collection. The rest of the group wore traditional New Guinean feathered hats on their heads and shorts and T-shirts, some camouflage patterned, on their bodies. To one side a cluster of women and children was seated, looking wide-eyed at our sweaty white faces.

The leader spoke and Kelly translated.

"We are all members of the TPN—the liberation army of West Papua. We are the military wing of the OPM. You are here to find out about the war and we will tell you."

I took out my notepad, ready to start writing.

Then the leader told me the story of the armed resistance. He told me about the waves of transmigrants stealing the Papuan's land and the way they treated the Papuans like monkeys; he told me how Papuan resources were stolen without any recompense, how swathes of ancestral territories were turned upside down and smelted into profit for outsiders. The leader told me that the Papuan people were angry and that they killed four of the Indonesian police right here in the Baliem and started a war. He told me how the Indonesians responded with machine guns and aircraft and troops, how they killed thousands of Papuans. He gave me names and dates and figures and I wrote them all down on my scrappy notepad. Then he told me about the people around me, how all the TPN guerrillas in this detachment were orphans from the war. He told me about another massacre in the Baliem near a village called Kimbim. The day of the massacre, only one survived, he said—an old tribal chief who feigned death until he was able to crawl out of the pile of bodies at night.

Another man started to speak and slowly the translation filtered back to me. His father, he said, was killed on that hill overlooking Kimbim. He told me that many of the elders in the area were brought to that place, where they were lined up on the edge of a pit by the Indonesian military and shot. His mother, he said, went to pick up her husband's body the next day, but she too disappeared.

The leader started to speak again, telling me how it was still going on. Papuan people were still being tortured, shot to death at rallies, beaten and tear-gassed. Unlawfully detained. And now they needed outside help—guns, training, NATO. He told me how only this could change the fate of Papuans. Only this would force the Indonesians out.

And only that could save Papua from ruin.

I then raised my voice to meet all of them. I told them that I hoped there was something I could do; that I would try to help the Papuan people. Speaking in my poor Indonesian, I told them that I would tell their story. I told them I would do my best to let the world know the injustices they faced and they started to clap and smile and stand up to shake our hands. One of the more frail looking elders walked towards us with two plastic bags in his hands. I noticed that one was moving. He passed them to Chris and I, and I thanked him.

After a few minutes, Kelly turned to us with a concerned expression and told us we should leave. I passed the message on to Chris, who was being hugged by a crying naked lady.

"Well, he knows best," Chris responded.

We were walking back through the sweet potato fields past little clumps of thatched huts, when I sneaked a look at the contents of my plastic bag. Inside it were some of the choicest cuts of pork; all meat, no fat, and still warm. Peering ahead towards Chris, I asked him what was in his.

"Don't know mate," he said as he climbed over an irrigation ditch, "but it's been clucking at me since we set off."

* * *

Back on our porch, Chris fried the pork on his stove and boiled up some more noodles on mine, while I cut the elastic bands on the chicken's legs. "What do you think we should call it?" I asked.

"Delilah?" he responded, after thinking for a moment.

"Too girly."

"It *is* a girl."

"Well, I doubt she really cares. What about Winston?" I suggested.

"No, too authoritative. We need a balance. A sort of matron-like name." He hummed for a moment, pondering, then said, "Audrey?"

"Suits me."

Audrey the Chicken nodded a few times, like chickens do. I let her loose and she started clucking about under the porch, pecking sporadically at the ground. Flicking through my notepad, I came across one of the figures I was quoted. "12,367 tribal chiefs killed—that's a hell of a lot."

"I thought the entire population of the Baliem Valley was only 100,000 at the time?"

"It was."

"So more than one in ten people in the valley were tribal chiefs? Given the number of kids I've seen, that makes every single adult a tribal chief."

"And every single adult dead."

I drained the noodles and added some spices, mixing them in with a plastic spoon. "Pork nearly done?"

Chris rolled the chunks of meat around the pan and looked up. "Yup, pop the noodles over here." He ladled the meat into the noodle mix and passed some to me. "Do you think they were lying?"

"About the death statistics, yeah. They must have been exaggerating. But I think the rest was largely true—it all ties in with what I've heard elsewhere."

"Nice guys, weren't they?"

"Yeah, to us at least," I replied, remembering that people from the same organisation were responsible for the kidnapping and deaths of quite a few outsiders in recent years—some European, as well as many Indonesians. I bit into a chunk of pork and decided it was the best thing I had tasted for a few weeks at least. "Think we need to verify what they said though."

After we finished the meal, we walked across to Paul's house for a hot drink and a chat. During the conversation, Paul explained a few things in his perfect English: "The Dani people have a thing they call 'mature speak' and I think this is what you encountered today. It is when a speaker uses irony and exaggeration to win over an audience, but not many foreigners in Papua realise this. It is a cultural thing, you might call it lying, but the audience is expected to work out what is true and what is not from the way the speaker says it. In the highland customs, the more confused the audience, the better the speaker."

"That doesn't make any sense!" I exclaimed. "Why tell us something that isn't true?"

"It is the same as sarcasm in English I think. Some cultures understand it, others don't. But you have to look at what they told you and work out for yourself what was true and false. A lot of bad things have happened here, and lots of people were killed; there are still many problems—alcoholism, prostitution, AIDS—and you could say these things are a result of the occupation because they never existed until Indonesia came, but you cannot exaggerate when you tell the story of Papua. Things are not as simple as the resistance believes." He paused, taking a sip of tea. "May I suggest a different point of view?"

"Yes, of course. Please do."

"Papua does not necessarily need independence."

"Really?" It was the first time we'd heard a Papuan say anything like this. "So what is the solution?" I asked.

"Education. What Papua needs is education. Not the kind of education that keeps people in line, but the kind of education that frees them. Allows them to run a business; the kind of education that gives them the integrity and confidence to govern a province."

Paul continued, "In Indonesia, there is an education system that rewards conformity. At school, students are taught to learn facts by heart and then not to question them. Discussion is discouraged and the student-teacher relationship is more like master-servant. The Indonesian phrase 'datang, duduk, diem' sums this attitude up: arrive, sit down and be quiet. The result is that those who do well in school, who are more likely to find employment later on in life, are taught to be automatons, faithful to their superiors. The reason for this is that Indonesia is a big place with many different peoples; teach students to be critical and maybe it will fall apart!" Paul laughed. "You are aware Papua has been granted Special Autonomy by Indonesia?"

"It gave Papuans control over certain parts of the governing of the province, right?"

"Correct, but it also gives us the opportunity for local indigenous leadership, as well as a share of the profits from Papuan natural resources. It is not much, but each part of Papua now receives some money from the Special Autonomy fund. It was a concession to stop the protests a few years ago."

"Has it worked?"

"No. If anything, it is working in Jakarta's favour."

Chris's eyebrows raised in confusion. "How?"

"Did you see the kiosks in Wamena?"

"Yes, but only ones that were owned by Indonesians," Chris said.

"Exactly. The Indonesians own all the places where Papuans can buy things. They have hundreds of years of practicing trading in their culture, maybe thousands; Papuans have not. If Papuans were given the skills they needed to run a business such as this, the Special Autonomy fund might improve our living standards—all it is doing now is making Papuans who receive it dependent on it…but this is a side issue. The main problem with these funds is the way they are distributed." Paul took another sip of tea before continuing.

"Papua is divided into smaller areas known as regencies. Money is given out in each regency. Because Papua has a legacy of oppression, the indigenous leaders who give out this money are often corrupt and keep more of it for themselves and their own families, so very little reaches the people who need it most. This creates suspicion and discontent and now Papua is being divided as more families and tribes try to set up their own regencies to control some of this money for themselves. The political map is returning to the lines of the tribal warfare that ended with the Dutch Christian missionaries. Facilities like schools and hospitals are going to waste because nobody will cooperate. Even some of the resistance leaders during the uprising have been bought out; now, they are the ones you see driving expensive four wheel drives through Jayapura."

Resistance leaders driving four wheel drives through Jayapura? It didn't make much sense. "Why is this? Don't Papuans want to help themselves?"

"Yes, of course. But you can see it in any place where people have been oppressed. They learn a master-servant relationship with those in power and so corruption and mismanagement are always in the mindset of the people. And this is why we need education; education can break the cycle of oppression and teach those in power to have integrity and accountability, teach them not to rush ahead wherever they can but to help each other. There is more opportunity for us now, but only once this step has been taken can the standard of living for all Papuans improve."

"Is that why this school is here?"

"Exactly. We are privately run, and our aim is to give students integrity and confidence to choose their own path and break the cycle of oppression. If we can teach our students to become the leaders and businessmen of Papua's future, Papuan people will be able to prosper."

"So what about independence?" I asked, taking a sip of the sweet tea.

Paul hesitated for a moment, then suggested, "If independence were to happen now, Papua would tear itself apart."

We chatted for a while longer and later on, Chris and I walked across to the school canteen—a wooden room with large tables and benches—and stayed with the students for the evening sermon. A few stood and read some passages from the bible, and then they all sang hymns in a local language. Their voices harmonised and it sounded beautiful, like a professional choir. But it also made me feel quite sombre, for I knew that our time in the Baliem was coming to an end.

Once the evening sermon was finished, the students filtered out of the room and went to their respective dormitories. With nothing better to do, we strolled back across the lawn just as the generator was switched off, enveloping the grassy campus in a blanket of darkness. We wandered to the edge of the embankment that surrounded the school and gazed over the wicker fence, looking out across the valley once more.

With no pollution the stars stood out like Christmas lights silhouetted behind flashing cumulonimbus at the far end of the basin, and the nearby hills seemed to be painted with a silver sheen. In the far distance, the twinkling glow of Wamena was the only indication that there was anybody else in the whole universe. I turned to the rough outline that I could just make out to be Chris. "I think I've got enough from here," I said slowly. "Maybe it's time to donate Audrey."

The outline replied, "Cool."

Some time later, when I reached my room, I lit a candle and noticed that Audrey had managed to climb onto the top of the wardrobe and was looking fairly miffed, so I picked her up and put her on the floor. Unfortunately for Audrey, she had good reason to be miffed. The next day, we had a goodbye feast with the students.

* * *

In the days and weeks after the chat we'd had with Paul, it all started to make some sense. Not only that, but the more I listened to the stories and spoke to the people, the clearer the ramifications became: the way Papua had been treated for the last half-century was the way much of the developing world had been treated in the past, and so the problems that Papua faced today reflected the infant stages of those in many other parts of the world.

Paul had suggested that the exploitative nature of colonisation caused far-reaching social scars that self-determination on its own would not heal. From what I learnt later on in the trip, it became apparent that the cycle of oppression in Papua meant that effective self-governance was almost impossible; where it had been granted, the social divisions that now existed often led to chaos, prompting racist myths that indigenous Papuans were too backward to look after themselves.

Despite the Special Autonomy funds that were finally giving something back to the local economy, it would take a complete change of mindset for prosperity to reach the Papuan people, and what Paul was suggesting was that a tailored education system might help. I admired him greatly—he was able to see a bigger picture, see the fact that Papuan welfare did not necessarily need independence anymore, but rather, capable Papuans.

It was in those weeks that I too began to see a bigger picture—one that built on what I had caught a whiff of in Borneo. Like the parts of Sarawak I had heard about, Papua was a valuable commodity simply because of the fact that consumers around the world, ignorant or indifferent to the social implications of their consumption, were willing to pay a combined fortune for the resources that came from Papuan lands. While many in Indonesia had prospered from this transaction, until recently it hadn't been the local Papuans. And now that something was finally being given back—even if it was arguably too little too late—it was becoming clear that Papua's colonisation had passed on one problem that virtually circumvented all others: corruption. This might well be *the* common denominator among troubled states across the globe today—an oppressive past and a corrupt future.

Papuans were angry with Indonesia, just as the Indonesians had once been with the Dutch, and this was obvious when I thought back to the footage of the violent demonstrations in Abepura. But again, just as with the Dutch, there were several ways in which the Indonesians, consciously or otherwise, kept the Papuans from being too much of a hindrance in this process of exploitation: the education system, grooming unquestioning, passive individuals for the higher echelons of Papuan society; the Special Autonomy fund to reward obedience; the use of violence and torture against those that did not comply.

I remembered the stories I'd been told by the TPN, of the mass graves and how the old guy had shown us the huts where Indonesian soldiers had allegedly raped local women. I thought of the detentions we'd heard about and the killing of a young Papuan demonstrator in Wamena two weeks before we arrived, along with the shooting of fourteen others in Enarotali, a village a two weeks' walk away, around the same time. Against such a backdrop, it was little wonder that brutality and a lack of accountability had been embedded in modern Papuan society. The longer the maltreatment continued, the worse it would become, unless people like Paul could expand the good work they were doing to counteract it.

In some ways, it was really quite ironic. The same forces that once repressed the Javanese had since washed their hands of the morally ambiguous title of coloniser and were now allowing Java to do the dirty work for them in Papua. It was indicative of the worst traits of mankind: greed, selfishness, cold-heartedness. And it made me feel uneasy. I didn't want to face it at first, but the trail lead uncomfortably close to home; Britain was part of the gang that had originally started this whole process off. Just as Belgium had once ruled over the Congo and Spain had galloped across South America, the United Kingdom had once held control over the largest empire the world had ever known. Now that unquenchable European thirst for consumption was finally saturating through to the final corners of the globe, and I didn't much like the look of it.

The more time I spent in Papua, the more I started to wonder if that was what development really meant. For the blessed few, who could reap all the benefits of the system, it was perfect. But for a tribal people who'd mostly wanted to continue to live as their ancestors had done for millennia, it was doing more than just stealing their land—it was tearing the fabric of their society. Destroying hope, ambition, pushing people towards alcoholism, dependancy and depression. The same as it had done to the aboriginal people of Australia, the American Indians; the bushmen of the Kalahari, the autochthon of the Congo Basin; even the Dayaks of Borneo, the Moken of Thailand, the Innu of Canada and Greenland.

Everywhere, the same story: ancient communities having their livelihoods destroyed by outsiders keen to profit from their lands. People being abused and tossed aside, forced away from the structures, traditions, even religions that once made up their natural lives, into an existence no one could ever want. They'd had their stool kicked away and were now being left to hang in a world that mostly saw them as backward and stupid; a pointless, whinging obstruction to the inevitable mechanisms of capitalism. Money is to greed is to exploitation, as exploitation is to oppression, corruption, desperation, and ultimately conflict: all this, because a minority were so desperate for wealth they were willing to turn a blind eye to the costs of their actions. And now, whichever way things went from here, the damage had been done. Change had happened, and things would never be the same in the last place in the tropics.

EIGHT

Time of Your Life

We spent more time interviewing in jungles and cities across Papua and Indonesia as a whole, and the hammock and boots were put to good use. But by the time I had left the Baliem, my project already had its answer; the remainder of our visa passed largely without incident. And so, with the remaining weeks before our flights home from Bangkok, Chris and I decided to take the opportunity to visit the Philippines. A confusion meant that we arrived a day apart, and the plan was for him to let me know where he was staying so we could meet for a quick breather before heading to the island of Palawan.

Simple plan. In theory. But four hours of walking up and down the clammy Manila waterfront suggested otherwise.

Looking at the scrap of paper that I had jotted Chris's address from an email back in Jakarta down on, I could only guess at the writing—the ink had smudged from the sweat in my pocket. Something about Beverly, maybe, but I couldn't be sure. It was no use; I would have to find him a different way.

So, as the sun dipped below the horizon, I took a turn away from the waterfront and the orange sky and back into the high rises and bars of downtown.

Earlier that day, Manila had been a pleasant place of friendly, well-armed security guards, crazy traffic and colourful jeepneys.* I

---

* Jeepneys are a form of public transport peculiar to the Philippines; converted from ex-US army jeeps, they have an extended passenger bay in

had been hassled very little and found the atmosphere highly agreeable.

By dusk though, the city had changed.

I turned onto the main street that ran parallel to the waterfront.

"Excuse me sir, where are you going?" asked a friendly-looking girl with a gentle stroke on the arm.

"Um, Malate." I slowed down and turned my head back as I passed her. "Just looking for a guesthouse." I tapped my small rucksack, to show that I was, indeed, just looking for a guesthouse.

"Okay sir, I can show you the way."

"Oh, that's fine, it's just down here right?" I pointed down the street, to where I was fairly certain Malate was.

"It's very hard to find sir, come with me and I'll show you." She took me by the arm and started to lead me back to the waterfront.

"We're going the wrong way."

"Come on sir, I just want to show you something."

"No, look, I want to find Malate." I stopped, and she pulled at my arm.

The girl lowered her voice. "Yes, yes, we go to Malate. But we can have some fun first," she winked, trying to pull me along again.

I held back. "Thanks, but I'm okay."

"Sir," she stepped close to me and whispered seductively, "only one thousand pesos for you, all night."

"One thou-" I was surprised, but I caught myself. "No! Go away."

"I make you a *very* happy man?"

"No." I pulled away from her. "Bye."

"Sir?"

I walked away from the girl as fast as I could, down the street towards Malate. Seconds later, two glamorous-looking ladies grabbed at my hands.

"Hey, you handsome. You wanna go?"

"No!"

"You have both at same time…"

I tried to act like I didn't hear. Ignore them and walk on, *ignore them and walk on,* I told myself, yanking my hands away.

"We show you best time your life. Together…"

"Bugger off!"

---

the rear with space for up to twelve, albeit small, adults. Usually, the style of driving is matched only in extravagance by the paint job on the outside.

Three metres was as far as I got before a stunningly beautiful girl brushed alongside me, looping her arm through mine, and started speaking in a sultry monologue.

"Hey, you very handsome sir, you want a massage? I give you a good price."

Ignore and walk on.

"Please, slow down, I will give you a very nice ending. Why you walk away? You will be happy man if you come with me."

Ignore. And walk on.

"Please, come with me handsome. Very special massage, just for you."

Ignore.

And.

Walk.

On.

I pulled her arm off mine and started jogging.

"Hey, come back—I fuck you! For free!"

"Leave me alone!"

Thirty-four similar encounters later, I found my way to the guesthouse in Malate that was recommended by the guys I'd met in Bangkok. It was a comfortable place, once you passed the guard with the shotgun on the ground floor and the sign that said, "Sex Tourist Not Allowed". Feeling reassured, I checked my email in the communal area upstairs.

There was one message, from Chris.

18 September, 5:09pm.

Shitface, didn't find you at the room earlier so I suggest we meet in town this evening. I'll be at the Hobbit House at 8. It's on the main street north of Malate, sure you'll find it.

I logged off and had a quick shower. The thought of going back to that street even later made me apprehensive, but the prospect of a house full of hobbits was something that no reasonable man could turn down. Thirty minutes later and I strolled down the stairs and past the armed guard, who woke with a start when I coughed loudly right next to his ear.

The amusement didn't last long though. Feeling a strange mixture of arousal and fear, I stepped onto the street. But this time things were different. This time, I made a friend.

As I walked out of the foyer, a kid stood in my way, trying to block my path with his grubby hands outstretched.

"No mate, I'm not giving you a pencil or whatever it is you want. Sorry."

"Peso?"

"No, go away."

"Peso?"

"Look kid, if you don't get out of my way, I will move you out of my way."

"Peso?"

"Seriously, I've got some hobbits to see, shoo."

"Peso?"

"Well, you're just asking for it now aren't you?"

"Peso?"

"Nope, no bloody peso. Go *away!*"

He paused for a moment to consider the options he had available to him. Then he said, "Peso?"

I picked the irritating little bugger up and placed him to the side, at which point he forgot all about the peso and started giggling. Confused, I looked at him and he grinned, gesturing for me to pick him up again. I obliged, which made him laugh even more, and he started running around me quite happily as I walked along, picking him up every few paces or so. A few moments later, another kid walked up and demanded a peso; my new best friend pushed him aside playfully and said a few words in Tagalog. The second kid then started giggling and gestured for me to pick him up too, but the first boy pushed him away again and he trotted off, cheerfully distracted by another foreigner across the street.

Up ahead, a young lady eyed me up as I walked along, but as soon as she saw the kid, she backed off. He shouted something at her and she giggled too, smiling at him and then at me.

This is brilliant! I thought as he ran around me, batting off prostitutes and small children at every turn. Here was my very own grubby little force field, my barrier against the hassles of Manila.

I decided to take the opportunity to ask my new friend where the Hobbit House was. He grabbed my hand and dragged me a hundred metres along the road, pointing to a small, round, wooden door. I thanked him, picked him up once more for good measure and when I put him down, he scampered away with a huge grin on his face and a few extra pesos in his pocket.

What a great kid.

A few moments passed, and I looked at the door, too self-conscious to open it. I knew I was early, so there was no way of knowing whether Chris was inside this place, whatever it was. And for all I knew, it could have been a hoax, a dirty trick played by Chris for his own amusement. He was probably in a bar across the street, snorting at me through a window. I scanned the street, but I could see no snorters at all, let alone a snorting Chris.

Hmmm.

Well, I was at the Hobbit House and it certainly had a Hobbit Door. *Why not live life on the edge?* I thought. So I grabbed the large metal handle and pushed it open, ducking down into a dark room, which at first glance seemed to be filled with hobbits. Genuine hobbits, not just short people.

This was strange. Hobbits in Manila? Surely I had got lost somewhere along the way and ended up in Devon.

"Dude! You made it!"

The voice came from the right, where Chris was propped against a bar, holding a beer.

"Mate, what is this place?"

"It's a pub! Cool isn't it?"

"Where did they get all the hobbits from?"

"I don't know, the Shetlands? Anyway, who cares, grab a beer."

Chris waved at one of the hobbits, who walked over to us. On closer inspection, the hobbit was in fact a Filipino dwarf dressed in a red T-shirt, which, if I'm to be politically correct, was not a let down at all. "What can I get you sir?" he asked in an American-sounding accent.

"A big cold beer please!" Chris answered for me.

"Sure," he replied, and walked around the bar.

"How the hell did you find this place?"

"I was walking about yesterday and needed somewhere to escape the ladyboys so I ducked in here. Pretty awesome isn't it?"

"Ladyboys?"

"Yeah, the ones who grab your hand outside here, they've all got todgers."

"All of them?"

"Well, no. But a guy I spoke to yesterday said that if they grab your hand or are at all aggressive, they're probably male. He was Scottish so I reckon he was talking from experience."

"I'm a bit Scottish!" I replied.

"Whatever. Anyway, he told me that the girls are never aggressive. Ever. And he also told me that there's ways they can have sex with you without you even knowing they're packing. They con hundreds of Western men into their bottoms like that."

"Who was this guy?"

"His name's Jock, apparently he runs a bar around here. I'll take you to it in a minute."

My beer arrived with the dwarf barman, the condensation already forming droplets on the brown bottle.

"Thanks buddy."

"You're welcome sir."

I turned to Chris. "What about if there are two of them?"

"Definitely male dude." Then he shot me a look. "Did yo-"

"No! I've only just arrived. *And* I've got a girlfriend, remember?"

Chris looked relieved, then mischievous. "Were you tempted?"

"No…but they *were* surprisingly hot." I took a swig and it turned out to be much more refreshing than I expected, so I extended the swig into a gulp. "For a pair of blokes at least. Were you tempted?"

"Hell yes, dude!" Chris grinned. "But before you ask, no I didn't. There was a much better, and free, option that I took instead."

"Oh yeah? What was his name?"

"*Her* name was…er, something Scandinavian. Helga or something."

"Helga. Sounds really hot."

"Yeah, she was…" Chris went all glazed for a moment until he realised he'd been staring at one of the staff, who started shooting him evil looks in return.

Then he switched into talk mode.

"You know, I actually hunted this place out." He leant back and swept his gaze casually across the Tolkein-themed bar. "I was reading a book about some guy who worked on rigs and he reckoned there was this wall you could throw the dwarfs against."

"Right."

"Yeah, you get a dwarf, cover them in Velcro and throw them against this wall that's covered in the opposing Velcro."

"Sounds PC. There isn't a wall like that in here is there?"

"Not that I've seen, but you could always ask."

"No man, they probably get that all the time."

Chris nodded his head in agreement. "Oh, and one more thing. I got us flights to Palawan for tomorrow morning at seven."

"You did what?"

"Well, it was a good deal, about four thousand rupiah cheaper and I thought you wouldn't mind."

"Rupiah?"

"Shit. Pesos. You know what I mean. Anyway, you can pay me back whenever." Chris took another gulp.

"Well, can't argue with that. It's going to hurt like hell on the flight though," I smiled.

Sooner than expected, we finished the beers.

"On to Jock's place?" Chris asked.

"Yup."

Chris led the way directly across the street, past a few mental drivers and several prostitutes, and followed the sidewalk (this being the Philippines, there were no pavements) until we stumbled past a small doorway with a glass window. He read the sign above the door.

"This must be it," Chris said as we looked through the glass window and tried to see past all the girls peeping at us from the other side, waving. Sensing my facial expression, he laughed, pulled the door open and said, "Look, have one beer, meet Jock, then we can throw some dwarves."

Inside, the bar was loaded with girls. It was a small place, maybe the size of a shipping container, and with only a dozen people it looked rammed. We squeezed past to reach the bar. From the corner, shouted: "Alright fellas! Grab yerselves a seat!" Where the voice had boomed over the music, there was an old thickset jock sitting underneath a nubile Filipino nursing blanket.

"That must be Jock," I observed.

"Yup." Chris plodded through the swirling, floating hands of the entirely female crowd. "Alright fella."

"How are ya! Grab yerself a beer. Eh, Daizeh," he shouted, "can ah 'ave two beers for these gentlemen please? Ah, an' one more for ma'self."

Daisy, who didn't seem too much like any other Daisy I'd seen before, thumped three lagers on the bar next to us and carried on gyrating.

"Cheers!" Jock gulped down a stubby.

"Cheers," we responded, taking dainty sips in comparison.

Jock sat back in his chair, which somehow lifted the bar girl up a few inches or so. I tried not to notice the mechanics. "It ain't a fancy joint, but it serves me well," he said, and I didn't doubt him. "What d'you boys think of Manila then?"

"Nuts," I replied.

"Way crazier than Bangkok," agreed Chris.

"Fuckin' right," Jock slurred, "ain't no other place like it." Daisy brought him another stubby and he gulped it down. "An' Bangkok's a fuckin' trap. *This*," he pointed to the bar girl on his lap, to the other girls around the bar, "is where it's all at." The bar girl laughed and stroked his knee. "Those fuckin' Thai bimbos ain't got nothin' on these. Look at her. She's got an arse like a ten-year old Cambodian boy."

He laughed, downed another beer, then said, "Ah fuck. Ah'm too pissed. There ah go, sayin' something like that!" The bar girl leant close to his ear and her mouth moved, then she giggled. He smirked. "Sorry boys, looks like I've got to hit the sack." He leant closer and winked. "Or the sacks's got to hit her, perhaps I should say."

The tiny Filipino on his lap got thrown a few feet when he stood up, and he staggered across the room and left through the curtain at the rear. The bar girl followed on.

"Nice guy," I said to Chris.

"Well, yesterday he wasn't so drunk. And he did offer to get us a free beer if we came to his bar."

"Did he tell you it was a brothel?"

"Nope."

"But he did mention the name."

"Yup."

"And you didn't guess it was a brothel?"

"Well, sort of. But free beer?" He looked at me with a pleading expression. "Anyway, I figured it would be an interesting addition to your quest for global knowledge. Don't tell me you wouldn't have taken up the offer."

"Good point."

Two girls slunk over, tittering shyly to each other, and tried to jump on our laps. We pushed them off.

"Ladies, sorry, we're not here for that," said Chris.

"Oh." They looked taken aback.

"Look," he continued, "we're just here for a drink. You are very beautiful but he's got a girlfriend and I'm gay."

They shot him a queer look. Chris clarified. "Fine, I'm not gay. I've got a girlfriend too."

"What is her name?" the shorter of the two girls asked.

"Helga," I answered for him.

"She sounds nice."

"No she doesn't, she sounds like a Viking," I blurted. But noticing the confusion on the girls' faces and the upset on Chris's, I felt obliged to clarify too. "But she *is* beautiful."

To distract them from the rapidly approaching tumbleweed, I attempted a quick turn in the conversation. *Think quick—what do you normally say to two girls you've only just met?*

"Um. So, what do you girls do for a living?"

They looked at each other.

"I mean, how old are you?"

"Nineteen," the short girl answered.

"Twenty-two," said the taller girl.

"Honestly?" Chris asked. "Look, it doesn't matter to us. We aren't customers or clients or whatever you call it."

"Well, she *is* nineteen, but I am…you can have a guess."

"Twenty-three?"

"Twenty-eight," said the taller girl.

"Jesus, you don't look it. Where are you from?" Chris asked.

"She from Luzon and I from Mindanao, the island with terrorists that cut off people's heads," laughed the shorter girl, presumably referring to an extremist offshoot of the Moro Islamic Liberation Front, whose unfortunate acronym made me chuckle whenever I thought about it.

"Right…Why did you come here then?" I asked.

"For money. I come from poor family and I must support them so…this is best money." She laughed again. "Best money in Manila."

"Still not good money, but it the best we can find," said the taller girl. "It is not enough for raise a family."

The sentence stuck in my mind, but I let it slide. "Don't a lot of Filipinos go and work abroad? You can get good money from that, right?"

The girls looked at each other and the taller one turned to us to speak. "I was an overseas worker. I was a maid in Malaysia."

"So why did you come back?"

She looked and smiled at the shorter girl and said, "The mistress hit me and the master try to have sex with me all the time." Then she laughed, "Now when I come back to Manila, I start doing this!"

They both giggled.

Wondering if Chris found the irony amusing or disturbing, I looked at him again and saw a mixture of sympathy and dismay in his face.

"Hey, you don't worry. You are nice guys, you want more beer?" she asked.

I glanced at Chris, who turned back to me.

"One more?"

"One more."

***

"Fuck, that was a heavy night," Chris groaned. "My head feels like I've got Barbara Streisand and Hitler singing a duet in it."

"Mine feels like I've got God jumping on it."

Chris unbuckled his waist strap. "Those girls were awesome."

"I know. Really awesome." I leant back against the headrest, but my forehead started pounding so I fell back into my hands again. "Did we eat something salty earlier? I think I can still taste it."

"We had that salted pig in the club, remember?"

"Oh yeah."

No matter how I shifted my head it still hurt, so I looked out of the window into the bright sunlight for a moment, which definitely did me no favours on the pain front, but there were some pretty islands that looked like blobs of green paint on a blue canvas that kept me occupied for longer than I originally intended. I closed the window cover and the pain that pulsed through my cranium retreated to a manageable level momentarily, then carried on, jackhammer-like, as usual.

I tried to piece together my night.

Live singing, I think that happened. And I think someone sang the song, "When You're Gone" by Avril Lavigne, and that had made me get all sentimental and miss my girlfriend for quite a long time, but now it was on loop in my head and was starting to piss me off. Then another club, and we walked around Manila and Chris nearly got into a fight by accidentally strolling into a scooter when crossing a road. Some pork, followed by more beer. By the time we had left the final club it was already light outside, so we had walked to Chris's place and mine, picked up our bags and gone straight to the airport, saying goodbye to the girls at the bar we had met them at.

That's a pretty good recollection. That kind of sums it all up, I think. Only a few more minor details to remember.

"Do you think they actually enjoyed themselves?" Chris asked, the words plopping out of his mouth like dung from a horse's bottom.

"Definitely mate, they had a great time. I don't think they get the chance to do that often."

"Nah, probably not." Chris rolled his head and groaned some more. "I can't believe she was twenty-eight. She didn't look it."

"I know mate, and she had a kid." I rubbed my eyes as a pretty stewardess walked past Chris. He didn't look up. My head felt compressed and my eyes may as well have been pickled, but I rubbed them again anyway. "She knew the clubs pretty well though. Do you think you would have considered…you know?"

"Going with one of them?"

"Yeah. I mean, if you were Australian or something and you knew you had to pay for it anyway."

"If I didn't know about the kid and all that other stuff, possibly." Chris paused, reconsidered. "Actually, no. Not now I've spoken to them. It seems too much like paying someone to be raped." Chris let his head flop back into the headrest. "God, they've been messed around."

"I know man."

"But they were so cool about having that job," Chris mumbled. "They had to deal with so much shit and they just got on with it."

"Pretty inspiring." I let go of my head, having started to feel like I was being a wimp.

"Awesome girls."

"Yeah, really awesome."

I closed my eyes for a second and looked back out of the window. Somehow, in that short space of time, we had got to Palawan and landed. From the airport, we took a rickshaw into town and checked in to another guesthouse, where, predictably, there wasn't much to write about for the next eight hours.

NINE

Karen

"Elnido-elnido-elnido! Taytay, Elnido!"

We piled out of our rickshaw and staggered towards the noise. A few torches waved about in the darkness, seemingly there to add to the sense of confusion as millions of people descended onto one helpless bus. As we neared, we could see plastic chairs, bicycles, bags of rice and a year's worth of supplies being wrenched up to the roof by an army of small boys, who climbed up and down the windows like macaques, hoisting rope and tarpaulins over the load. Voices were everywhere, surrounding us in the dark, crying out names and directions. The shouting and flashing torches reached out like tractor beams, pulling us through our daze towards the rusting carcass of public transport. I wiped the sleep from my eyes as I stumbled along, pushing my way through the crowd and picking a place to sit on the side of the aisle. Chris wasn't far behind; we ended up diagonally opposite each other, perched into impossible spaces between rows of rusty metal seating that seemed to have been designed to only accommodate employees of the Hobbit House. My knees were by my chest and although we hadn't even started moving, I could already feel the pain in my coccyx.

Gradually, the chaos decreased until it hovered around the level of mild panic, and this was obviously the sign for the driver to start up the beast. With a deafening wrench, the engine roared and suddenly my seat was transformed into a vibrating massage chair, only the experience wasn't quite so pleasant. I could feel my rump being tenderised, and given the cannibalistic history of some of the islands of the Philippines and the Filipino bus safety records, I wasn't sure if this was coincidental.

There was some more shouting outside, seemingly directing the monkey-children, but the bus's internal lighting made it impossible to see what was going on. I could hear one more item being hoisted on to the roof and a few more people stepped onto the bus. Then, with an almighty crunch, the whole chassis lurched over on its left side, throwing a few of the standing passengers off balance. Instinctively, I reached across and held on to one of the metal seats on the far side of the aisle to save myself from pushing my neighbouring passenger through the window.

Then, as if nothing was wrong, the driver cranked the beast into gear and set off through the dark, empty streets of Puerto with the cool wind blowing through the open windows of the wonky bus.

Somehow, I drifted off.

When I woke, I woke with a start.

We were tipping dangerously, leaning way over to the left. At some point I had obviously let go of my handhold and slid into my neighbour, who sat in politely stunned silence. I could see that we were driving around something, some obstacle, and it took me a few dazed moments to see that we were edging past a large mound of sand that had spread right across the road from a construction site opposite us.

The bus inched forward as I re-found my handhold, just behind Chris. He was looking wide-eyed at the road ahead, trying to work out what was coming and whether we would tip or not, holding onto a vertical bar that ran between the floor and the ceiling of the bus. Seeing the concern on his usually chirpy face like that unnerved me so I looked in a different direction—the direction we were precariously tilted.

Not the best idea.

We were on a ridge. A ridge with a steep drop-off. Through the foliage, it was difficult to see where it bottomed out, but it certainly wasn't close. And the foliage was not quite thick enough to catch us.

How far can this bus lean?

The driver was struggling with the clutch; he jumped the bus a few inches, making the tilt that little bit more precarious, and I heard a few gasps of breath from the otherwise silent crowd of passengers around me.

Slowly, the bus eased forward and with each centimetre, the tilt grew more severe. I gripped harder and my brain, useful as it could be, filled with images of people being sliced in half as they were thrown through the glassless windows of the tumbling bus. Images of the crumpled chassis filled with a human soup, sloshing about and leaking into the forest. I had visions of the relief effort, people being pulled from the jungle ravine and placed on a black tarpaulin, their limp torsos and heads covered with blankets and coats. Blurry photos, and YouTube videos shot from bystanders' mobile phones. And the headline: *Red Faced Tourist and Usually Chirpy Mate in Philippine Bus Carnage!*

It didn't take long to realise that not only was this a poor headline, but that my imagination was really not helping anything.

I started trying to think of a plan, a way out of the bus if it were to topple. But there was no way; each door had three or more people between me and it. And the bus would topple fast. The windows, following on from my daydream, didn't seem like such a viable option either. In short: if the bus rolled, I was screwed.

We all were.

The gears crunched and the bus edged further. I felt my hand tighten before I noticed the tilt swing further over to the left and then the screams started. Short, involuntary wails, like the screams you'd hear from a cinema audience during an especially jumpy scene. Only, unlike bus passengers in the Philippines, cinema audiences don't tend to get violently killed.

One more inch.

The vehicle hovered, perched on its suspension, deciding which way to roll. Another centimetre. The audience waited with baited breath. The silent tension had all but drowned out the sound of the engine.

Toss a coin. Heads; survive. Tails; die.

Heads or tails, heads or tails…

Right or left.

And then the bus made its choice.

With a tremendous thump, it swung down onto all four wheels. A simultaneous exhalation and we were back on the ground. The engine roared like a disgruntled wookiee and Chris glanced over his shoulder at me.

We started laughing.

My seat neighbour turned and smiled at me and I grinned back. The sandy obstacle was cleared; we were on our way. On our way to paradise.

* * *

For a while, the engine roared some more, as engines often do, but a few hours passed and the bus began to slow, as broken buses often do. We were going uphill now and I could almost taste the burnt rubber and fuel as the gears wrenched mightily, straining against the weight of the load. The effort of the engine was sending shockwaves through the metal floor of the bus, right the way up my legs and into my knees.

Thanks to the vibrations, my coccyx was now in agony. I had damaged it during a rugby match against Yeovil—the pleasant town full of friendly people—three years before and I still hadn't got anyone to check it out. Just the thought of how someone might try to readjust it was enough to scare me into a lifetime of discomfort on long-distance journeys. I still stand by the decision.

Clunk!

The engine fell silent and the bus jerked to a halt. We were halfway around a bend but this time we were leaning into the hillside and there was no sandcastle to topple us into the ravine. This time, it was just the bus that was screwed.

For a few moments we just sat around, wondering what to do. Was the bus broken or did the driver just switch the engine off? Was this a lunch stop or what? Are the buses here really that bad?

It quickly became apparent that we weren't going anywhere anytime soon when the other passengers started stepping down onto the road. Initially, they stood, chatting idly as a few people crawled about under the engine. But then bags were offloaded and small gatherings materialised by the side of the road. If it wasn't for the greasy black crankshaft that had now fallen from the bottom of the bus, anybody could have been forgiven for thinking it really was just a picnic break.

"Well mate, what shall we do?" I asked Chris, taking a seat next to him on the roadside. "I think the bus is a non-starter."

"We could walk," Chris suggested, and in hindsight this was probably as bad a joke as the one I just made, but I took it literally.

"Yeah sure, let's do it."

I stood up, hoisted my bag and set off up the hill. Not being one to back down from a challenge, Chris followed.

"If we see anything else, we could always hitch a lift."

As it turned out, the rumours that Palawan was quite rural were, indeed, based on reality. For miles, there was nothing but rice paddy and jungle lining the empty winding road. The air was still thick enough that we were covered in sweat, but fortunately, the bright morning sunlight had started to lose its sting as a cloudy haze spread across the stratosphere above us. If we had been looking carefully, we would have recognised the change as an ominous sign.

With nobody around, I took my T-shirt off and walked barefoot for a while, clipping my flip-flops to my bag. I could feel the stones under my feet and the breeze on my clammy skin. We were stretched out and moving through the countryside in such a way that we would at least have *some* control over whether we plunged into a ravine or not.

After the cramped bus, it felt good.

Some time later, maybe an hour or two—we didn't keep track—we came across a small cluster of simple wooden huts by the side of the road. It wasn't much of a surprise to us; the increasing frequency of lone cattle chomping grass along our path gave us a hint that something must have been nearby. Stopping at one of the huts, we asked a friendly man how far it would be to walk to the nearest town.

"Walk?"

"Yeah, our bus is broken. How far?" We gestured walking with our fingers and he muttered something in Tagalog, the Filipino language. At least, it was probably Tagalog—for all I knew he could have been talking Aramaic, but I used my powerful reasoning skills.

He paused for a moment.

"Three-wheeler?" He revved an imaginary throttle and made a noise.

"Yeah, that would be great!"

The man ran off, leaving us standing by the roadside for a few minutes once again, and when he returned, he was spluttering down the path in a farty rickshaw.

Perfect.

Half an hour more and we were in Taytay, only a few hours from our destination. We thanked our driver profusely, but he only allowed us to give him some money for fuel. With a grin and a wave, the little rickshaw farted off back down the road, leaving us in a pleasant café in which we could chomp on a snack while we waited for sleep or the only other bus of the day to take us the rest of the journey, whichever came first. I had long-since forgotten the morning's terror and by then we had both learnt that the small victories in life were worth cherishing: I had a Snickers, I had seen some beautiful countryside *and* I had a great little story that I could embellish to my heart's content when I got home.

It was a good day.

I felt happy.

"How come things always seem to work out so well?" I asked Chris.

"We nearly fell off a cliff and our bus just broke down…I don't know, maybe we were just born lucky."

"Yeah, I'm starting to think that too." I finished off my Snickers with a hiccup and a smile. Then Chris pulled his "I'm listening to something" face that he often pulls when he's listening to something. If you didn't know him, you'd be forgiven for thinking he'd just had an accident.

"Dude, what's that sound?"

I strained to hear anything for a moment, then picked up a faint growl. I listened some more, waiting for the noise to register in my head. Suddenly it clicked: it sounded like a bus.

Radically, I said, "That sounds like a bus," just as a bus turned up and pulled into the café courtyard.

Chris stood up. "Wait here."

"What? Where are you going?"

"Shops." Chris trotted off down the street. "Back in a sec."

"There's a bus here!" I shouted after him.

"Chill, Winston! I'll be back before it leaves," Chris called, darting around a corner.

"I am not called Winston and I will *not* chill," I muttered spitefully under my breath. Our luck had just jumped up a notch and there goes Chris, sauntering off for a shit or whatever it is he does. Bloody perfect timing. Now don't get me wrong, Taytay seemed lovely, but I wanted our luck to continue. I wanted to get to El Nido before tomorrow. Or next bloody year.

Well, sod him. I wasn't going to let his bad timing ruin my chances. Not that day. As soon as the bus came to a halt, I looked inside. People were on top of people who were on top of people, who were on top of bags of rice and bicycles. These, in turn, had been placed on top of people. There was maybe one litre of spare air within the confines of the metal cage and an elderly lady was using that; I shouldn't really take it from her—she would probably die.

Still, worth a shot.

I wandered up to the ticket seller that was hanging from the door and asked him if there were any spare seats on the bus.

"No sir, we had one break down before so now everybody got on this bus."

"I was on the last bus too and I walked here with my friend."

"Walked all the way?"

"Yeah, sort of. Are you sure you don't have anywhere we could sit? I have a spare Snickers…"

"You can sit on the roof if you want?"

"Perfect."

Now, was I being a bad friend, ditching Chris so suddenly? I had no idea, but as a saving grace I decided to pick up his bag and sling it on the bus just in case he did manage to get back in time. As I climbed up the side, the ticket seller grabbed my leg.

"We are having a food stop. Come back in twenty minutes."

I sat back down.

When I saw Chris galloping back to the courtyard, I was grumpy. I had nothing better to be. He had judged the situation much better than I had and I felt ashamed by my self-righteous assumption that he was about to jeopardise our chances of getting to El Nido. I felt guilty that my first reaction was not to give my loyal buddy the benefit of the doubt. I had been a bad friend and I knew it now. *I'll make it up to him*, I thought. *From now on, I'll be super nice.*

Chris waddled up.

"Where the fuck have you been?" I barked at him, pleasantly.

Chris stood there with a gleeful expression and a plastic bag. "Well, if you don't want a beer, just say so. There's no need to get all menstrual."

"Fine," I said, sulking a little bit more. "I'll have a beer."

Chris tossed me a can and the ring pull pierced the cap with a hiss. I drank it down, savouring the taste; pure, fizzy, warm refreshment—the perfect way to top off our walk. A few gulps and another cheeky Snickers later, and my mood was back on track. I decided to let Chris know the local gossip. "We've got to sit on the roof because there isn't enough space and at least one old lady will die."

Chris and I climbed up the side of the bus, using the open windows as hand and footholds, and perched ourselves against a few bags of rice. "Ahhhh," I said, leaning back and topping up my happiness tank with more beer.

So there we were, sitting on the roof with our beers, sipping contentedly until the bus started on its way once more. The breeze whistled through our hair and kept us cool, and we finally had space to stretch our legs. Aside from one incident where I got cocky and nearly fell off, we were fairly safe; there were railings on the edge that seemed to fit the purpose of keeping roof-dwellers such as ourselves in the right place. Even low hanging wires and trees became part of the excitement, as Chris and I started playing "Duck-Chicken", a largely poultry-free adventure whereupon the first person to duck was a chicken. Unfortunately, despite the fun, we did stop playing after Chris was lashed across the face by a high-velocity leaf. This, he argued, made me the chicken.

But it didn't matter—we were having a great time. My frame of mind was lifted such that I almost could have enjoyed a Shakespearean tragedy and as we passed through hamlet after hamlet, laughing children gathered on the dirt roads and waved at us ecstatically, almost as though we were Danish royalty.

Strange.

Then the beautiful countryside resumed—shimmering lakes and lush green rice paddies, all surrounded by hills and thick jungle; a nature lover's dream.

Sitting on the roof, you no longer felt enclosed, secluded, confined. You no longer felt detached from the environment, stuck in that roaring little box of heat and fumes and sweat. Now, you were a part of your surroundings: you saw everything; the world around you stretched from periphery to periphery—the trees, the birds, the fields, the colourful old ladies by the bus stops—and you could feel everything; wind, sun, flies, rain…even the colourful old ladies if you were quick enough. It was all there, battering your grateful pink face.

Like going commando to an interview, it felt dangerously liberating. You were outside and being outside was *fun*.

Saying that, it was getting cold, and not long after we set off again did I feel the first wave of goosebumps crawl up my arms. The bus charged on though, making the scenery fly by in a blustery blur.

***

"It must be getting on, look at the sky," Chris shouted over the noise of the airstream.

"Oh shit yeah, looks like we're going to arrive after dark!"

"Sweet, an eight-hour journey that took us from dawn to dusk! Haven't done one of those before." His voice quietened, lost its melody for a moment. "That happened really fast."

"It's because we're near the equator mate, the earth rotates faster at the equator. That's why it gets dark really quickly here," I said, by way of explanation. "Surely you're used to that by now."

"Really quickly," Chris repeated, ignoring my nugget of knowledge. I briefly glanced across at him, sitting there with his hair flapping about like a Londoner with a broken Blackberry, but the wind was blowing hard into my right ear so I looked forward again. Something cold hit my cheek with a slight sting.

Then Chris said, "It was sunny just a minute ago and now it's virtually night." His face turned towards me. "What *is* the time?"

I peered into my watch, tried to read it but there was a bit of water splattered across the face. Another cold sting, this time on my right arm. I wiped the watch face.

"It's half-three," I shouted to Chris over the howl of the wind. He ignored me.

"Dude, look at the road."

The cold wind buffeting my face, I squinted ahead.

"Oh shit."

It was only slightly more translucent than a thick mist, but you could easily make out the dividing line. Grey isn't the right colour; then again, neither is white—only the darkness in the sky above us revealed what lay ahead. The road itself was a smudge, a colourless blur; it was as though someone tried to erase it with an old rubber and had given up just before the job was done. For a moment, I had a brief image of Angela, the Canadian girl I had met in Kuala Lumpur a year earlier, sitting on her bed next to her bag, with her face all creased.

I braced myself, then it hit.

Along with the freezing cold, two sounds became noticeable. First was the loud *shhhhh,* an amalgamation of the sound of a million droplets of water hitting millions of other droplets of water. Then there was the thudding sound, which is probably like the sound you'd hear if there were a hundred chimps with small, powerful hammers repeatedly hitting your head and body. The deep muffled thump that lets you know that the sound waves your ear drums are registering have travelled through you.

As raindrops the size of fists slammed into every inch of my body, I felt like I was eleven again, getting pelted by my older brother's BB gun, cowering, doing my best to minimise the pain. I tried to shout something sensible to Chris, like "It's rainy now isn't it?" or, "This is probably why the sky was so dark!" but when I opened my mouth, it was bombarded by gallons of water and I spluttered.

Shielding his face with his hand, Chris turned to me; I could barely make out his voice above the din: "…can't see…'ucking thing…how…odge trees?"

He had a point: occasionally, branches would jut out only a few inches across the roof of the bus and with the ability to see ahead, it was easy to shift to the other side of the roof before they swiped you off, but that wasn't possible now that facing ahead with your eyes open was no longer an option. There had to be some way of getting around this, I knew, so I tried everything I could think of: holding my hand in front of my face, wrapping a thin piece of cloth above my eyes and stretching it, sunglasses, tantric meditation; nothing worked. Nothing could stop the pounding of water droplets into my eyes. Then I stumbled upon another idea.

"What th…re you doing?" Chris yelled.

"I've stumbled upon another idea!" I shouted back, forcing the words through the torrent, fishing in my bag. When I found what I was looking for, the hiss drowned out most of his laughter and I could only just hear him shout, "…brilliant…photo!"

I fished around some more until I found my waterproof camera and passed it over.

Then, Chris took a picture of me sitting in torrential rain on the roof of a bus in the Philippines wearing a pair of rolled-up trousers, a T-shirt, and a snorkel and mask. It's just a shame you couldn't see the beer.

When in Rome…

"Hmmfffhheerrrmffuurnnmmeggnneee!" I said. Which, if you translate it literally from Snorkelese means, "Watch out for that tree!"

Thwack!

By the time we had arrived in El Nido, it was still possible to make out the craggy limestone cliffs in the low cloud, just.

I was shivering.

In fact, I couldn't stop shivering. Everything was soaked through and it was difficult to climb off the bus—as though my limbs would give way and I would collapse to the floor in a bleak puddle of hypothermic misery. I struggled to keep my grip on things and my fingers were slow to react. All I wanted was to curl myself up and sit in the end of a giant's hairdryer for a day or two. It didn't take long to find somewhere to stay, but we did not know how long we would have to remain there. Nor did we realise that the storm had been given a name: Karen.

It took me a long time to stop shivering that night.

***

Along the northern coast of the dagger-shaped island of Palawan lies a pristine archipelago of towering limestone and sparkling crystal waters; a place where deserted white sand beaches and hidden lagoons give way to coral reefs that house a marine ecology more colourful than an eighties music video. It is a tropical paradise of fishermen and coconuts, where the pace of life is slow and the grass always green.

In short, a great place to fanny about with a hammock.

To get to El Nido, I had flown from Sorong in Papua to Jakarta, via Sulawesi, then on to Bangkok, taken a train down to Kuala Lumpur, caught another flight to Manila, then one more to Puerto Princesa, where we caught a bus to somewhere near Taytay, from which we had walked to a place where we found a rickshaw to take us all the way to Taytay, and finally hopped on one more bus from Taytay to El Nido. A total journey time of about five days. Now that we had arrived in El Nido, our mission was simple: get out.

Pleasant as the small town was, what we had actually come to see was the stunning Bacuit Archipelago, the scattering of emerald islets that spread out from El Nido as though God had once stood over Palawan and sneezed violently into the sea. After the difficulties of travelling the length and breadth of Papua illegally, we wanted to find a place where we could relax in our hammocks with a bottle of rum and some char-grilled fish without being stared at by hordes of curious locals.

Unfortunately, we were still in a part of the world where things are rarely that simple.

"This'll pass; it's just a bad spell. Wait for this afternoon, it'll be sunny—you'll see."

"If you say so dude."

Chris splashed into the water towards the bangka, the small traditional-style boat we were taking out into the bay, and put our bags into the hull. I waded in after him and held onto one of the outriggers, partly to keep it steady while he climbed in, and partly for another reason. Then, with the average water temperature in El Nido's bay ever so slightly increased and everybody else boarded, I gave the outrigger a shove and sloshed alongside the hull, where Chris helped pull me in.

Landing with a flop on the narrow decking, I nodded to the boatman. A swift yank on the starter cord and the boat came alive.

Put put put…

With that noise as our companion, we chugged away from the beach, drawing parallel to the misty limestone cliffs that surrounded El Nido and provided shelter for the bay.

"I don't see what all the fuss is about anyway, the sea is pretty calm today," I said as we neared the edge of the cliffs.

"Well I suppose sooo-" Chris's last vowel was elongated as he momentarily became weightless. "Shit me!"

A jet of salty water coated the occupants of the boat—myself, Chris and the boatman, as well as a German guy who had tagged along for a spot of snorkelling. The bangka rocked back, making our bags fall further into the rear of the hull as green sea splashed and frothed all around us, the foam being blasted along the wind-swept crests of waves. Between each dip and ridge, the little boat was being tossed about like a pancake, smashing into the swell, bouncing through the rain.

Up the crest, down the trough, splash, repeat.

The boatman turned the bangka around the corner of the rocky headland towards the hazy outline of the craggy limestone islands as a gust of wind, thick with salty spray, pushed into our faces and nearly knocked off the German's cap.

"Scheiss!" he exclaimed, gripping onto his head.

With the strength of the wind, the rain was now horizontal and it cut through us like a cold knife. I started welcoming the spray from the waves—it felt warm compared to the rain. We were soaked through and although I knew all my camping kit was sealed in waterproof bags, I didn't have much in the way of spare clothing.

Up the crest, down the trough, splash, repeat…

We managed to get a surprising distance in the little bangka before we noticed that it was beginning to fill with water. In fact, we were way out in the open, equidistant between three potential landing points. In one way, this was a good thing since we had several options open to us. Unfortunately, every silver lining has a cloud and all of these options were shit.

The boatman passed me a bucket via Chris, since I was in the best place to start bailing water from the hull. I took to the task with exceptional vigour, whispering a discrete prayer under my breath. Only once my body started to warm up did I slow down to a reasonable level, but it wasn't much use. Hard as I tried, the bangka was starting to sink. Realising this fact, we also sensed something else. Barely a hundred metres from us, there was a person standing on the water.

"Look," I shouted over the hiss of another wave breaking on the boat, "Jesus has come to save us!"

"Oh my!" shouted Chris, "It *is* Jesus!"

The German guy said simply, "I don't think it is Jesus."

"Oh look," Chris said, spotting another figure, "Jesus has got a girlfriend!"

"Good lad, maybe that's where he went wrong last time!"

"Yeah, and they're both holding snorkels! Must be a honeymoon or something, maybe the Sea of Galilee is too cliché nowadays!"

Doing his bit for our quest for divine knowledge, the boatman had started turning the bangka around, towards the couple standing on the water.

"You Englanders are so dumb," said the German in his German accent, "that is not Jesus and his wife. There are more than two of them."

I squinted and held my hand up to stop the spray. He was right; his efficient German eyesight had served him well, for there were two heads bobbing in the water next to Christ and his missus. Not only that, but Jesus seemed to be panicking, waving at us with uncharacteristic terror. His powers were obviously getting weaker—

the water was now around his knees. For a moment, the engine cut out and we heard the word, "Heellllp!" floating through the gusting rain. The couple were waiving at us now with their flippers, stumbling, trying to maintain their balance.

When I lay in my guesthouse bed early that morning, I remembered hearing the sound of one boat leaving the beach. I had heard or seen no others since and as far as I knew it was the only other boat to leave the bay that day.

"Hey," the boatman shouted at me, "water!" He pointed to our boat; it was filling up again. I caught on and started bailing as though lives depended on it. Which I suppose they did. A few seconds later the engine spluttered but I heard the starter cord wind back into place. A second wrench on the engine; again, nothing happened. The boatman said something that sounded very similar to "duck" in Tagalog. At least, I think it was Tagalog.

I bailed harder, throwing gallons of water into the sea around us. A slow minute passed and the water level finally started dropping. The boatman gave the engine another tug and this time it coughed back into life. Feeling less biblical, we reached the stricken couple soon after.

"Our boat sank!" shouted Jesus in an American accent. Now that we were closer, we could see a light-coloured shape hovering just below the surface of the choppy green waves; two Filipino men were clinging to it. "My girlfriend is getting really cold. Can you take us back to El Nido?"

"No," shouted the boatman. "We cannot take any more or our boat sink too. We will call help. You must wait for rescue boat."

I turned to him, "We can't abandon our mateys like that—she's getting really sick."

"Aye," agreed Chris.

Sailing the rough tropical seas on the search for hidden lagoons and coming across stricken vessels was affecting us, it seemed. And, short and blue as she had become, Jesus's girlfriend was slowly starting to look like a Smurf.

"Listen up crew, we'll be taking these scurvy dogs back to port, savvy?" I said, or words to that effect.

"Please," the American deity begged.

"Okay," the boatman relented.

"Arr," I concluded.

"Hold yer sail, what about those landlubbers?" Chris pointed to the two Filipinos bobbing in the water beside us. They smiled and wagged their heads as though there was nothing wrong.

"They must stay with the boat—we go now and get bigger boat. Their one made from wood, it will float," the boatman said. He waved at the men and they waved back, exchanging a few sentences over the sound of the idling engine. The American swam across with his girlfriend and Chris helped them into the boat.

The boatman, who I then decided to nickname Barry (Barry Boatman or Barry Bastard, depending on how the next hour played out), revved the engine and chugged off back towards El Nido. With the swell now on our side, we made good progress and the extra weight was offset by manic bailing from all. Once we had reached the headland, no more water was splashing across the sides of the hull and the rocking motion became more subdued. Barry coasted the bangka into the sand and threw an anchor behind us. After helping the Americans out, he trotted off up the beach, returning by the time we had unloaded and waded ashore with our bags.

"It's okay, I go now with a bigger boat and we, um…"

"Tow?" Chris suggested.

"Yes, tow the other boat back." Barry Boatman smiled, "Don't worry, it is safe."

Down the beach, a crew had started loading a much larger vessel which appeared to have a cabin and a roof. Still made from wood and with the same outriggers that characterised Filipino boats, this bangka was clearly the toughest beast in the bay.

"We will be back in one hour, maybe two."

"Do you need some help?" Chris asked.

"No, it is okay. We do this many times."

Chris and I sat down on the sand, looking out at the sea with the rain washing away the salt water from our faces. A mild sense of relief kept us stationary for a short while. Chris rolled down onto his stomach and said, "I'm not sure this storm is going to pass that quickly dude."

"I think you might be right."

I lay back and closed my eyes, feeling the raindrops slap heavily against my skin.

"Hey guys," the American said as he padded across, "thanks for helping us out back there."

"No worries Jesus, couldn't leave a smurf behind—but thank Barry when he gets back too, savvy?" I said, without opening my eyes.

"Huh?"

"Oh, er, you're welcome mate."

TEN

Tanduay Times

Chris pulled up a chair and so did I.

"So you were the crazy idiots who went out into the bay today?"

"Two of them, yes," Chris responded.

"You know this is a typhoon that's hitting now right?"

"Really?" I looked at Chris. "Well that makes sense."

"So when's it going to end?" Chris asked.

"I don't know man, few days maybe. But look, don't worry. Tanduay is only seventy pesos from the shop here."

"Tanduay?"

"You don't know Tanduay? It's the best rum. Tastes like a baboon's arsehole if you drink it straight but it is good with pineapple juice."

"Nice."

Another lad walked in.

"Hey, this is Leo."

"Hi, where are you guys from?" asked Leo.

"England," we replied simultaneously. "You?"

"He's from here too, he's one of my fellow tour guides."

"Ah okay, sorry, you sounded American. So you weren't running the tours today?"

"No man, we'd die! Times like these, we call them Tanduay Times, don't we Leo?"

"Yeah, you can't go into the bay right now. The boats will sink."

Emmanuel turned to Leo, "These crazy fuckers did!"

"No way!" A look of astonishment washed over his handsome face. "You went in today?"

"Yeah, but we didn't get very far."

"Oh shit," Leo laughed, "Were you the guys who got rescued?"

Chris looked taken aback. "Hell no, we *did* the rescue." Then he scratched his head. "Some of it, anyway."

"What happened to that boat?" Leo asked.

"They towed it in about an hour ago man." Emmanuel shouted something in Tagalog at the bar girl and she wandered across with a can of pineapple juice and a cup. He then fished about under the big wooden table, brought out a dark brown bottle, poured some into a cup and handed it to Chris. "Try this dude."

"Thanks fella." Chris took a swig and instantly gagged. "Gah! It tastes fucking horrible!" Then he tried to pull a smile, but it still looked like a grimace to me. "Only joking," he gasped, "it tastes really nice, honest." He passed the cup over and I took a cautious sniff.

"Gooh, fuck. It smells like Ricky Gervais's jokes."

"Have a swig you pussy!" Chris jived.

"Yeah, English wuss!" agreed Emmanuel.

"Drink!" shouted Leo.

I heaved the glass back and gulped it down. Chris was right, it did taste unconventional. "That tastes like diarrhoea!" I shouted.

The table went silent for a moment.

"Too far?"

"Too far," replied Chris.

Before long, the cup was filled again, only this time the pineapple was poured in. "Now try."

I took a sip. The sting of the rum was completely gone. "This is lovely," I said. "How much of this is pineapple juice?"

Leo pointed halfway down the glass. "Doesn't take much to make it good, man—that's the beauty of Tanduay. Hey, do you guys want to come to Balay Tubay?"

"What's that?"

"It's a bar, but there's live music."

"Leo plays there on the guitar. He's fuckin' good!"

"Nah, I'm not, I am just learning," Leo said, shying away. "But I like playing." He paused for a second, looked at us. "There are some really good guys who play there though, you have to see it."

"Sure."

***

Tanduay count: 3

The room was dark and the music was loud—loud enough that we had to raise our voices to be heard by one another. That wasn't an issue though, Leo was practically shouting anyway.

"The Philippines is America's bitch man, we do whatever they say. You know what, it's really screwing us."

"What do you mean? I thought the Americans had left the Philippines ages ago?"

"No dude, I'm not talking about the army. It's the government that keeps getting pushed around. The US tells us what to do and we do it."

"Why?"

"Economy—America is controlling our economy. You see the guys in here? They're all activists."

"Activists against what?"

"The neoliberals man, they're ruining this country."

"Look, Leo mate, I have no idea what you're getting at here."

"Sure, sorry." Leo paused, took a quick sip of his tanduay and pineapple. "Look, what the West wants is a place where they can get cheap labour—bigger profit margins, you know, the American dream right? So they pressure the Philippines to make sure there aren't taxes on foreign companies. Neoliberalism—it's all about free trade. Free trade means deregulation, deregulation means the corporations that turn up here can do whatever they want without the government getting anything from it. If the government disagrees, the US pushes us about."

"How?"

"Loans—the IMF and World Bank have got the Philippines by the balls and they are controlled by America. America controls the IMF, the IMF controls the Philippines. And then there's the aid."

"Aid?"

"Yeah, because the Philippine government is in so much debt with the IMF and World Bank, it relies on aid. So America gives the Philippines aid to help run stuff like education and healthcare as long as the Philippines government does what America says—promote corporate investment and deregulate the market. And you know why that's a bad thing right?"

"Um. No?"

"Because of what the corporations do to us. They force us to sell our land and resources for a price we have to accept so they can make money from it without giving anything back. If they employ Filipinos, they pay them as little as they can, and they don't always bother to do that anyway. Some people here, they think they are getting a good deal, but that's because they don't know how valuable what we have is. This is the simple truth man: those internationals don't care about what happened before they came or what will happen after they go, they just want to make as much money as they can in as little time as they can. You deregulate the market; these fuckers can get away with anything. In the neoliberal world, worker's rights don't exist. Environments, people—these are just resources to be consumed. This kind of shit is making poor people poorer and rich people richer everywhere, all over the world."

"Oh," I suggested, gulping down some of my drink to distract from the fact that I was starting to feel slightly guilty.

"We're activists because we don't want to be the place where the West—sorry man—get's its fucking underpants stitched together. This is a beautiful place and we are talented people. We are clever people. We don't want our environment destroyed and our brothers starved so some fat guy can buy a yacht and join a golfing club and fuck his plastic wife in a huge house ten thousand miles away. Cheap labour, man, that's what it's all about. It's economic slavery: keep us poor and them rich. If this neoliberalism shit worked like they say it should, we'd all be rich by now already."

"But the more investment you get, the richer you guys become, right?"

"Wrong dude! The only reason the West is so rich is because others are poor. That's the way it works. You think everybody could consume as much as the West does?"

"I guess not."

"You see, the people who have the money have the power to make sure the system keeps running like it should, because if everybody got rich, the world would be screwed. Everything would run out. And look, it's not just about that—we want to stand up for ourselves. I don't care what it takes, I don't want to be America's bitch anymore."

The musicians had stopped playing for a moment and were shouting something. Leo turned around. "What?"

"Get up here!"

"Oh, right." He faced me again, standing up. "Sorry to get heavy. But that's why I work in tourism; it's the only way I can learn to speak English fluently and fund my education." He stepped away, paused, then looked back at the yellow-brown liquid that sat in a small plastic cup on the table in front. "Look man, finish this off. I can't drink any more." Pushing it over to me, Leo stood up from the table and walked across to the small stage at the other side of the bar, grabbing a guitar from the stand by the side. As I picked up the cup, smelling the sweet aroma of pineapple, someone counted to four and the band started playing a cover of "Wonderwall" by Oasis.

I took a sip and decided it was my favourite song in the world.

* * *

Tanduay count: 5

We paused to listen as Leo cranked out one of the best covers I'd ever heard of "Hotel California"—one of the classic Eagles tunes that somehow surfaced quite regularly in beachside backpacker hotspots like this. While the band was singing a number of great local songs, I had taken in the surroundings. The bar had been garnished with wooden and rope artefacts—playful handicrafts and knickknacks that suited the artistic décor down to the ground. Everything had a natural, handmade feel about it. Even the heavy polished-timber tabletops were held up by thick sections of tree trunk. It was as though the whole place had been made from the same group of trees by the same group of people, for exactly the same reasons.

Around the band, colourful paintings and portraits of famous people—Bob Marley, Tracy Chapman, even Jesus (who didn't look much like the American guy earlier after all, even if he was somehow as white as the pope)—hung against the bamboo and wooden-slat background. The warm tones of the moody lighting that bounced up the walls helped add to the sense of homeliness and welcome, but the band were painted in a different, lagoon-blue stage light; dancing and moving with the music, they stood out well.

The guys who built the place had clearly put a lot of thought into what they wanted, because in Balay Tubay, we weren't just sitting in a bar; we were sitting in an ideology. A way of life. A different outlook on the world. One where anything was possible if you were creative enough. It felt inspired and for me, inspiring. It almost made me want to grow a ponytail, just for the hell of it. Or a shit beard, like the kind of beard Chris would grow if he ever went to Cuba.

"I had to find the passage back to the place I was before..."

Emmanuel turned back towards us. "I told you he was good!" Chris and I nodded enthusiastically, but we were too busy singing along to the music to answer him verbally. We all looked back towards Leo, who was filling each lyric with the emotion it deserved.

"You can checkout any time you like, but you can never *leave!"*

Another phenomenal piece of guitar work followed. Possibly the greatest piece of live music I had ever heard, ever. Either that, or I was starting to feel the spirited passion of the Tanduay. The small crowd in the bar—a masala mix of locals and foreigners—whooped and cheered as the piece seamlessly merged into the first chords of the acoustic version of "Layla", the best rendering of Eric Clapton's most famous song. I was impressed; the guys clearly knew their stuff.

Together, illuminated in the heavy stage lighting, band members hammered out the music with rhythm and feeling, smiling at each other as they each showed their flare on the instruments. Combined, the effect was astounding, and my foot started tapping away involuntarily. In the moody darkness, I could see that Chris was playing the drums on his arm. Emmanuel, on the other hand, was singing through a grin that made it seem as though the Hoover Dam had been built under his nose.

***

Tanduay count: 8

"Sho, where are you from?" asked the Dutch guy in a near-shout. It was his turn in the conversation to find out about me. You see, I knew that he was from Holland, here for two weeks with his three children and wife, and they were planning to go "shnorkelling" in the bay but were "shtuck" in town until the typhoon had moved on. After their two weeks here, they would go sailing around the world or swimming to Mars or something like that. I think.

"England," I responded.

"And you are jusht on holidaysh here or shumthing?" he followed on, with the familiar Dutch lisp.

"Yesh. I mean, yes." I replied. "Well, sort of. I was doing some research for my degree thesis."

Degresis, I thought, predictably.

"That sounds very intereshting! Where was that?"

"In Papua."

"Where?"

"Um, Papua. West Papua."

"Papua New Guinea?"

"No, West Papua," I shouted inaudibly over the sound of harmonising voices. "It's part of Indonesia. It shouldn't be really, but it is their easternmost province. Also called Irian Jaya?"

A blank expression with yellow-blonde hair stared back at me.

"Just to the left of Papua New Guinea?" I suggested.

"Ah, I think I know where you mean. With the monkey people who live in trees. It is very remote, no? What is it like?"

"Oh, it's incredible—really really *really* incredible. And beautiful too." I paused for a hiccup. "But the culture and everything there is being destroyed. I mean, it's so horrible to think that this is one of the last places where people can live like they always have and it's being *destroyed*. God it's sad."

"Really?"

"Yeah! These people, there's still guys in tribal clothing, like with *penis* gourds and shit, and this is the only place outside the Amazon or the Nicobar Islands where you'll find tribes with no outside contact who still use stone axes instead of machetes, and it's all being pillaged and all this *civilise the savages* bullshit; it's just killing off the last truly free people on the *planet*, you know? They don't want that—they don't want to be *civilised*. Are some people really arrogant enough to think that chewing the world up and turning into blobs of fashionably shiny shit in the name of greed is civilised?"

I knew I was slurring, but I didn't really care. I wasn't *drunk*, drunk. Just passionate, filled with the spirit of Filipino rum.

"Yah, I think it is a shame that people have to do this."

"I know, and it's *our* fault man! It's *our* ideology that's destroying someone else's culture just to satisfy our craving for having loads and loads of pointless shiny stuff we could easily just live without. It's fucked, man, I'm telling you. The world's just fucked."

"Wow," said the Dutch Flash Gordon, gulping down some of his drink. "That sucks."

"Sorry. Maybe I went on a bit."

"I need to go to the toilet," he said, standing up from his wicker chair too quickly, almost knocking it over.

"Okay, buddy. Take it easy," I tried to shout after him, but he was already gone.

Shit, maybe I went too deep too soon?

"I hate it when that happens," Chris said, leaning across from me—obviously I had been thinking out loud again.

"What do you mean?"

"Don't worry dude. Bad memories. Just ignore me."

I did.

Then I hiccupped again.

* * *

Tanduay count: 11

Our second bottle of Tanduay was running low by the time the band had stopped playing and was packing up. The mixes had been getting progressively weaker, so over the course of the night we had remained just about legible. But I was getting danger-close to the point of no return. Or complete return, depending on how you looked at it. Whatever it was, I knew that I needed to slow down or I'd be speaking Vomitese—a chunky language I'd already perfected in Malaysia and needed no reminding of—before the night was through.

"I know this feeling mate, we need to get out of here," I told Chris, as I watched the outline of his twin creeping out of him.

I closed my eyes.

Focus. Not again. *Twice in one book is too much,* I probably thought.

When my lids heaved themselves open, Chris was standing. "Let's go. I need some air."

We waved goodbye to the band, telling Leo and Emmanuel we'd see them tomorrow, and headed out onto the street behind the bar. Combined, the irregular padding of our footsteps must have sounded like Meg White drumming for the White Stripes—there was no rhythm to it whatsoever. I veered to the sides of the street like a circus amateur perched on a monocycle. When I looked down, I could see that my legs were just a convenient obstacle between the ground and me. Self-consciously, I corrected myself into Chris's path as soon as I noticed my direction.

"I think I need to stop drinking so much," I slurred as I bounced into Chris for the fourth time.

Chris paused for a moment, considering the information I'd just imparted on him so eloquently, then veered forward as though he were being driven by a malicious four-year old with a remote control. When he caught up with me, he said, "I think I left my flip-flops behind."

Which, more than anything else, summed up how I felt at that moment too.

* * *

Chris padded along the beach, leaving a trail of footprints that led back to the reception of our old guesthouse. Over his shoulders, the detachable pouches from his rucksack were casually slung. Like me, he had left everything at a storage facility in Bangkok and only had what he needed for the trip: hammock, machete, lighter, toothbrush and for now, a few days' food and a pot.

The sun was shining bright and without any breeze, the air was already hot. I could feel the sweat collecting like condensation on my chest. From here the sea seemed calm, but the storm had pushed a murky layer of silt to the surface of the water in the bay. On top of the shimmering latte-brown, the flaking bangka bobbed happily, like a puppy about to be taken for a walk.

"He's coming now!" I shouted at Emmanuel, who ran down to the beach from the restaurant and started wading into the silt. Chris strolled over, his shadow slanting out towards the water.

"Room all sorted?" I asked.

"Yeah dude, no troubles." Chris stood next to me and we both peeked at the bangka with eyes shielded under our hands. "Is she good to go?"

"Think so." I shuffled my feet in the sand, enjoying the sensation as the tiny grains pushed through my toes. The top layer was hot and dry, but under the surface, I could still feel the cool moisture from the rains sticking to my skin. "Emmanuel says if it gets too rough around the headland, we'll just head back in. But it's looking good."

"As good as it's looked since we got here."

I shouldered my small rucksack and trudged down the slope until I felt the cool splash of water wash the grainy sediment away from my ankles. "Hey Emmanuel, how is it going?"

"Yeah man, come on in!"

I jumped into the bangka and climbed to the front, flopping my legs over each side of the wooden bow. Emmanuel helped Chris up, grabbed a bamboo pole and started punting the boat around to face out from the beach. With the cloud finally gone, I could see how remarkable the bay was. To the left, a limestone precipice projected itself straight up from the village at the far end of the beach; compared to the small shacks nestled around their base, the cliffs were infinitely more imposing than any castle I had ever seen. But it was obvious that they served a protective purpose, for the site of the village had clearly been chosen to maximise the shelter provided by the craggy outcrops. They were a safeguard, a shield from the violent storms and typhoons that often lashed against the reaches of the shore during the monsoon season.

To the front, another limestone hill jutted out of the sea, its elongated spine thick with greenery—an island sheltering numerous protected beaches and secret coves. There was something primordial about the way it raised itself up from the waves; I could easily imagine it swimming across to New York and smashing down all the tourist attractions, just for the hell of it.

As we started put-putting into the archipelago, the water blurring under my feet changed colour from milky brown, through grey-green, to the same deep emerald as the foliage on the hillsides around us. I could see my shadow outline jutting out from the bow, cutting a dark silhouette through the depths in front of me, contrasting against the iridescent sea and the tiny particles of plankton that whizzed under the boat. By the time we had reached the headland, the warm wind had all but dried the sweat from my skin and the sun felt pleasantly hot on my back. Small waves slapped unthreateningly against the hull; occasionally, one would spray my hovering feet. The bow rose and dipped with the gentle swell—not a jumpy movement this time, but more relaxed, like an old rocking chair swinging back and forth over the glistening ocean.

We were passing a small beach that lay under the shade of overhanging palm fronds, translucent water lapping the white sand, when Emmanuel shouted over the engine, "This is where we can drop you off tonight." I raised my thumb without looking at him. I could see a few coconuts scattered along the beach—perfect to supplement our water supplies.

I had to be honest with myself, this place was a cliché. Nobody should be lucky enough to live here. Unspoilt beaches, hidden lagoons, crystal waters, azure skies. The storm, while it had been an interesting experience, had totally blinded us to the sheer splendour of the archipelago on our doorstep. We had been forced to spend our days sitting on the porch of our beach hut, nursing residual hangovers and waiting for the rain to stop as we increased our tolerance to rum, talked politics or just joked with Emmanuel and Leo. It hadn't been a dull time by any stretch; I had really enjoyed their company and the opportunity to stay in one place for a while, soaking up the local mentality on life. But now, we were getting on with what we had first intended to do. The days spent in the rain only made the experience all the more agreeable, all the more enriched.

Here, the beauty felt different from the Papuan highlands in a way that was hard to describe; in the mountains, we were witnessing the scenic attractiveness of a populated land superficially unchanged for millennia, and yet there was an undercurrent of gritty hardship that seemed to pervade life there. Perhaps because I had spent time looking into the politics of the area, I found that it was a tough beauty, where people had to put up with the harsh realities of tribal life under occupation—disease, insecurity, the threat of violence. It was a rewarding place to be and an exciting one—after all, we were exploring one of the last frontiers on the planet. But I couldn't say it was relaxing.

Now, on our bangka, everything was designed to be pleasing to the eye. Pleasant to the touch. There was no hardship, not in our little bangka. The weather was fine; we had food, shelter. We had water. We were no longer under constant threat of being caught doing anything illegal, or being offensively smelly. *And* we were pottering through one of the most dazzlingly beautiful island groups in the world. What we had, right there, bobbing through the islets of the Bacuit, with the wind in our hair and the spray on our feet, was freedom. Pure, undiluted freedom.

Nobody should be this lucky, I thought to myself again, as a shoal of flying fish leapt out from under the advancing bow.

For a while, I got lost staring at my feet, watching the glitter of spray coat them, watching the water change colour yet again, from green to aqua blue. Swimming-pool blue. The blue that makes you sign up to every tropical beach holiday you'll ever go on.

The boatman shut off the engine and Emmanuel chucked an anchor over the side; it pierced the surface of the water with a splash and I watched as it floated down to its impact on the sandy bottom. I stood up and Chris threw me my goggles. "Last one to catch a shark buys the Tanduay."

By the time the bangka dropped us off and we had waded ashore with our bags held above our heads, it was late afternoon. The sun was still bright, but it no longer held the heat of earlier on. While the boat drifted off, the sound of the engine slowly evaporating, Chris and I sat on a log that had been dumped on the beach by the tide.

"Not a bad day," Chris said, as the noise all but disappeared.

"Hmm," I said thoughtfully, looking at the islands scattered like polka dots in the bay in front of us. "Not a bad day at all. Fancy a coconut?" I got up, a large grin on my face.

"Fuck yes dude."

I grabbed the knife from my sack, tied it onto my waist. Turned around and started trudging up the beach.

Stretching out from my feet, the shadow on the sand in front of me told me everything I needed to know to understand what I was doing here: an outline of a skinny guy with unruly hair, dressed only in ragged shorts; a hammock slung over one shoulder and a machete tapping against his leg. It was the shadow of someone who had everything he needed and—for the first time since he got a train set on his sixth birthday—everything he wanted.

As I climbed up the bank and set my hammock down on the floor between two palm trees, a breeze drifted through the fronds above my head and a thump sounded out a few metres away. Walking over to it, there was a green coconut lying on the ground so I picked it up and bashed it a few times with the machete until a splash of liquid poured onto my hands. Holstering the knife in its wooden sheath, I trudged down to Chris, who hadn't moved a centimetre.

"Here you go, sugar."

"Thanks sweetie."

Chris took a swig. "Ahhhh."

"Any good?"

He passed it over and I gulped the coconut. The warm, sweet liquid was perfectly refreshing. So I used that as an excuse to take it with me and start setting up camp while Chris made a small fire on the beach.

* * *

Because we had not taken any bowls, I was holding a water bottle cut in half, inside which steamed a mixture of noodles and tinned fish. The sun was dipping below the ridge of an island in the distance, the air was still warm and our hammocks were up and dry, ready for the night. Embers glowed and the occasional flame licked up the side of the blackened pan. Neither of us looked at each other when we spoke in between the odd mouthful—the orange sky was far more appealing.

"This is what it's supposed to be like, isn't it?" Chris mumbled.

"What?"

"This life thing."

"In what way?"

"Well, this place is stunning. That helps. But it's not that, it's…stuff happens here. You don't need anything else to keep you occupied. I mean…ah, fuck. I don't know what I mean." He looked down. "I'll get back to you on that one dude."

"I think I might know." I shifted my feet in the sand, hearing the splash of the surf lapping the shoreline.

"Yeah?"

"Well, maybe. I was thinking about it all earlier—about that silly bus ride here, the sinking boat, Karen, and then this. It's just right. In a way that home isn't."

"Yeah, exactly. Nobody is trying to make this place into a utopia, and maybe that's why it works. Being here, it's like life without armbands—when you sink, you drown. And when you don't, fuck me is it worth it." Chris put his noodles down for a moment and leant back, looking unusually contemplative. "I wouldn't change where we are right now for the world. It just fits. Everything fits."

"The simple life, right?"

"Precisely dude."

A while later, I walked back up the bank and left Chris on the beach, contentedly poking the fire. And as my feet imprinted themselves on the warm sand and I thought about what he'd just said, I realised that the Philippines had become more than just a filler between Papua and our flights back home. Our conversations with the prostitutes in Manila as well as Leo and Emmanuel here had helped fill the next blank in what Chris now only slightly mockingly called my "quest for global knowledge". There was something else too though, something more subjective, more qualitative that built on what I'd found in Borneo—this idea of the simple life. And the basic premise was this: when life was reduced to its bare essentials, happiness was easier to come by. It was an interesting theory, and one I would have to test, but not here. It was too cloudy here—not just meteorologically. There were too many confounding variables. The rum, the company, the sense of freedom. There were too many other possible reasons for our contentedness, so I'd have to find out if I could recreate the same feeling elsewhere.

I climbed into my hammock; under the flysheet, I could see the last of the pink sky fading into darkness and the silhouette of the islands reflected in the water.

This was the view I fell asleep to.

* * *

"PISSONASHITTINGWANKYFUCK!" I screamed through clenched jaws. "FUCK!"

"Dude, what's up?"

"OH, SHIT. Ah, God!" I fell back into the waves. "FUCK!"

Chris jumped out of the boat and splashed his way across, the others following after him. "What's happened?"

"My foot. FUCK!"

"Dude, chill. What's going on?"

"Fucking stood on something. Shit me." My right foot was searing with an unbearable pain, and it was starting to shoot up my leg. "Ah shit. Bollocks. Shit!"

"Calm down dude," Chris said as he reached me. A young Filipino guy had run up the beach and shouted something back. "What?" Chris yelled at him, helping me up.

"Fuck," I said again, balancing precariously with one foot perched in the rocks and Chris supporting me against the swell.

"Sonfis. Comhea!"

"Ah, fuck, what did he say?"

"Stonefish. We need to get you on to the beach."

The pain was excruciating; I could practically feel it throbbing all the way up to the back of my neck. When we got to the young

Filipino lad, he was busy blowing on embers, using sticks to try to get the fire going again. Chris put me down and I lay back, squirming, trying to find some way to relieve the agonising sting. With a hiss, the boatman turned up and extinguished the efforts of the other lad, pouring liquid onto the struggling embers. "Get back," he said, producing a lighter from his shorts. The young lad took a few paces away from the overhanging rock wall that sheltered the fire from the wind.

Whoomph!

The boatman jumped as flames flashed up his arms. The choking smell of burning petrol, and my pounding foot was grabbed and held against the fire. I could feel the heat scalding the skin in every part of my foot, except for the agonising throbbing on the front sole.

"You lucky, jus' wan spine."

I tried to rest my head and ignore the blazing furnace that raged inside my foot, but it was too intrusive, too invasive. Whatever I did, the pain was there, throbbing, grabbing at my attention. I squirmed against the sand, but each time my foot left the flames, it was pulled back, yanked towards the heat. Chris leaned over me, a concerned look on his face. "Keep your foot in the fire dude, it neutralises the poison."

Fuck. *Get a grip.*

I stopped struggling, let my muscles relax. Squirming wasn't helping anything, I needed to zone out, empty my mind of anything.

The burning clawed at my leg, struggling to climb its way back into my awareness, but I let go. Five minutes, ten minutes passed; the burn was still there but I was winning the battle. A piece of driftwood was hoisted under my calf muscle to keep the leg bent and my foot above the glowing blaze.

I could tell that the concentrated sting—the solid, swollen lump that felt like an acid tumour had infused itself just beneath my toes—was merging into the rest of the foot. The whole base had reached the point where my nerves could no longer distinguish whether they were registering extreme heat or, strangely, if they were actually pressed against something painfully cold.

Fuck it hurts.

More time passed and the others were seated around the fire, beginning to look concerned.

"Jams, how it? Still pain?"

"I don't know, maybe a bit better. My whole foot feels like it's on fire though."

"Okay, we stay longer. But soon must go, too much waves."

I pulled the now largely useless appendage away and bent it back so I could look at the sole. A large white area had formed, solid, swollen, surrounded by redness, on the base. I could see the tiny puncture mark in the centre of the inflammation—just a small red dot, although the swelling had closed it completely. As the area around it cooled, the throbbing resumed, clawing its way back up my leg. I put my foot back into the fire, sensing my powers had started to wear thin.

The more the foot burned, the less it stung. Take the burn away and the isolated pulsating would resume, like some kind of fucked up seesaw of agony. But the longer I held my foot in the fire, the more I could tell that the sting was losing its power. It wasn't me that was winning against the pain, but the flame.

After what must have been nearly ninety minutes since I had first stepped on the stonefish, the boys started getting back on the rocking boat. I was loaded on with them.

The boat had picked us up later than agreed that morning—Emmanuel and Leo hadn't come along this time and two other Filipino lads were with us today, along with an assortment of tourists who had taken advantage of the break in the weather to get out into the bay. This, we presumed, was why we had been loaded onto a tour to get us to our next camping spot, rather than being taken individually. Everyone had the same idea and there simply weren't enough boats to go around for us to claim any kind of special treatment. We couldn't complain, not just because we were getting another view of the beautiful bay; again, the weather was perfect.

As the afternoon had progressed however, the familiar clouds started swirling around the highest of the limestone towers and we had been forced to anchor ourselves in the cove by a heavy shower. We took the opportunity to have a food stop until the shower passed. But the swell picked up and started to toss the boat around the stony bay, lashing it against the anchor line, and as the vessel veered dangerously close to the rocky cliffs that formed the cove, pushed by the wind, we decided to load ourselves back on for a quick exit. I was holding the bangka in place, balancing and hobbling on the rocks as the waves splashed over my thighs and against my waist, trying to keep it steady, when I stood on the stonefish.

While I lay with my foot in the fire, oblivious to the activities around me, the team of Filipinos and tourists had tethered the boat down, drafting out lines here and there. For the most part, it was kept from harm and once I was back on, we left the cove.

For the rest of the afternoon, it became apparent that there was going to be no significant improvement in the weather. With one last night before we were due to begin the long journey home though, there was little debate. We would camp again.

***

Lashing tropical storms battered the hammocks all night, but we somehow remained dry in our shelters and the next day didn't start out badly either. Only a mild sniffle accompanied my shuffling attempts to pack up the kit and get on the bangka. I felt relatively strong, pretty rejuvenated, and happy. Most of all, in fact, I felt happy.

Our stay in Palawan had been perfect—exactly what we were after. The weather, once again, wasn't too bad either. The storms of the night had moved on, allowing us the much-needed time to get back on the bus to Puerto Princesa. Even the bus was fine. No worrying lean on this one. Still, we elected to sit on the roof as the weather was looking good and the scenery was worth it.

My sniffles increased, but for the time being, there was nothing sinister going on. Only when we got off the bus and caught a rickshaw into town did I notice that for some reason, I couldn't clear my sinuses. No big problem, just a bit of swelling in the nose. It would be gone in no time, I thought.

By the time we reached Manila, I could feel the first onset of a fever—the achy muscles, the decreased resistance to pain, the general weakness. And the pressure in my sinuses was building into a throbbing headache that had started spreading across my face; it was not helped, of course, by the flight. One more to Kuala Lumpur, then another to Bangkok and my face felt likely to explode.

I arrived in Khao San bleary eyed, cowering in discomfort, and hobbled my way to the nearest hostel. The pain had taken on a different status to the stonefish sting—less intense, but this I couldn't zone out of. I lay for hours on the bed, desperately trying to clear my head, fighting the build-up of pressure against my eyes and behind my cheeks. There was a cavity inside my face, bulging like a water balloon, ready to explode. But when it did, there came no relief; only a thick stream of dark red fluid that kept pouring relentlessly, for hours.

When I boarded the next plane, my condition deteriorated further; I landed in Mumbai airport feeling *very* sorry for myself. But the final flight back to the UK was by far the worst—indeed, it was the worst flight I have ever been on. My headache soared, my fever raged, and my nose continued to bleed dark red. I took paracetamol—something I never normally do—and was quite impressed to see that it actually worked, after half a packet had gone down my throat. But still it was not enough for me to sleep. One week later, my GP diagnosed me with Acute Bacterial Sinusitis and prescribed me some antibiotics. Five days after that, the pain was gone. Apparently, my GP told me, it's normally "not that bad", but "flying doesn't help". I didn't question her.

But I was relieved to see that this time, English people *had* noticed I was gone. Indeed, they had been waiting the whole time for my return by the looks of things.

The economy was in *tatters*.

ELEVEN

You Used to be Cool

Term had already started when I finally arrived back in Exeter. My sinuses were almost normal again, but my foot still ached when I put weight on it. When I described my ordeals to my sympathetic housemates, they were quick to point out that my hair, too, had gone an even redder shade of blonde than usual. "But it doesn't matter," they said, "most gingers smell of piss and biscuits, but you're okay."

Only Kate disagreed.

So there was a plus side, and on top of that I still had my girlfriend to see.

Actually, what the hell was I talking about? I had tonnes of stuff to be pleased about. I had a load of great research, I still had some good friends and a brilliant house! Chris lived just down the road! Guy's blue van now had a specific compartment just for his tools!

Life was *sweet.*

It didn't take me long to get out of the victim mentality of a week or so before; more than anything, it made me realise that I clearly wasn't learning the lessons of Papua. I had witnessed firsthand how life can be much, much tougher, so how could I complain? With the events of the Philippines—being battered by the odd typhoon, getting stung by poisonous fish here and there, dealing with the occasional facial implosion—I hadn't really reflected too much on what my new findings meant for my own world standing. I felt a few pangs of guilt subconsciously, but it was only when I drank that anything started to make any sense.

In the first weeks, I often thought back to the bar in El Nido, where Leo had yelled at me about the injustices of the developing world, and I made a point to look into it. See whether he was correct. And as I assimilated the notes from Papua, read over my journal entries in the Philippines, I began to realise how lucky I was. Simply by being born on the right side of the global economic divide, I had so much more opportunity. I was not lucky because my lifestyle was any better necessarily, but lucky because I would always have a choice. I could *choose* to travel in the Philippines, *choose* to spend my time chasing sharks and stamping on dreadful spindly killer fish; I could *choose* to saunter off into the highlands of New Guinea and eat chickens and play with rebels' spears in the least euphemistic sense possible. And then I could choose to come home and carry on with my degree, or get a job.

Leo, on the other hand, couldn't. Nor could Emmanuel, or Paul. Or Kaka. Or Nikson. The family in the jungle, the prostitutes in Manila; the best they could hope for would be to work extremely hard all their lives for a wage closer, but never that close, to the one I would get if I walked into the corner shop at the end of my street and asked for a spot of part-time.

I *was* lucky. I lived in a free society, where most people could choose to do almost anything they wanted to do, as long as they were disciplined and put their mind to it. Me and my fellow citizens—almost all of us, we could have a TV and a hot shower. We could watch movies, afford at least one pair of shoes, eat the occasional ice cream. We could go out and find a career—not necessarily the perfect career, but a career nonetheless. And as long as we were careful, as long as we worked hard, prioritised, we could generally achieve whatever it was that we wanted to achieve, even if that sometimes meant ending up in so much debt that our lives resembled those of the beggars on the outskirts of the world's worst slums—but it was still our choice.

Apparently, though, this free society had now been smashed by a financial earthquake, a disaster of epic proportions that had plunged the country into the worst recession in living memory. It was terrible; the government simply didn't know what to do. It stuttered and slouched and blamed greedy bankers for the mess, but mostly it just panicked. The shit had hit the fan and for the first time in my lifespan, British people were facing extreme hardship.

Apparently.

Now maybe that really was the case in some circles, but as hard as I tried, I couldn't find it anywhere. We were in the worst economic depression since World War Two and nothing really seemed to be happening. Sure, people were losing jobs, struggling to pay bills, and plenty of families could quite rightly claim to be having a much tougher time than they were before, but very few people were actually *starving*. Very few were *dying*. In fact, if some newspapers were to be believed, the mortality rate was lower now than ever before because fewer people could afford the alcohol levels that allowed them to do reckless things.

It was confusing.

And it was at that moment that I realised one of the most underrated facts of life: *Everything is relative*.

It's a fundamental, right? No matter how high you are, it will always suck to fall. And no matter how low you are, every step up must feel great. Or, at least, that's the only way I could get my head around the panic that consumed the British media and the fear that had wafted up the noses of the British public.

***

I'll admit, when I got back from Papua and the Philippines, I was different. My lifestyle shifted; I spent more time alone, more time reading and listening to music. More time exercising, cycling, climbing. I took up a self-defence class for three evenings a week, relishing the opportunity to vent some imaginary anger at something I didn't really understand. I boxed, punched bags until the skin on my knuckles cracked, then punched some more, leaving dark shiny flecks on the red vinyl. Then, with shaking hands, I'd sit and read something, maybe do some writing. Try and work out what exactly my role in the world really was.

I had my little routine, my way of moving the days forward, but deep down I had started to feel quite unsettled.

It was noticeable to others too. I turned down offers to go to the pub, I never really went partying. If I somehow ended up near a nightclub, I'd get away as soon as possible—the loud music, heavy atmosphere and flashing lights just made me feel aggressive. Quite often, while my friends staggered on to the next watering hole, I would find myself walking through town alone, strolling purposefully away from the laughter and merriment, back to a pizza and a spot of late-night softcore.

It was a strange time; I felt like I had started taking myself quite seriously—something I had always tried to avoid—and it was certainly having an effect. My friendships started drifting; eventually people I'd had nights out with in the years before no longer sent me messages letting me know where the meeting point was or how many "lash tokens" I needed to bring. Presumably, they knew my answer would be: No. Sorry, I'm busy tonight.

Even things with my girlfriend started taking a turn for the worse. We still got on, but the chemistry was different. Half the time, she seemed aloof, unaffectionate, and I couldn't help but think that maybe it was a reflection on me, of how I seemed to her. I still liked her a lot, but like everyone else in their third year at university, she was working hard and playing hard—going out and having fun, ringing me at the end of the evening, telling me that I should have been there with her and that she's just had the best time with her friends, that she misses me and wishes I would come out with her too sometimes and could she please see me, yes, now, please.

Usually, I'd agree. But my reluctance rarely went unnoticed and we had our first arguments in the few months after I got back.

I remember one night that summed it all up; having walked back from one of the more smelly clubs in Exeter, I was sitting down in the living room with a pizza. Some useless crap was on the television—probably *Sexcetera* or something equally educational—and I was counting down the housemates as they returned from various nightspots around town. Amber was out, probably seeing her boyfriend. Kate had rushed upstairs, presumably on a post-binge purge, and I'd sniggered as I listened to the footsteps thump through the house, wondering when she'd discover that I'd maturely placed her cuddly toys in compromising positions on her pillow.

Grumpy or not, I *was* still a student.

Guy, who had contributed a few latex props for the scheme, joined me in the living room and flopped on the couch, chuckling to himself too. That left only two more—Venetia and Mark.

Venetia, a drama student in all senses and yet possibly one of the loveliest people I have come across, danced into the lounge a few minutes later. "Hi guys!" she sang. "You just missed out on the most *wonderful* night."

"Hey Venetia," we groaned.

She stood by the door for a moment, shifting her weight from one foot to the other, looking, as usual, as happy as she did pretty.

"Well?"

My mouth barely opened. "What?"

"Don't you want to hear about it?"

"Not really V," I grumbled.

"What are you watching?" She hopped onto the settee next to me and curled her knees up. "Oh, guys, this is *disgusting*."

"It's very educational."

"Oh. My. God. Why would you *ever* do that to your boyfriend? Doesn't it hurt?" She looked at the plate on my lap. "Can I have some pizza please Jamie?"

"No."

"Thanks J-dog!" she said in a tuneful voice, grabbing a slice and ruffling my hair. "I don't know what I'd do without you."

"Bugger off."

Venetia stuffed half the slice into her mouth and looked around. "God, you guys are so *boring*," she said once she'd finished laboriously chewing the pizza. She glanced at us with a playful sneer and looked back at the TV. "That girl's not going to put that there is she? Oh my, that would be wrong even if he wasn't sixty-million years old! That. Is. *Gross!*"

Mark, the final housemate, walked in and took a seat next to Guy.

"Marky!" Venetia shouted.

"Sharky!" Guy concurred.

"Evening," replied Mark with a cheeky grin.

"Wasn't that just the *best* night ever?" Venetia rolled her eyes, smiling at Mark.

"Wasn't bad was it!" He leant back into the couch. "Where the hell did you go, Jamie?"

"Went home early," I said, through a mouthful of pizza. "Wasn't really feeling it."

"You never come out anymore." Venetia brushed the crumbs from her lap. "I think you've turned into a loser."

"I think *you've* turned into the loser," I replied, wittily.

"Seriously Jamie, what has happened to you? You used to be fun."

"Yeah, now you're really boring."

"Dunno. Just not that into it anymore I guess."

"Don't worry, you'll be back with us soon, right Jimbo?" Venetia ruffled my hair again. "Right J-dog? He's just manstrating. We've all been there." She paused. "Well, not me. But you know what I mean."

"Shut up Venetia."

"Yeah V, be quiet."

"Okay!"

The conversation died down for a while, with Mark, Guy and I all staring at the TV. Venetia winced, occasionally saying things like "How many *what* can she fit in *where?*" and "Seriously, what is the age gap *there?* Dis-gus-ting." I could still see the silicon girls with their prosthetic tits as they pranced around on the TV in front, but a sentence kept flashing up in bold neon across the screen: *You used to be fun.*

YOU USED TO BE FUN! Now, you're really boring.

I used to be fun? What's that supposed to mean? That I'm now a granddad? I'm still at uni for God's sake, I'm having the time of my life. I *MUST* be fun.

Everyone is fun at university.

They were, of course, right. It was true. I *did* used to be fun. At least, whatever the grammatically correct version of that sentence was, it was true. What had got into me? In fact, ever since I first started travelling, I'd slowly found myself turning more introspective, more introverted. For whatever reason, I was now a lot more *intro*-everything. And I had started to appreciate people who had longer hair and wore bead necklaces like Richard Hammond from Top Gear did after his rocket-car crash. That couldn't be a good thing. What could possibly make that seem like a good idea? Does travel really make a person less sociable? Has it made me more boring?

It didn't make sense.

Really? I'd done so much stuff—I couldn't be boring! *Could I?*

I hadn't a clue. But I knew I needed a change. The longer I remained in my room, wallowing, doing my little routine, staying in at night, the more I began to find Exeter claustrophobic. The more I disliked student life. The days were getting shorter, the nights longer, and my patience was wearing thin.

Maybe, I wondered as I sat on the couch, maybe I was getting too bogged down in all this moral stuff. All my life I'd considered myself a nice guy; I'd open doors for people, I'd help old ladies with their shopping if they needed it; I'd go out of my way for a friend.

Because I was a *nice* guy.

Now, like a poison, something had made me question that. Subconsciously at first, but I must have made the connection back in Balay Tubay, swaying with the passion of Tanduay. And the more I thought about Papua, the more I read about the Philippines; the more I looked at statistics and my mind processed how those statistics would play out across the world, the blacker my mood became. Before, it would bounce off me—those things were miles away and even the glum voiceovers on adverts with black children and flies and sad music couldn't convince me otherwise. Now I knew that those people were just like me, only less fortunate. It felt like a ridiculous cliché just admitting it, that it was true. But it was: people were starving, parents forced to watch their children die of some disease or other because they couldn't afford the cure—a cure that would cost less than the pizza I was eating, and yet here I was, still eating that pizza.

How could I possibly be a nice guy? How could I possibly live, knowing that I was so much more fortunate than most other people in the world and not do everything I could to help them? How could I even justify my own existence when all I did was live off the economy I'd been jammy enough to land in? What had I contributed? What had I ever done to make this world a better place?

Bugger all.

Because, in reality, I wasn't a nice guy…

No.

No, that couldn't be true.

I *was* a nice guy.

I am a good person.

I couldn't face the world on my own, nor could I blame myself for how it turned out. Just like the rich man who won the lottery over more needy people, sometimes it's just the way things went, right? I couldn't bear the weight of global poverty on my shoulders and why should I? It wasn't me who was putting all these trade rules in place, it wasn't me who took slaves and pillaged colonies. I didn't cause any of this shit. I was just a twenty-year old who was doing what every other twenty-year old should be doing. And I wasn't even that rich. All the money that I did scrounge together came from rich people via part-time jobs and bank loans and went to poorer communities anyway. Wasn't that the sort of thing that made Robin Hood so famous?

I *was* doing some good.

I had done some good.

And with my report on Papua, maybe I could continue to do some good.

"Jimbo?"

This was getting too heavy. I needed to backtrack.

"J-dog?" *Prod.*

I needed to get out.

Another prod. "Jamie?"

I was back in the room. "Yes?"

"Are you all right?" Venetia had switched into her Caring Drama Student mode now and was using the Soft Voice her elocution lessons had taught her.

"Yeah V, fine. What's up?"

"The TV's off and we all decided to go to bed about twenty minutes ago. I thought you might want to know."

"Oh, right. Okay."

I wandered up the stairs and fell onto my mattress. As I lay there, I started pondering, poking around for a solution. How could I get out of this? How could I stop being so stupidly glum?

Well...there was *one* way. It might not help that much in the long run, but it would distract me at least. Because really, that's what I needed: a distraction. A diversion—that would settle my mind. One more jaunt, one last stage on my quest for global enlightenment, then I'd be able to relax, get back to my usual self. Be *fun* again. Be interesting. Get me ready for leaving university and finding one of those *real* jobs that everybody raves about.

That would be a *good* idea.

Suddenly, startlingly, my phone started to ring; the Nokia tone, yelling at me with the loud obtrusiveness of a teenage mother shouting at a child in a supermarket. I picked it up.

"Hello?...Yeah, I'm alright...Okay, see you in a minute..."

TWELVE

The Promised Land

Over the next few months, I started planning, and a few months after that I decided I wouldn't plan. No, no more plans—this trip would be totally spur of the moment. I'd play it by ear and do whatever it took to get myself back out of the rut. I was craving a bit of edge, a bit of grit, and I knew that if I left it up to a whim I would end up somewhere I could learn to stop taking myself so seriously again.

In the void of what had become of my university life, somewhere between the blur of essays and dissertations, a flight was booked. I was excited and that excitement grew as the days inched closer. All too soon, I was sharing an almond croissant with my girlfriend in an airport café, then I was watching the clouds float over the Mediterranean like suspended fluff underneath me, then it was dark and we were descending into a strip of lights in blackness and when I finally stepped out of the airport, I instantly felt like something in me had reawakened. The air felt exotic, cool, dry, inviting for the sole fact that it was different. The characters hanging around the taxi stand looked shifty and sinister in the orange streetlight. They eyed me suspiciously, and the more they did, the more I knew that *this* was what I had been missing. *This* was what I had been craving.

It struck me.

All those months, I had been wrong. I wasn't just grumpy because I thought I was a nice guy. No, that's bullshit. The real reason?

I was grumpy because I was bored. And I was bored because I wasn't travelling.

I spent my nights watching Sexcetera on TV because nothing, *nothing* interested me anymore. Whatever I did, it seemed like there was no danger, no risk; there was never the possibility of any real excitement. The more punch bags I hit, the more futile it all seemed.

It was so obvious; how had it taken me this long to work out? There I was, on the verge of having all the opportunities of a society with all the choices in the world laid out and presented to me—and I found it tedious. I didn't want to go and make shit loads of money and live in a nice house with a really shiny car like everybody else seemed to want to do. I didn't want to stylise my life so I could improve my workflow, or buy watches that people would remark upon at board meetings, or wear brightly coloured socks under my suit trousers so I could subtly reveal a slither of my cheeky inner self to those that looked hard enough.

The ups and downs, that's what I craved, not some corporate internship that would pay me fuck all and still make out that I was the one getting the good deal. Not some financial job that, sure, would give me all the women and cocktails I could ever get my face around, but only to distract me from the fact that I was making shit loads of money for people who had far too much already.

I didn't want that. Hell, I didn't even want to be a nice guy anymore. I just wanted to get out, go somewhere where stress meant more than having four hours left to write two thousand words. Where stress didn't mean a deadline, but death.

Plain, simple, glorious death.

I wanted to put things back into perspective, back where they belonged. And now I was going to do just that; I was going to a place where people didn't express their anger through letters of complaint, but through petrol bombs and tear gas and bullets. And I was excited because one big piece of my puzzle was still missing. And so I enigmatically sidled through the night towards the sinister-looking group of men.

"Can somebody take me to the bus station for a reasonable fare?" I grinned.

The nearest of the men mumbled something and it sounded remarkably like a northern-accented "fook off", so I took a few steps away, looking across the car park until I saw what looked like a blob waving at me.

"Yes, yes!" A fat man waddled in a half jog, shouting, with his white shirt barely covering his paunch and his arms in the air. "Taxi?

You come here!" he panted. "Come, come. Taxi? Yes. Come. I take you to the bus stop, yes?" As the Egyptian Jabba the Hutt neared, I began to walk towards him, slowly at first, like a mysterious, danger-seeking chunk of iron being pulled towards a hairy, overweight magnet, but then he turned and I broke into a near-run. He waddled some more, leading me to the taxi, and I got in.

The taxi driver, bless him, had all the natural charisma of a garlic burp, but he did get me where I wanted to go, and two hours and one bus later, I was standing on the rocks, listening to the wind whip up the swell, savouring the moment I had been waiting months for. I couldn't see it, but in front of me, over the dark, windswept waters of the Red Sea, lay the Arabian Peninsular and the deserts of Saudi Arabia and Jordan. Somewhere off to the left, near the shadows of jagged sandstone mountains, lay Israel and a land that had been a source of conflict for millennia. And in a matter of hours, I'd be in amongst it all.

It felt good to be back.

***

Maybe I should elaborate a little.

I had been to the Middle East before, just under a year ago. I had been through Syria, Jordan, Palestine and Egypt and although my time hadn't been without incident, it had been rushed. Well, less rushed—more cut short. But, simple as it was, there *were* some memorable moments.

One such moment was on Mt. Nebo, famed for being the ridge where Moses was said to have looked out across the "Promised Land" many thousands of years ago. It was a cold day, which wasn't aided by the fact that construction work was going on noisily around the main compound of temples and churches so there weren't many other tourists about. I remember looking from the edge of the ridge towards the dusty valleys and terraced hillsides to the west—the same view that millions of people had seen on pilgrimages that went back thousands of years. I as I stood there, the clouds parted and there shone a single beam of light across the sweeping hills in front; for a moment, it looked like God Himself was actually reaching out and poking the landscape.

But the biblical setting contrasted so greatly with the heavy metallic rattling of jackhammers and generators in my ears that it made me laugh. Here I was, watching a timeless scene unfold across a timeless landscape and it was impossible to even hear myself shout.

Even God can't shut these bastards up, I remember thinking, quite blasphemously.

And yet it didn't really detract from the significance of the place, for I was much more interested in the modern history than the ancient. The jackhammers, the construction; they were all part of it. This little patch of land was still a focal point, a centre of passion for so many. Coming from Britain, the land of staunch agnosticism, I found it hard to imagine that even now there were people out there—vast numbers of people—who still had solid beliefs, who were still certain that it was *their* way; *their* way, or no way at all. People who would give up their lives a thousand times over just to see this collection of dust and olives remain in the hands of men who believed in the same book as they did. And all this, despite rampant development and the Petri dish spread of Western culture—the culture in which I had marinated for two decades, where the dominant religion was no longer Christianity but Consumerism, and the most common way of dealing with questions of mortality and existence was the "out of sight, out of mind" approach. Really, the closest we've got to that kind of passion back in the UK is football, and half the population thinks even *that* is a load of shite.

When I walked around the buildings that weren't under construction, I saw that they were indeed good, and I was pleased, for they were tastefully laid out; there were candles, and archaeology, and tapestries, and for a moment, the combination of these things nearly threatened to rouse the religious upbringing in me. In fact, it got me thinking about all the forces that had come together to bring me to the same place that Moses had visited all those thousands of years ago. It made me wonder what he thought when he looked out across the dusty valleys and the hillsides and the clouds doth part and God commandeth unto him, "Go forth and seek out thine promised land," and whether he thought of replying, "But I am the leader, Almighty Lord; shouldn't I go first?" and whether the Almighty would have found this in any way amusing, or, as I suspected, whether he would have just turned Moses into a smouldering pile of ash with a bolt of heavenly lightning. But it also made me wonder if Moses, too, would have been impressed by all the nice monuments and stuff. All the pretty stonework. I mean, really he was just there for the view, right? I guess he'd probably have thought the sculpture depicting his staff was pretty cool though.

Now, it was all very tasteful and the plaques were interesting and readable. But to me, they seemed to be missing the point. If the story *was* true, and Moses was taken up to Mt. Nebo, then it must have been for the view. And that view alone was enough for anybody who visited to understand the significance of the place without needing a plaque to explain it. Must be the modern fascination for information, I'd guessed, when sometimes information is simply a distraction from what really counts.

I stuck my fingers in my ears and wandered outside again, looked west, into the blinding sliver of a sunset sandwiched for a brief moment between cloud layers. I could feel a sense of empathetic pride for the Israelis for whom this was, in their religion, the Promised Land. But in that empathy, there was more than just a twinge of sorrow for the swathes of people who had died fighting what they saw as an unjust occupation.

The hills, the light: it was incredible.

***

The days spun by; like I said, the trip was a short one. But after visiting Mt. Nebo, and upon returning from my brief tour of Jerusalem and the West Bank, I accidentally, anticlimactically got banned from Syria, cutting the journey short by some weeks.

I suppose it's worth mentioning how, and this time, unlike the many times I'd explained it to my friends back home, I will avoid the temptation to say something cool like, "They thought I was a spy, so they tortured me for eight days before I managed to break out of prison and escape in an abandoned mule cart," because if I'm being honest, I didn't. That wasn't true. I didn't even do anything radical at the border like remove my clothes and shout, "Jesus loves me just the way I am!", which I now partly regret because the outcome would have likely been the same.

This is what happened.

On my way to Lebanon, a Syrian border official correctly guessed that the marks on the back of my passport were from baggage stamps at the Jordan-Israeli border that had been pulled off in haste on the drive through Jordan, and, maintaining the policy of ensuring that nobody who'd been to Israel could ever enter Syria, turned me away.

Rubbing the marks off with alcohol, I tried again at a different border post the following day, only to be formally blacklisted.

It *was* a tad stupid really—the cancelled Jordanian exit stamp was an obvious enough clue about what had happened the day before and even without any marks on my passport, it would have taken little more than a dunce to have worked that one out. This was proved by the fact that the border official at the second post was little more than a dunce and he did work it out. Gutted, I drove back down to Jordan and set about leaving through Egypt instead.

So it was, in all honesty, a bit of an appetiser for the Middle East. A taster menu, if you like. Therefore, in the spirit of the trip, here are a few of the dishes presented to you as they flash up in my memory.

For the starter, I am lying in a sleeping bag set out on rocks and sand. Somewhere nearby, a dog howls in the darkness, but it is impossible to guess the source and proximity of the sound, or even whether it is just one dog or several. The sky is a pinpricked sheet of black in front of a lamp; the rough ground is greyscale iced with the silver sheen of moonlight, and the air is cold. Freezing, in fact. In front of me, the rocks have been arranged into crumbling towers that now resemble humungous termite mounds and either side, hills rise high. The crumbling edifices give off an eerie vibe; rightly so, for they are the tombs of the ancient Roman city of Palmyra. But in the moonlight I just can't stop wondering if the dog is a dog or dogs.

Time for an appetiser: I'm on a small plinth of rock with my back against a wall that juts out a few hundred feet above the timeless landscape below. The sun is the warm red of glowing embers in a fire, vague in the dusty air, and it is hovering just above the distant horizon. Some genetic throwback from when humans evolved from moths keeps me staring at it, captivated, despite the blind spot it paints in my retina after a while. Tiny flurries of a gentle breeze occasionally ripple through my shirt, but otherwise all else is calm in the vast hazy orange-brown of towering sandstone and sweeping plains, and the silence is absolute to the point of deafening.

The Entrée. The window bay is broad—broad enough for me to sit in and write my journal entry for the day using the orange streetlight outside. A small white paper box that used to house an assortment of once delicious, now sickly baklava has been swept off my knee and onto the floor next to the one that has a partially eaten portion of kanafeh, the delicious but filling Palestinian sweet for which Nablus is renowned, still in it. It loses its appeal rather quickly when the cheese cools down and solidifies and in my laziness, I haven't yet picked either box up and taken them to the bin in the far corner of the room—I'll do that when I've finished the next sentence. At least, that's the thought that's going through my head when I hear the metallic ker-klunk of a pistol being cocked and the sphincter-clenching pop of seven gunshots fired in quick succession down on the street below, no more than ten metres away, and by the time the brass casings have fallen on the floor I've jumped down from the window ledge and am grinning like a schoolboy who'd just got laid, but in all honesty, I can't remember if I actually got around to tidying the boxes away that evening.

Dessert. Now there's a hilarious sand-based joke in there somewhere, but it's just not going to work written down. So, instead, I'll offer a selection of alternatives: seeing the sun glinting off the Dome of the Rock in Jerusalem for the first time; looking up through the steep aqua topography of Dahab's Blue Hole; chatting about movies and celebrities with a young Palestinian boy during the weekly Friday protest near Bethlehem while Israeli snipers on the terraced hillsides to the north train their scopes on shouting demonstrators all around us; eating chicken by the Mediterranean in Syria...It's your choice. If I were you though, I'd choose the Blue Hole, because it's the best way to round off a great taster session.

So that was my trip.

Fun, yes. But it was just a taster, a glimpse. This time, I was going to try to understand the place a bit more—ask some questions, find out what was going on. Discover the viewpoints that newspapers are scared to print for fear of seeming anti-Semitic or unsympathetic enough to the Palestinian plight. This time, I'd fill that gap in my jigsaw properly.

But first, I had a theory to test.

THIRTEEN

Hostage to the Sands

The window rolled down and I stooped to look inside. "Do you want a lift?" asked a thickly accented voice wearing a red keffiyeh headscarf and immaculate white robes. There was a bundle on the passenger seat, wrapped up in another headscarf, and it took me a moment to realise it was a baby, only it wasn't moving at all. I remembered rule number one of maintaining personal safety in unfamiliar places—don't accept lifts from complete strangers—and figured that this rule is probably amplified tenfold if there's already a dead child in the car. Then again, it was really quite hot and I didn't have much water left, so bollocks to it.

"Yes please."

The man in the headscarf reached back and opened the rear door so I climbed inside. "For how long are you here?" he asked, slowly accelerating down the desert road.

"Don't know, a few days, maybe a week or two."

"It is not enough," he said curtly.

"Oh, right."

We drove on in silence for a few minutes, until he stroked his moustache and asked, "Maybe you could help me?"

"Um, sure. What would you like me to do?"

"We can discuss it later, but for now you may stay in my desert camp for free."

Rule number two: don't stay with complete strangers. Especially if the offer sounds like the Bedouin version of Hotel California.

"Brilliant, thank you."

Ah, well. There's always next time.

The car pulled up by a herd of camels that was wandering lazily down a backstreet and my newfound kidnapper led me into the large communal room of his mud-brick house. "Now you drink tea, I will return later."

"What do you want me to do?"

"An exchange. You help me, I help you. We discuss tonight. Then we go to the desert camp." With that, he walked out of the house and got back into the car, and I listened to the vehicle start up and pull away.

Now, if this really was a kidnapping, he was going about it in a strange way. I knew that I could pick up my bag and leave any second, but something was compelling me to stay. Perhaps this was the legendary Bedouin hospitality I had read about in guidebooks? To give up such an offer would be tantamount to unnecessary littering in the Travellers' Code. In other words, it would be unthinkable—especially for an open-minded, freethinking, butterfly of a person like me. So I sat there, patiently sipping tea, waiting for my new friend to return so I could utilise my skills.

What skills were they anyway?

***

Rum Village, Jordan. 1 April.

From what I've gleamed around town today, the man who gave me a lift from the Aqaba-Amman road earlier this morning is kind of a big deal. Local rumour has it, he has many leather-bound books and his tent smells of rich mahogany. Some also say he can't turn left, but I think they've confused him with someone else. His name is Eid-Ali and he has three sons, the youngest of which turned out to be alive after all. The elder two are roughly my age. Like most of the Bedouin I've met, Eid-Ali is tall, thin and somewhat reserved. He didn't return to the village until well past sunset, and I was in two minds whether to split and run or stay and potentially end up living the Bedouin dream. The offer still stands, it seems, and it's not the kind that I should really turn down.

But I'm still waiting.

As it turns out, my fears of kidnap have largely been dispelled, for I am not the only Westerner living here. In fact, it seems like the communal room in Eid-Ali's house is a staging post for tourists who want to visit the desert, most of whom are paying large sums of money to stay. Yet I am being fed and accommodated for free. This is puzzling, but I think the key to solving the mystery lies with two enigmatic characters who floated past me earlier this evening and with whom I am sharing a room tonight: Yuki and Ellie. I'm still not sure who they are or what exactly they do, but it appears they are not paying to stay here either.

Only time will tell.

2 April.

Here is what I know: Eid-Ali is a tour guide and he takes tourists from his house in Rum Village on 'safari', where they spend the nights in the camp listening to traditional music and eating chicken and potatoes. His family are conservative Muslims, but his two sons are confused. I have only been here one day and have already caught both of them looking at porn at various times on the house's only computer, despite the diligence with which they seem to perform the salat prayers. When Eid-Ali comes near the computer room, the screen magically switches to Qur'an research. Neither of the brothers will speak to me though, perhaps because they know that I now know that they are just as perverted as any other male on the planet, despite the religious pretence.

I'll be honest, I don't really care.

What I do care about though is what is going on with the girls, because it is the best clue I have as to why I am here and therefore, whether I should stay.

Yuki is a stereotypical Japanese girl; quiet, giggly, shy. With the comically tilted glasses and the thoughtful "hmmm" she injects into conversations at random, she gives off the impression of being quite intellectual. Ellie is an English ex-vegan who has been to India, where she apparently found herself, and has the key to her heart hanging from a chain on her right ear. She dresses accordingly. Again, she seems nice, quite chatty, good sense of humour and very friendly with the boys. From what I've seen, they spend their time tending to a small garden each day. I'm not quite sure if the two sons are part of their duties or just a hobby, but there must be more than just cuddly friendship going on there.

Here is what I don't know: what it is I am expected to do and what gives Eid-Ali the impression that I'd be able to do it. The man is still showing me plenty of generosity by letting me stay at his camp for free. But everyone else who gets the same deal is watering the plants or shagging his sons. And I'm rubbish at gardening.

So I can't help but wonder what it is that makes me so special that he needs my help over and above everybody else in the village. The more I think about it, the more sinister it seems. Either I've landed the jackpot, or I am about to be rogered by two Bedouin teenagers.

Only time will tell.

***

That night, the second since I arrived in Wadi Rum, we drove into the desert until we reached Eid-Ali's camp. Several groups of tourists were staying at the place and I was still being treated as one of them—only I wasn't paying. After dinner in the communal tent, I took the opportunity to speak to Yuki and Ellie, because it was the only way I was going to understand whether I had landed a good deal or not. Unfortunately, that was what it boiled down to; Eid-Ali's thus far regal, uncommunicative air suggested I was simply being given hospitality as one half of a transaction, but I still didn't know what the other half was.

I shuffled across the rug to where the girls were sitting.

"Look, what's the deal here?" I asked.

"What do you mean? We've been wanting to ask you the same question for two days now," said Ellie.

"Hmmm," said Yuki, pushing her tilted glasses up her nose.

"What? I don't know. That's why I'm asking you."

"What are you actually doing here?" Ellie asked.

I was taken aback. Surely Eid-Ali had mentioned something to them? They must know who I am!

"I was just hitchhiking up from Aqaba and Eid-Ali picked me up at the Rum Village turnoff and now I'm here and I'm not paying and I'm really confused!"

"Ahh," said Yuki, and I began to wonder if she'd mistaken the conversation for a firework display.

"So, you're what—a volunteer?"

"Volunteer for what?" I replied.

"Wait—you really don't have a clue do you? What's he said to you?"

I explained our conversation in the car, the dead child, the kidnapping, followed by the realisation that it was all just the product of a paranoid mind obsessed with finding fun in danger, and, crucially, that Eid-Ali had mentioned an "exchange" and that I'd answered in the affirmative. Yuki's glasses actually dropped an inch when I told them that, but it could have been coincidental.

"So you *are* a volunteer!" Ellie explained.

"No, what? I'm not a volunteer, I don't even know what I'm supposed to be doing. I just thought he needed some help with a computer or something technical in exchange for a bit of goat and a bed. Maybe putting up a firewall or something to stop, you know, whatever it is people might be doing or looking at on that computer."

"And he hasn't even mentioned what me and Yuki do here?"

"No. What *do* you do here?"

"Well, we're helpers. The computer thing is one part of it, I normally do that, but we do whatever it is he needs help with. Gardening, dishes, emails. Make bookings, take reservations. Talk to the clients." *Shag his sons*. "Basically, we help him run his business."

"So did he kidnap you from the road as well?"

"Hmmm."

"No, we signed up on a volunteering website. We've been looking for one more volunteer to help out with extra duties and we thought that was you but if you don't have any idea about this, maybe he has special plans."

"I've got a girlfriend so I can't do anything like that."

"What?" Ellie looked perplexed.

"Don't worry. Look, I just came here to spend time in the desert and I thought Eid-Ali needed someone with my expertise for some specific task he couldn't otherwise do."

"Well, you'll just have to ask him." Ellie looked sterner and suddenly I started to feel naïve. "But somehow I don't think he'd recruit a hitchhiker he happened to pick up on the Aqaba-Amman road for their 'expertise', whatever that might be."

"Ahh," Yuki grinned, nodding.

The next day, leaving my rucksack in the camp, we were driven to a recently constructed building on the far side of Rum village—a bumpy drive of roughly thirty minutes through the sand—where my expertise was put to good use.

It turned out Ellie was right.

It also turned out that Yuki couldn't really speak English too well, and when I thought about it, both of these things made a lot of sense.

I had already done enough travelling to know that the golden rule, when presented with an opportunity, is to ask yourself the following question: is it too good to be true? Now this works on a scale—the further towards "no" you get, the safer the opportunity. The further towards "yes", the riskier. If the answer is an outright yes, no matter what the offer, or how good it could be, turn it down. Otherwise, chances are, you'll end up either getting forced into being a drug mule until you are arrested and given the death penalty in Bangladesh, or find yourself doing filthy things to British stag party members in Prague in return for the next shot of heroin.

Now, to be fair, it's not always going to be as bad as that (or good, depending on how much you like execution, poverty, willies or heroin). But generally, if the answer is closer to yes than no, there's going to be some kind of catch. So this process must have gone on in my head and I must have thought, somehow, that it wasn't Too Good To Be True. For that to be the case, I must have thought of some logical reason why I had been given the opportunity to stay in a desert camp for free.

Help, wasn't it?

Trouble is, "Help" is a pretty broad umbrella for all kinds of things. Was I really naïve enough to suppose that a man like Eid-Ali would need the help of a random hitchhiker for something he couldn't achieve himself? I began pondering this as I picked up a hose and splattered the dust into brown globules of gloop around a few weeds. How could I possibly help him more than anyone else in Wadi Rum, and how could this possibly be obvious to him from the few words we spoke in the car before he recruited me into his little desert commune of potatoes and porn? How had I justified this deal to be realistic enough to sit on the "no" side of the Too Good To Be True scale?

Much as I racked my brain, the only thing I could think of, really, was that maybe he had noticed that I was foreign, and young. And, being foreign and young, I was probably good with computers and technical stuff, and all those other things that young Westerners are good at. I was probably *way* better than all the other local boys, which is why he needed *me* and not *them*. At least, these were the tacit premises to the argument that I should help him as far as I was concerned; these were the things that tipped the balance for me enough to agree to it. And he, being a simple Bedouin man, probably wouldn't be able to pay a rich Westerner like me the kind of wage I'd expect for my powers and I would therefore have to accept his desert hospitality as a humble compromise. A gesture of appreciation for my noble efforts, if you will.

This I must have assumed, albeit subconsciously, when I sat in his car. Because this would have led to me getting a good deal, without being Too Good To Be True. The chance to stay in a Bedouin camp in return for giving a few lessons on IT. Not too bad. Otherwise, presumably, I'd have thanked him for the lift and gone about my dusty business, knowing that something didn't quite add up.

Because, really, something didn't quite add up. It wasn't big, but it was enough. Now that I'd seen how skilled some of those local boys could be with computers, I started to realise how destructive subconscious racial arrogance could be—for I had been tricked. The white supremacist in me, the one that assumed I would have certain useful traits by virtue of being Western, and that these would be obvious to any desert-based Jordanian solely because of my age and the colour of my skin, had been conned into thinking I was going to get a good deal and that I was being treated well because I had something *valuable* to contribute to his backward, technologically-impaired community.

In other words, somehow I had landed the traveller jackpot.

As I reluctantly splattered another plant with the steady dribble of the hose, I realised that the joke was on me, for this was no jackpot. I looked across at Eid-Ali, who was lying in the shade, dozing with the mint tea we had made for him, and realised something.

I didn't have any special skill that the locals needed.

I couldn't do anything more than they could.

Despite my flash background and my natural affinity with keyboards and screens, I was no more technologically advanced than his sons. This was all the more apparent when Ellie enlightened me to the fact that there was a firewall after all and they had somehow managed to get around it—which I couldn't do. So what was so special about me that he'd been able to notice when I was stood, stinking, staring wide-eyed at his potentially deceased one-year old son in the car on that lonely desert road?

First, that I was foreign and travelling, and thus probably quite rich.

Second, that I was hitchhiking, and therefore not so rich that I would splash the cash on silly things like buses or taxis or desert safaris with potatoes and chicken and porn.

Third, that I was coming to Wadi Rum, and thus wanted to spend some time in the desert.

Combined, these three facts were enough to make it a reasonable deduction that I'd be willing to work for no money, because I already had enough to travel anyway, in return for food and accommodation and the chance to live in the desert instead.

Now, there was nothing at all wrong with that assumption. It would have been true for ninety-nine percent of tourists in a similar situation. But me being me, I already had all the food and accommodation to last my time in the desert stashed away in my backpack. So the only incentive to work for him was the chance to spend a bit of time learning about Bedouin culture in a traditional Bedouin camp, which his tourist-tent empire most certainly wasn't, even if it was comfortable and very pleasant. What it boiled down to was this: anybody could splash plants and do dishes, but the only unique service I could offer him was the willingness to work for free, just like Yuki and Ellie were doing.

"That'll do, they don't need too much. Now you can carry on painting the doors," said Ellie, taking the hose out of my hands.

I turned to her. "Ellie, why are you doing this?"

"Because I want to spend time in the desert," she replied matter-of-factly. "I've been here five months and I couldn't afford to do that otherwise."

We walked across the courtyard of Eid-Ali's new house, the one we were now tasked with renovating, and stepped over Eid-Ali's snoozing body where, inside, I was greeted with the semi-pleasant smell of solvent and varnish.

I knew I may have been overanalysing it all a bit. But seeing as this wasn't quite such a good deal for me anymore, I started to question Eid-Ali's motives. The tourists had told me they were paying between fifty and ninety dollars a night, per person. Even with the overheads—food, petrol, materials for the tent, car repairs, off-season survival—that still meant there would be a considerable amount of money left over. Presumably, sufficient money to hire enough local people to help run the business and renovate his house without using volunteers. But apart from his two sons, who acted as Bedouin guides and drivers, and a cook, there didn't seem to be any other paid staff.

Funny, that.

I put the brush down, resting it on the lid of a paint pot. "Ellie, you do realise this is just a way of getting cheap labour don't you?"

"What?"

"All the money that he's saving by having you and me and Yuki helping him is money that goes on things like *this* instead of saturating through the local economy." I pointed to the recently plastered walls of Eid-Ali's newest house. "We are his sweatshop workers."

"Yeah, I guess so. You know you don't have to stay though, don't you?" Ellie replied.

Once I'd finished the door, I told Eid-Ali I didn't want to work for him.

In all honesty, I felt a bit ashamed. Sure, I'd done a fair few hours of painting and gardening, probably enough to justify the food and accommodation, but I shouldn't have agreed to his "exchange" in the first place and it was only my arrogant naïvety that had made me do so. And when I woke him from his nap, he had nodded and looked surprised, but I suspected that he'd also been disappointed but was too sleepy to protest, which made me feel sorry for him.

Then I quickly realised that that was silly, feeling sorry for him; something like Stockholm syndrome, only less severe. Because, when I thought about it, it was quite late in the afternoon by now and he didn't really need to be napping. Also, he hadn't made any attempt to tell me what exactly it was that I'd be doing, despite my questions, so it wasn't *really* a fair deal. And he *was* using free labour to keep as much of the tourist dollar as he could to himself. That, in itself, wasn't right. That wasn't something I was ready to help him out with. So why should I feel sorry for him? Why should I feel like I still owed him something?

I started walking.

***

There's no other word for it: the desert around Wadi Rum is spectacular. Tall, red-brown sandstone pinnacles rising like castles from vast sandy plains. If you took the Bacuit archipelago and drained it, then stuck it in an oven for a few thousand years, this is what you'd end up with.

Open plains of sand, scrub, rock.

By the time I'd walked back to camp and picked up my bag, a blinding ball of orange was slicing lines of gold across the tops of the mountains and sending shadows sprawling out over the valleys. Tiny lizards scattered all over the place as my sandalled feet broke the hardened crust on top of the sand and the wind was blowing warm against my chest. Slowly, the sky turned dark blue and the first stars appeared.

As the noises of the camp were carried away in the evening air, I actually began to think of Eid-Ali in a more positive light. I'd seen how he'd behaved among his guests—polite, respectful, kind. To me, he'd been generous, if a bit aloof. He wasn't a crook, he just didn't want to waste unnecessary money by paying people to do something that others would do for free, just for the opportunity to live in this fantastic place.

If I'd had longer, months maybe, I'd have considered staying. But I didn't have months. And although there were plenty of tourists to go to the other camps and have their money filter back down the food chain, I didn't want to be the one to encourage this one not to. I couldn't hold it against Eid-Ali though; this was his business model and it was working. And it was a lot fairer than almost any corporate business ethic in the Western world. He hadn't been an ogre to me at all—quite the opposite. He'd given me a lift in the first place, given me food, the chance to spend a night in a Bedouin tent, and at no point had he even mentioned money. It was just a shame that I didn't make my decision sooner, before I'd let him think I was keen to volunteer.

I walked south across the silver plains, feeling the warm sand between my toes, savouring the refreshingly cool wind that I knew would not exist during the day. I walked until I was well within the protected zone of Wadi Rum—an area where jeeps and tent camps gave way to rare herds of Arabian Oryx, eagles and a multitude of lizards and beetles; where the orange sand turned white and the Saudi Arabian border was only a stone's throw away, albeit with a trebuchet.

By the time I had set up camp (read: taken my sleeping back out of my rucksack and placed it on the ground), I was completely alone—no people, no roads, nothing for miles around. Just sand and mountains and stars. Exactly what I wanted when I travelled to Wadi Rum, because now I could finally test my theory. Now I was free to live the simple life again.

I set up my stove, got a meal on the boil and sat, absorbed, staring while the blue and yellow flame licked up the side of the small pot and danced to the wind. No noise, apart from the faint roar of the hexamine tablets burning and a strange buzz that seemed to flick around my ears every now and then.

Hmmm, as Yuki would say.

Still, no matter. What could possibly follow me all the way out here, right into the middle of the desert?

Whack!

Something smacked into my head at an alarming pace and I emitted an embarrassing squeal. What the hell was that? Someone with a bunch of small rocks? Someone hiding in the desert flicking camel shit at my face? The bastard!

Thump!

There it was again! What the hell was going on? I stood up, flashed my head torch around. Sure enough, I was clear on all sides. Even if someone had wanted to sneak up on me, they couldn't and—let's face it—I was probably the only one in the desert who'd do something weird like that anyway. I heard a low buzz resonate through the silence, then… *Whack!*

"Shit!" I shouted, to no one in particular, which was in no small part related to the fact that there was no one in particular to shout it to.

What the hell is this thing?

What looked like a small bird zipped in front of my face and came round for another swoop, but I ducked and it hit my hands instead. *The little shit*, I thought, only it really wasn't that little: by the looks of things, I was being attacked by a moth the size of an ostrich.

I immediately switched my head torch off, but the fire from my stove was still going. And this thing, this creature, seemed to have the quantum probability of an electron—somehow it was everywhere and nowhere at once, emitting its faint deep buzz and smacking into my face like a violent, insect-based version of Chinese water torture.

I kicked over the stove and put the fire out. Still the beast whirred menacingly, so I ducked and dived just to reduce the possibility of more merciless attacks, but to no avail.

Smack! It hit my arm this time.

Thwak! Now my cheek.

I couldn't take any more of this, not knowing where it would be coming from next, or what velocity it was travelling at. If I didn't take cover, this thing would gradually beat me to death over a matter of weeks.

I was in for a long and irritating end.

I jumped into the sleeping bag and drew the hood tight over my head—safe, at last, to eat my beef burger and beans. But the menace was still out there, lurking, waiting to inflict minimal pain and maximal terror on its hapless victim in this lonely corner of Arabia.

My head didn't leave the hood all night.

***

The days were long and hot, dry, and soon enough my lips had started cracking painfully every time I squinted at the blazing sun. The sand got everywhere: between my toes, in my crotch, ears and nostrils; everywhere. I'd walk until it became too hot, then I'd find somewhere to sit for a while, and when it became cooler, I'd walk some more. It was impossible to keep track of the number of lizards I saw; they had at first just amused and fascinated me, but after the first night I saw them as useful allies in the war against the horrible bastard moths. Hopping up rocks, eyeing me with an inquisitive tilt of the head, scuttling off, they became my friends. My substitute for human company.

The evenings were always the best. With the light casting gold on any surface it touched, the high cliffs of Wadi Rum became the colour of the setting sun. Warm winds would blow across the dunes, cool enough to be refreshing, not so cool that you felt any discomfort sitting still for a while.

I always made a point of climbing as high as I could for the evenings. Hiding my rucksack in a bush, I'd set off, bounding from handhold to handhold, up the sandstone outcrops with a bottle of water and a camera. The reward was always worth it: a red snooker ball being pocketed in slow motion over the edge of the desert. Then followed the exhilaration of a difficult climb in reverse and the peacefulness of walking through the silver landscape at night, navigating by stars much brighter than those anywhere else in the world.

Camping was a gamble; moths gave way to mosquitoes, which gave way to beetles that were happy to trample across my head while I slept. Amazing, how much life there was in a place so apparently inhospitable. Amazing also, how much of that life seemed to have developed over millions of years of evolution an innate fascination with my face.

In the morning I would wake, shivering, well before first light and watch as the most magnificent night sky slowly turned to dark blue, purple, red and pink. Then, with the sun almost horizontal, cutting through the crisp morning air like a warm knife through butter, I would laze, basking like one of my lizard buddies, soaking up the rays while warmth was still something to be treasured. Snoozing for an hour or so, I would finally arise as the sleeping bag started to fill with sweat and eat a banana for breakfast.

Then I'd start walking.

But after a while, it all started to merge.

The sand, the sky, the rocks. Lizards and me. The truth was, only a week into my first conscious stab at achieving contentedness, I was already getting lonely. Lonely, and a tad bored. Well, not in the evenings, because there was a magic you could never get used to in the evenings, but during the day, sat in the shade, too hot to walk, there was little to keep me entertained. Playing cards by yourself isn't as fun as it sounds and it doesn't sound that fun, but once I had finished all my fruitless soul-searching, that was what I was reduced to. My water had been holding out, just, but the longer I stayed in the desert, the easier it was to carry my bag as I drunk my supplies and ate my food. This became as good an incentive as any to drink and eat more, and so I stopped holding back on my consumption. Still, as much as I drunk, I never felt like I would be able to take in enough water to feel hydrated again, such was the dryness of the environment. Then, sitting under a small overhang one blazing afternoon, feeling my lips crack as they parted for one last date, with only the sound of the wind whistling through the rocks for company, I had a realisation.

I'd failed. It was time to leave.

FOURTEEN

The Waurist

You hear enough traveller types banging on about it, but alone, the word is nothing: experience.

Experience.

Crossing the road is an experience. Scratching your bum is an experience. Being dumped—that too, is an experience.

But in my own opinion, what makes an experience an Experience, in the travel sense, is that it is out of the ordinary; it is memorable, unique. But it is more than that—for me, it is the string of memories that becomes the spell that binds a person to a place. The way I'd walk past a restaurant one day and a wafting scent of fried noodles would send me straight back to the streets of Jakarta, or I'd be in a pub somewhere and I'd hear a song I'd last listened to in the Atlas Mountains of Morocco and the spell would grip me once more. With enough experience, life is enriched; it adds an extra layer to everything that happens thereafter.

So for me, the more depth a place has—the more unique it is—the more experience it offers. And this, more than anything else, was the reason I was back in Jerusalem. Because, although I had been here before, there was nowhere in the world quite like it. Walking through the narrow, quirky streets of the old city, you were traversing the political world. And no matter how many times I went, it would always be an experience. It would always be memorable. It would always be unique.

The new city, West Jerusalem, could be anywhere in the Western world. Tree-lined shopping districts and clean, tidy streets, filled with commerce and traffic. Cars like you'd find anywhere—new, shiny, elegant. Tanned, trendy types walking around in huge sunglasses holding shopping bags full of expensive-looking items. Only the occasional armalite strapped to the back of a passer by would rouse suspicions that this was not just any nonspecific Western urbanisation.

Merging into the new city almost imperceptibly at first is the traditionally Palestinian neighbourhood of East Jerusalem; very much a contemporary place complete with a modest nightlife; white stone housing, modern buildings—but still home to the terraced hills and open donkey-grazing areas that seem to be lifted directly from nativity paintings. Obvious indications that this was the less well-off part of the city—scrap metal, an old broken bus chassis, the occasional smattering of litter. Older cars, rusting. Groups of young guys hanging around like young guys do when there is no work; kicking dirt, staring at passers by.

While the borders between the two neighbourhoods overlap, the cultural differences between East and West Jerusalem are stark, and at times, threatening. But if you arrived here blindfolded, only the uniform housing built with white Jerusalem stone would tell you this wasn't just anywhere in the Arab world.

Where Jerusalem truly becomes a mosaic though is among the cramped labyrinthine streets of the old city. Walk for five minutes and you'd pass a rabbi, an imam, a priest, along with a billion tourists, holding the hundreds of video cameras that would account for thousands of hours of boredom in millions of polite relatives' homes. Then there's the food; falafel, humous, bagels, shawarmas, hot dogs, pizzas. The smell of blood in the butchers' souq; the backgammon players drinking tea; tradesmen, craft shops, money changers. Churches, pilgrims, temples, mosques. Policemen, soldiers; guns—everywhere, guns. Narrow lanes that unfold into busy passageways, leading to courtyards and stairways and thick wooden doors with Narnia on the other side of them. Turn a corner and you're in a different country; Syria, Armenia, Greece. Then step around another alley and you're in somewhere that can only be Jerusalem—cobbled, medieval streets; Orthodox Jews with their tall hats, fixed gazes and strides that always seem a few inches too long. Eventually, all streets lead to the Wailing Wall, the Dome of the

Rock, the Al-Aqsa Mosque. Go there, stare long enough and you almost begin to understand why so many lives have ended in squabbles over their ownership; you'll start to know why Jerusalem is as relevant today as it was two thousand years ago. Walking through the old city, you're walking through a multilayered, multi-sensual maze of history and religion and culture. And it's endlessly fascinating.

But as always, there's a darker side to all this—a side that would provide yet another perspective on my home culture. And that was why I was here.

***

To understand the Arab-Israeli conflict, we need to look into the past in more detail. For Israelis, this past starts many thousands of years ago, back in the days of Moses and Noah and David and Solomon. But more importantly, it branches out to include the history of Europe in the mid-20th century and the rise of global anti-Semitism. For Palestinians, the relevant history is more recent, contained in the years and generations since the British Mandate of Palestine. And yet nowadays, both sides seem to overlook one significant detail: Jews and Muslims once coexisted. It was not always peaceful coexistence, or even coexistence free from discrimination, but coexistence it was.

Someone once told me that to fully comprehend the situation in this part of the world, the secret is to ignore the opinion of everybody else and delve as far back as you can. But, this being a synopsis, I'm not going to go much further than the time just after the breakup of the Ottoman Empire. Being British, it was all my fault, or so the story goes. Britain helped the Arabs overthrow the Ottomans back in the days when T. E. Lawrence was floating around Wadi Rum, but it was the Balfour Declaration that earned us the reputation we have today. In 1917, the British government decided that Palestine, a territory in the Arab heartland, should become the national home for the Jewish people. Nothing official came of it, but the Arabs were understandably miffed by any unwelcome meddling in their affairs by what they saw as an arrogant foreign power. Especially so by the 1930s, when anti-Semitism was pushing European Jews away from Prussia, France and Eastern Europe and into Arabic areas, where they often established Jew-only farms and businesses that excluded the majority Arab population. The kibbutz culture stirred up trouble and soon enough local grievances simmered into outbreaks of violence.

In a predictable Catch-22 situation, the more Jews moved into Palestine from Europe, the more the tide started turning against the Arab Jews who had been living across the Middle East too, despite the fact that these people were traditionally something of a protected minority in Muslim states. Arab nationalism, fuelled by a new anti-Western outlook, spurred the xenophobic violence that caused many Arab Jews to flee their ancient homes and head for the hills of Palestine. For those Jews, gone were the days of barbecued fish on the banks of the Tigris, of watching belly dancers with other Arab friends, as fascist propaganda loaded with anti-imperialist sentiments hit the receptive ears of Muslim and Christian leaders across the Arab world. In 1941, the Farhoud massacre in Bagdad killed around 170 Jewish Arabs, and it wasn't an isolated event.

Then there was the conclusion of the Second World War, the Holocaust, and the more widespread international agreement that Jews needed a home. The Jewish community, once disjointed, was now largely united in the realisation of the dangers of being a stateless minority after the persecutions of Europe and the Arab world. What followed was an even greater surge of Jewish immigration to what was once Palestine, and a flip in the centuries-old status quo that had kept Muslims and Jews at peace—the status quo that meant Jews were often the educated and business-minded underdogs in Arab Muslim societies.

After much fighting, Israel was born. Finally, Jews had their state. And with it, their opportunity to fulfil not only a religious dream, but a more immediate one: to be free from persecution. Trouble was, to avoid being the persecuted minority, they became the persecuting majority. But for Israelis this was irrelevant, because they were unified under a shared ideology and a religious dream: what could be better than to escape anti-Semitism *and* get to live in the Promised Land?

They needed to do whatever it took.

And yet to the proud people of the Arab world, the creation and international acceptance of Israel was one last slap in the face from an arrogant colonial power—namely, Britain. Jews were no longer the neighbours they once had been, but were now a facet of European meddling in the region. Indeed, as far as many Arabs were concerned, Jews were the occupiers of a white-supremacist state in the heart of the Muslim world, a slither of unwelcome Western influence in an Eastern land.

So it was that Israel became the refuge for the persecuted and the thorn in the side of Muslim Arabs. The creation of a Jewish state and the widespread maltreatment of Palestinians had given birth to a suspicious anger that spread across the Middle East like a plague—an anger that only deepened and strengthened the more it met with the other. Soon, anger gave way to bitter resentment and with it came the first war of many.

By 1956, the world was polarised, with Arab Muslims not only battling against Israel, but France and Britain too, and entangled in all this was the growing issue of nuclear competition between the USA and the USSR. By the time Israelis could say "next year in Jerusalem" with any truth, things had got messy. The successes of 1967 were a humiliation that left the Arab world reeling, and the Yom Kippur war of 1973 only added to frustrations as religion warped to match politics. Extremism on both sides grew along with hate and irrationality; Jew and Muslim became fundamentally, religiously opposed to one another.

Then things got even more complicated.

Vocal Jews in America, with the terrors of the holocaust still burning in their minds, had all but eroded the ability of successive US presidents to do anything but wholeheartedly support Israel, yet the amount of military aid the Israelis received from the US was seen in terms of the effect those weapons had on Muslims as far as the rest of the Middle East was concerned. Still, at the time, the US was arming whomever it saw as more ideologically aligned to their neoliberal model of free-market capitalism, with a Hollywood fairytale-like ignorance of the dangers of international double standards.

Saddam Hussein in Iraq, the Mujahideen in Afghanistan and, of course, Israelis in Israel. It really doesn't get messier than that.

So this was how America became known as another unwelcome meddler. No doubt the invasions of Iraq and Afghanistan had something to do with it, but the seeds were sewn decades before. And by now, by extension, or association, this meant that virtually all NATO-aligned states were in some degree of conflict with the Muslim world.

For me, this fact alone made the Israel-Palestine issue the last essential piece of my global jigsaw.

In each region I'd travelled, I'd seen the West in a variety of ways. I'd seen its effects through various alternatives and confrontations, for instance with the struggle to save the ecology of Borneo, or the sociology of Papua. Even the economics of the Philippines. I'd seen how these encounters had supplied ammunition for indignation and strife. Yet here, because of this history, this legacy, the divergence between the Arab world and the West was not only economic and sociological, but also ideological and religious. If there was such a thing as an ultimate clash, a "clash of civilisations" to use Huntington's term, the Arab-Israeli war was it.

Still, before I got embroiled in all that, I went to do the touristy thing. See the sights, take some pictures. Get some more of that wonderful experience that Jerusalem dishes out like steaming falafel.

* * *

"Psst."

I put my camera down and turned around. "What?"

"I think you are Israeli."

"No, I'm not Israeli."

"Why are you here if you are not Israeli?"

I stammered slightly. I wasn't planning on lying, but the thought of seeming under-confident in my answer left me under-confident in my answer. "I'm doing research for my degree."

Yes, that old chestnut again. Maybe I was twisting the truth a bit.

"So you are studying. From America?"

"No, Britain."

"England?"

Here's a tip—if someone in Palestine asks where you are from in Britain, say Scotland. Or Ireland. Not England.

"Scotland," I said.

"Ah, Scotland. So you know what it is like to be under occupation?"

Strange, the perceptions people have. Maybe it is still going on in Scotland, but I doubted it. Then again, maybe London had just put a tax on Irn Bru while I was in the desert and I just hadn't found out about it yet.

"Um, sort of. It isn't that bad anymore though."

Pause. "Are you Jewish?"

"No, I am not Jewish."

"Are you sure? You look Jewish."

If there is one thing I do not look, it is Jewish.

"I have to go." I turned to leave, smiling as I did. Keep them sweet for as long as possible. I could feel the alarm bells ringing, even though I knew this guy was winding me up. He didn't think I was Jewish, that's just a way of trying to mess with me, I thought, but that sort of person wasn't the kind I wanted to be chatting to, not here. Really, it wasn't him, but his friend. His friend, sitting there, staring at me, talking under his breath. Harmless, possibly—but possibly not.

"Hey Jew, come sit with us. Let's have a conversation," he called over.

I started walking marginally faster.

"Talk with us, Jew."

They weren't big, these guys. But from my past experience, I knew that there was a reasonably high chance they'd have some kind of weapon. A pocket knife maybe; possibly something bigger. Moments like this, I hated being a solo traveller.

"Hey, why don't you want to talk to us? You think you are better than us?"

I kept walking, trying to put a few casual paces between me and these guys who seemed intent on causing grief.

"Come here you fucking Jew!"

Now it was clear; there was no subtlety to it anymore. He wanted to put me on the spot. Might be just to find out what I was made of, or possibly he's just messing with another tourist, one more ignorant foreigner who didn't give a fuck about his life. But it was not him I was concerned about, it was his friend. His friend with the slick black hair and the pointy face, the yellow sweater pulled up in the sleeves to reveal his gangly forearms. Jeans, trainers. Glaring, whispering under his breath and slowly standing up. His scrawny little friend with far more confidence than his weedy frame could deliver.

"Come back here, pussy Jew."

Now I might as well have been jogging. We all knew what the stakes were. They knew I knew they were going to do everything they could to screw with me; I knew that they knew I would do everything I could to get rid of them. I also knew it was not quite the time to turn around, rip my shirt apart and roar, "Let's dance, dickweeds!" like I always wanted to do—I had to be the bigger person, at least until I knew if they were armed.

"You think you are too good to talk to us don't you?"

Really, I should just play it cool. Keep walking, ignore them. Give them nothing to go on. But I needed to know—was I about to get a punch in the back of the head? A rock in the neck or worse? Trouble is, the more I looked back over my shoulder, the more I was starting to look like quarry. I started down the steps, the long winding path that led down to the main road and most likely the nearest place I'd find some help if I needed it. From there it was just a short hop to the Armenian Quarter and these guys wouldn't follow me in there.

From behind, something shouted—not in Arabic, but similar. Then laughing. It was blocked in part by the walls that lined the stone path down, but it was clearly getting closer. I didn't think it was jogging towards me yet, but it wasn't far off.

More laughing.

They were at the top of the steps now, leaning against a railing that overlooked the path, screaming at me and laughing to each other.

"FUCKING JEW!"

Incidentally, the railing also overlooked one of the most famous views in the region—Jerusalem from the Mount of Olives—but I was not really sure if they were appreciating it as much as they should have been. Halfway down the path now, and as far as I was aware, they were still near the top, shouting obscenities at me from the railing.

"I want to fuck you!" yelled the scrawnier of the two. It's true what they say—the quiet ones are always the dirtiest.

"I bet you do!" I shouted back, because, in truth, this was starting to piss me off. For a while there's silence, until I heard footsteps running around the corner and there they were, slowing into a walk.

"What did you say, Jew?" the chatty one uttered. "What did you fucking say?"

The other was whispering still, like the dirty little pervert he was.

"I said, fuck off."

Stakes raised once more.

I turned around and stopped and in a deliberate voice, said, "Do not follow me."

"What?"

"You stay here." My voice grew louder. "Do Not Follow Me. Understand?"

My shoulders were tense, my hands clenched tight. White-knuckle tight. "Stay the fuck here."

The boisterous one snapped first. "FUCK YOU!" he screamed, running at me. He jumped into the air and his foot punched my chest; by then I was so wired up I hardly noticed it, but I still pushed into him and this put him off balance, making him stumble. The other one ran up and tried to do the same—a jumping kick into the chest. I stood firm and he bounced off, with his wiry frame and slick greaseball hair.

I knew I could defend myself, but there was no need to up the ante just yet. Not until I knew what they were carrying.

"STAY HERE," I said.

The quiet one started reaching behind his yellow sweater, behind his back. Reaching into the top of his jeans.

"Back off. BACK OFF." My voice was shouting now, not stammering like before. If anything, I was moving towards them, safe in the knowledge that if the stakes were equal, I'd put these two fuckers in a coma. But my eyes were fixed on that hand, reaching behind his back, and I realised that if he pulled a knife, I'd have a bit of a situation on my hands. Still, I took a step forward and pointed at him. "BACK THE FUCK OFF."

"Fuck you!" shouted the greaseball in his piss-yellow sweater.

I looked at him. Talking deliberately, with my left hand pointing towards him and my right behind my back as if ready to pull something out, I said, slow and calm, "Back the fuck off. Now."

I was wearing a hoodie and I knew there was no way they could tell what I was carrying, so I stood in this position for a few moments and they started to step back. They turned to each other and laughed, walking away. Once they were out of sight, I continued walking down the path. Not rushed, but slowly, casually. Not looking back. And I kept walking until I hit the road, and when I did finally look back, I didn't see anyone.

Then, more out of habit than anything else, I walked straight into the old city and bought a kebab.

For what seemed like hours, I sat there, nursing my fat juicy kebab, thinking back to the last time I was in East Jerusalem. I remember, even then, coming across a hostility that I couldn't really place. For whatever reason, there seemed to be more suspicion, more aggression. More thuggery. Perhaps it was due to the resentment of being so overtly dominated by the Israelis, of having friends and relatives being forcibly evicted from their homes by extremist Jewish families on an almost daily basis, of being separated from the rest of the West Bank by the Wall. It was possible. More likely though, it was just the Palestinian equivalent of chavs. Bored, disaffected youth, fed on a diet of resentment. No jobs, nothing to do but stir up trouble. Places like Jerusalem, where there were plenty of targets in the form of hapless tourists, trouble was easy to stir. Still, whatever the cause, it clearly didn't help having Palestinians and Jews living so close together.

After I polished off the remaining meat, I smiled, walked the old city again, trying to absorb the sense of calm that now pervaded the streets. The bustle of tourists and shoppers was gone, replaced by the late-evening street-sweepers and the butchers pushing pools of blood into drains. I walked through the Muslim quarter with the sweet-iron smell of carcass and the soft orange light on cobblestones. Clunking and sweeping: the sounds of the last of the day's traders closing up shop. It didn't take me long to find my guesthouse—a grimy but atmospheric place in which I shared a dormitory with a schizophrenic tramp and a friendly local guy with some kind of compulsive disorder. It wasn't the classiest joint, but it was cheap and what I saved on accommodation, I could spend on kebabs.

I strolled upstairs, where my two roommates were agreeing with each other about the need to close all the windows in the building, and sat on my bed. It had been a good day. I'd eaten my body weight in falafel *and* I'd bought a cake. Shame about the misunderstanding earlier, but it gave me an idea. If things were like this in Jerusalem, where the Palestinians and Israelis were separated only by districts, how bad would it be if they were separated only by house walls?

As the light switch was flicked on and off at three-second intervals for exactly two minutes, I decided it was probably a good idea to get out of Jerusalem, for the time being at least. Go and see somewhere I hadn't visited before. Somewhere like Hebron.

"Yeah!" shouted the tramp. "Goddamn Martians everywhere."

He had a point.

* * *

I have always found potential to be an interesting concept. Today, it was the potential of objects that got me. A beer bottle, for instance. That had a number of possible applications—liquid storage, for instance. A cement block: the potential to construct a house. A metal pipe; well, the metal pipe has all sorts of uses.

Mesh, too, has many uses, but I'd never seen it used like this before. Now there's a reason behind the wire mesh that lies above the marketplace in Hebron. Several reasons, in fact. And most of those reasons can be seen sitting on top of the mesh, all heavy and inert. Harmless, really, like that. Nothing intrinsically damaging about them at all. But think of all the potential—all that liquid that could be stored, all those buildings that could be built. And the length of metal pipe that sits by the side of the road, just *imagine* the scaffolding: incredible! And not just scaffolding—it's a pipe right? A long, heavy, inert metal pipe.

All *sorts* of uses spring to mind.

And the people of Hebron are certainly ingenious. In all the places in the world you see objects used in ways that amaze and surprise you. The people of Hebron just take it to the next level.

Now the IMI Galil assault rifle that pumped 5.56 x 45 mm NATO ball through crowds of Muslim worshippers at the local Ibrahim Mosque, that had an obvious purpose from the start, but the metal pipe, the bottles, the bricks? I guess that happens if you can't get your hands on a rifle. They say necessity is the mother of invention, which might explain the mesh, but it isn't the question of whether the bottles and bricks and all the other half-smashed shit that spreads itself across the mesh are really necessary—clearly, from the volume, they are. What concerns me is the potential of all that stuff. The latent possibility.

Thanks to the mesh, the people of Hebron could pass through the narrow streets of the market area without having their head split apart by a beer bottle thrown from the window of an Israeli settler's apartment, or their shoulder smashed by a brick dropped from the hand of an American college kid on vacation to see his Israeli relatives.*

Just imagine it though. Fill the marketplace with shoppers, families, children in prams, fathers, mothers, traders; take all the crap

---

* After Israel annexed the West Bank and Gaza, a number of isolated Israeli communities in the Palestinian Territories sprung up. Some Israelis moved into these areas for economic reasons, others for religion. Illegal under international law, these settlements, and the settlers within them, have significantly heightened tensions in the region. Hebron, a holy site for Jews, has more than its fair share of settlers, and is one of the few places where settlers live inside the town itself.

on that mesh and lift it twenty feet. Then, remove the mesh and drop it all again, see what colour the cobble turns.

Fortunately for me, I could only imagine it. The people of Hebron didn't need to though, they had seen it happen. Just like they'd seen the potential of petrol and a lighter—and the occupants of those houses had felt that potential too.

One week, a settler gets into a fight with a Palestinian. The next, four Palestinian youths smash up a settler's car. The settler shoots two, killing one. The week after that, a relative of that kid stabs a settler in the street—it doesn't matter which one. Any of the fuckers will do, because, as he sees it, they are all responsible for the death of his ten-year old brother. And then, it turns out the man who was stabbed was a popular man, liked by all, and now those settlers want revenge. Now those settlers want to kill that Palestinian thug and his whole extended family of cousins and half-uncles that probably spreads all the way to Gaza Fucking City. So fifteen of the settlers rampage the streets with metal pipes and bricks and stones and beat the hell out of all those Palestinian thugs and their families. In return, the Palestinians pick up knives and whatever guns and grenades they can get hold of and kill a few of these settlers, until one settler gets an assault rifle and wanders down to the local mosque. This doesn't solve the problem, but that doesn't really matter anymore because now, very few can remember that not all settlers are fuckers and not all Palestinians are thugs.

Unfortunately, this isn't helped by the fact that a significant portion of the Israeli settlers in the area are extremist Zionists, who have come to realise their dream of a "Greater Israel" by causing havoc in the old city of Hebron. So when a load of violent Israelis turn up on your doorstep looking to kick you out of your house, beat the shit out of your kids and smash your uncle's face in with a discarded beer bottle in the name of the Torah, you could almost be forgiven for thinking all Israelis were evil, even if this really wasn't true. Especially given how at first glance, the Israeli Defence Force seems to protect them (although, from what I saw, they seemed more inclined to hold them back).

And nowadays, it's almost as if the settlers live there simply to stir things up with Palestinians. I'm sure there was some other reason the settlers turned up in Hebron initially, but when I think of what that reason was, all I can remember are the lyrics of the *De la Soul* track "Held Down", where Kelvin Mercer raps about all those people sleeping on the floor covered in red, who were looking for God but found religion instead. That's as good a summary of Hebron as I have ever found.

So here I was, trying to search out the next piece of my global jigsaw puzzle, and I found myself contemplating that religion thing. It was, after all, the reason those people turned up in the first place, kicking Palestinians out of their homes and acting violently towards anyone who disagreed. And in Hebron, it bugged me. Think about it long enough and it all seems so irrational, so futile—there was no real absence of shelter, no drought, no famine to speak of. There's enough land to go around. People *could* live side-by-side with no harm done to anybody. That's until religion swanned in with its beard all curly and decided what everybody really needed was a great big fight. I mean, if God had a favourite joke, it would have to be religion.

I had been brought up a Christian, but I never really got into the whole institutionalised side of it; personal faith is about as far as I ever went, and I would be lying if I said I had much of that left. Still, I saw nothing wrong with it. At times, I even wished I had the mental discipline not to question things all the time, not to invent arguments for why I should be morally permitted to what I was always going to do anyway. To me now, religion is just a nameless sort of guilt that somehow attaches itself to anything enjoyable, but I think that comes with being a Protestant in these immoral times. Live life like an atheist and renounce your sins at the last possible moment. Heaven? Thanks very much.

God's *so* forgiving.

Catholics have it slightly stricter—sin as much as you like, just don't forget to Hail Mary each time. What is that if not the spiritual equivalent of the phrase, "Just kidding!"? Still, wars have been fought and people murdered for less. I'm sure God forgives that too, because after all, He created it, set it all in motion. And well done to Him. I mean, you don't praise the bowling ball when it hits ten pins, do you? Of course not, you praise the bowler.

What if people could just turn around, see how this institutionalised religion thing added nothing but the excuse for elaborate ritual and unnecessary violence? What then—would Israelis and Palestinians be able to live together? Or would they just find another reason to fight?

In honesty, I could not slate religion that much because I had never truly been convinced by an atheist either. Deep down, I knew that like most people of my background, my aversion to religion was born out of a desperate craving to get laid as much as possible; anything that got in the way of that was to be shunned. So as a rule, I was mostly happy to float on the noncommittal moral-vacuum that was agnosticism, but that didn't mean I wasn't emotionally involved. In reality, I was very emotionally involved, walking around Hebron, seeing the areas of the city closed up from violence, seeing the soldiers march a procession of Israeli tourists through the old city, keeping all onlookers at a safe distance with voices and weapons raised. Perhaps I was even a little too emotionally involved.

During my time in Hebron, the locals had pointed out the areas of the city where the settlers lived, where the snipers had operated from; which parts of the city saw the most violence during the uprisings. They took me into rooms that had been set on fire by their next-door neighbours. They showed me the houses that'd had the Palestinian occupants forced out at gunpoint to make room for settlers. They pointed out where relatives had stabbed or been stabbed. For me, it was more than depressing; it was infuriating. It made me want to give up everything and take up a rifle. Find all the people who were causing this violence, people on both sides of the religious divide, line them up and keep shooting until nothing moved.

That would *definitely* solve the problem.

It took me a while to realise that I wasn't even a part of it; why, then, did I care so much? I could go through life without even smelling a whiff of this kind of hatred and probably die a happy man, wrapped in a fluffy blanket of social cotton wool.

Was that what I wanted?

Wasn't that what I *should* want?

Really, I wasn't enjoying it, seeing all this injustice, voyeuristically watching the lives of the people who had to put up with death and violence so often. It wasn't fun, speaking to the mother of a murdered son, walking through the charred remains of a bedroom. And the most infuriating thing of all is that, during my time in Hebron, nobody ever seemed to speak of anything other than peace. That, more than anything else, made me want to get out of there. Because after a while, I could no longer see the bigger picture. Even I didn't want peace. After a while, all I could think about was revenge for all this madness.

It wasn't until I left Hebron that I started to lose the cloud of anger that had started to soak up all reason, eliminating the strength of mind and character that allowed the people I met to talk of reconciliation, while I could only think of rage. I had been in Hebron when it was largely peaceful. Everywhere I looked though, I could see the potential, the history, and it angered me. But more than that, it worried me—because I knew now that this potential existed in me too.

As concerned and angered as I was though, after Hebron, I was starting to glimpse the reality of the Israeli-Palestinian issue. As much as anything, it was a conflict fought over emotions and ideas. Not land, not resources. Not even greed or wealth. Just abstract thoughts and immediate passions; tales of injustice and bitter vengeance that separated one man from another, one tribe from another—that turned two groups of fundamentally similar people into an "us" and a "them". And the only way I could think to solve the problem would be to wipe the memories of every person involved. Unfortunately, this made it as ridiculous as it was persistent—how each person I had spoken to had wanted peace and how achievable this could be if people just forgot past misdeeds and moved on. How even a minority of troublemakers could sustain a conflict that had gone on for more than half a century. Remembering Jerusalem, I knew this minority existed on both sides of the fight. It wasn't just limited to angry Hamas fighters and trigger-happy Israeli Defence Force soldiers either, it was bitter Palestinian youths and hardline Jewish extremists. It was old men and young boys, mothers and sisters; brothers, cousins. But this minority, in many places, had been incubated by the tacit consent of the unhappy majority. The majority whose dream was peace but who had long since accepted the fact that dreams rarely came true.

And this was what scared me most about Hebron: after only a short while, I knew I would not be part of the unhappy majority. I would be the violent minority if I was placed in the same position. I would be one of those angry Hamas fighters. I would be a trigger-happy IDF soldier if my parents had been killed in a suicide attack. From the outside, it's so much easier to point fingers, but if I was Israeli, if I was Palestinian, I would do the same.

If I was Israeli, if I was Palestinian, I may even do worse.

FIFTEEN

Tea with Terrorists

The sign to the guesthouse didn't have any new bullet holes in it. I took this as a good omen. Not as good an omen as the scent that wafted past my nose, however, and I was hungry.

The bus north had given me the time to think. I say bus—what I mean is the bus, followed by a checkpoint, followed by another bus, then one more checkpoint, and finally a taxi. Still, it had allowed me some perspective. This was not my war, I told myself; it had existed before me and would no doubt continue without me. I needed to take a step back or I would end up wearing a balaclava, acting all mysterious in shadows and that. Clearly, that would be a bad idea.

In fact, you could see how bad an idea that had been for several other passionate young lads on the drive in to Nablus—rounds from a large-calibre weapon had punched holes through the walls of several houses on the road and posters of the martyrs who were previously not martyrs before those bullet holes had been bullet holes were spread across every available surface. Thinking objectively, I had realised that martyrdom was not something I was particularly up for just yet, not until I had finished my studies at least. So I decided I'd approach my time in Nablus with a pinch of caution. Rather than just focusing on what people had to say about the conflict, I would simply chat. Discover the conflict indirectly, find out about it through the psyche of thc people, the way of life in the city. Instead of interviewing everybody I came across, I would try to become a resident of Nablus for a short while.

My first priority as a resident was to eat, so I followed my nose through the darkening streets to the central roundabout and headed towards one of the shawarma restaurants that lined the pavements. If my memory was anything to go by, the next five minutes after ordering the shawarma would most likely count among the best of my life.

Something like the snack equivalent of Penelope Cruz, a shawarma is a saucy, delicious type of wrap, inside which is the best possible combination of meat, vegetables and relish, along with a few French fries just to add that little bit of bulk (the likeness to Penelope is strictly in its deliciousness, not—I'd like to stress—its bulk and contents). Although there are shawarma stalls and restaurants all the way across the Middle East, right up through Turkey and no doubt a smattering in Egypt too, the ones in Nablus are something else. You could describe them as a singularity of taste, for the amount of ingredients they manage to cram into the pitta is nothing short of galactic. You are forced to eat them quickly or your arm will simply fall off from the weight of carrying it too long. Several people, I am assured, have died this way.

Actually, I made that up.

But they *are* huge and irrespective of all the other things I wanted to do in Nablus, eating a kebab the size of Mike Tyson's thigh was right up there.

"As-salaamu alaykum," I said with a grin. "Minfadlik, wahed kebeer shawarma."

"Wa-alaykum salaam, what would you like my friend?" asked the vendor.

"Uh, wahed shawarma. Kabeer. Please!"

"Ah, one large shawarma?"

"Yup!"

"You know this is not how we say it in Palestine, but it doesn't matter. You are trying very hard and this is good."

"Oh. Sorry."

"What would you like in the shawarma?"

"Everything," I replied in a sinister-sounding Movie Bad Guy voice, yet feeling like a child on Christmas Eve. Or a drunk at half-three in the morning, I couldn't quite decide. I suppose a shawarma is essentially a kebab, but the likeness to the mashed up baby-meat you get on British high streets is virtually nonexistent. To tell the truth, since eating my first shawarma, I have never touched a British kebab.

I passed over a few shekels and, receiving the shawarma with two hands to ensure I didn't drop it, left the restaurant a happy man.

I'm not going to describe the pleasure I was in when I ate it, save to say that anyone who spends their life chasing sex is truly misguided, but with my primal cravings largely satisfied, I started to notice my surroundings. It must have been roughly this time last year that I was here before, walking the same streets, but there was something radically different now. The air was warmer, much warmer—that wasn't it though. It had a totally different feel; the generic orange light, the groups of paramilitary Fatah police standing in the nighttime shadows, they somehow looked different. People were greeting me as they walked past, but it wasn't what they said, it was how they said it. Actually not even that, but the fact that there were people.

Lots of people.

In fact, the whole place was buzzing. Strolling through the souqs, the Arab pop sounding out from CD shops, I was doing something I knew from the advice I had received last year was unsafe to the point of being suicidal: I was walking through the old city of Nablus after dark, and somehow, I didn't even care. Because that was it—Nablus felt *safe*. Shops were open, men were laughing and holding hands in the largely heterosexual way Arab men do. Even groups of girls—some dressed in jeans and T-shirts with only a thin shawl covering their hair—were out and about, giggling, gossiping. After the grittiness of Hebron, it was all the more obvious that here, people were living. Sure, there were still pockmarks on every surface you could see—bullets, explosives, shrapnel—but the city was no longer gripped by fear.

It seems obvious to say that it wasn't always like this. Just one year before, the souq was an empty place. Having one of the largest and most labyrinthine of all the West Bank bazaars on their doorstep presented Palestinian militants with the perfect place to hide out, so the old city of Nablus had been the sight of a staggering amount of firefights between IDF troops and militias. Though my previous visit was brief, I had still somehow managed to sleep through an Israeli snatch operation that had entered the floor below mine; a different time, I had heard gunfire a few metres away—to this day I have no idea if it was for dramatic effect or intended for somebody, but I didn't pop my head out to see. And on the final night, a Palestinian teacher had, through an incredible show of generosity, put me up in a hotel far out of my price range because it was not safe to stay near the Old Quarter at the time. I didn't hear or see it, but people died in the city that night.

Apparently I can be a deep sleeper.

Scorch marks and crumbled buildings served as a reminder of what went on, but the fighting had moved elsewhere. Nowadays, the Israeli incursions were into the refugee camps, not the city itself. Obviously this meant I had to visit the refugee camps at some point, but I wasn't in such a hurry. Nablus had been transformed from a dangerously exhilarating place to a pleasant city, and I intended to take full advantage of that fact.

When I awoke early the following morning, I did so to the smell of cigarette smoke and the realisation that I had done it again; my large, two-bedded room now had an extra occupant, in dainty white Y-fronts no less, and I had no idea when he had turned up.

How is it that in Nablus, I could sleep through anything?

* * *

It was on the walk to An-Najah University that I met Safa.

An-Najah: home to the closest I was going to get to the Palestinian equivalent of me, and a Public Relations department that was able to provide student guides for foreigners visiting the city—a win-win situation for students who could practice their English, and foreigners who got to learn about Nablus firsthand.

I had bumped into her on the main road. I must have been looking truly lost because as she walked past, I tried to avoid her gaze out of macho embarrassment. A crack in the pavement took on an unbelievable amount of significance and Safa noticed this; walking straight up to me, she asked, "Are you looking for the university?"

Safa was an English teacher with a class of about twenty students that operated from a school just outside the university gates. Although it wasn't part of the campus, most of those studying English were doing degrees just around the corner at the same time. It was ideal for me, the perfect setting to meet fellow students, see what they felt, and Safa was the perfect guide. She was also a feminist in the truest sense—a powerful, ambitious woman with confidence and poise, and to her students, an inspirational leader. Unconcerned about petty things, she had the perspective and the capacity to see the bad with the good, yet she remained patriotically Palestinian: proud, educated; traditional, yet forward thinking.

In Nablus, there were many people like Safa.

My first days in the city were spent with her, walking the town, discussing things—life, history, traditions. For the first time for me, the place came alive.

It turned out Palestine was not all guns and stones and bombs; the West Bank is one of the most historically rich places in the world. Jericho, Bethlehem, Jerusalem; household names to those who have been raised in Abrahamic cultures, but Nablus had a biblical significance that went back to the first books of not only the Bible, but the Torah and the Qur'an—the City of Shechem, once the home of Jacob, was here.

The place was full of stories; if it wasn't for the conflict, tourists would flood Nablus. Safa didn't tell me this, but it was obvious. Everywhere, there were things to see and do: the olive-oil soap factories for which Nablus was famous; the churches, Joseph's well. You could eat the best shawarmas and kanafeh; smoke sheesha and drink mint tea looking across the beautiful hills and valleys surrounding the city. You could walk the bazaar, meet the people, buy the knockoff DVDs. Safa showed me all of these things and more, taking time out of her busy schedule to teach me about the Nablus you'd never understand from the news—and the history and way of life here.

Then, through Safa, I met Ala. And Yasmine.

* * *

One evening, Safa had invited me to her parents' home in the new city—a large, open apartment with a balcony facing the twinkling orange of the Nablus night. Her parents, part of the older, more conservative generation, talked for a while, about the immorality of alcohol, the way the British had sold Palestine to the Jews and how Israel controlled America "like a boy on the back of an elephant", in their words. For a while, I was kept on the defensive, asked to justify why the West waged war for oil, why Israel was being allowed to break international law without consequence; asked how people back home could justify doing whatever it is they were doing (drinking beer and having extramarital sex if reputation was anything to go by) while NATO bombs hit Iraqi families and ruined lives. And the truth was, I didn't have any real answers; I couldn't admit that all Westerners were greedy bullies who liked forcing other people to do what they wanted so they could continue to prosper, but the more I tried to shield my culture, my government from criticism, the harder it became.

"I think maybe everybody has too much," Safa had said.

"Maybe it is that they are never satisfied," her mother replied. "Perhaps they just do not know the consequences of their way of life."

I had responded that very few people actually supported the war in Iraq and that not all Westerners were slutty drunkards. I told them that it was only a few who gave the many a bad name. I did not say it, but I remember thinking how the same stereotypes worked in reverse, how the simplistic media in the UK and USA had convinced so many Westerners that all Arabs were either peace-loving hippies who secretly wanted to live in Western-style democracies, or Evil Terrorists who wanted to feast on the blood of the innocent when the moon was full. I did not say this too, but I remember thinking how at different stages of my life I'd been exactly the kind of person Safa's family was talking about—careless, ignorant, hedonistic. If that made me a bad person, and this I really didn't want to say, I wasn't sure I'd take it back either.

Safa and her family, although inquisitive, did not mean anything by these questions—they just wanted to hear my answers, to see the other side of the story. But the responses I gave barely convinced me, let alone them. It made me think about how my culture must seem from outside; carefree, morally depraved, greedy. And then the war, that bloody war. How that must have seemed—one of the wealthiest nations in the world, prancing about in a far-off country on the pretext of "liberating the people", only to plunge them further into poverty and mindless destruction, and then the coincidence that this country had one of the most sought-after commodities in the motorised age. How incredible that must have looked to anybody with the remotest shred of cynicism. The body count must stand at, what, a few hundred thousand? And if you made the not-unreasonable assumption that these deaths largely happened for economic reasons (implanting a favourable regime in the centre of an oil-rich area), what then did that mean? Hypocrisy breeds hatred, as many like to point out, and there's plenty of that to go around nowadays.

Fortunately, once my allegiances were broken down and I had accepted that the collectivist culture of the Middle East was less immoral than the materialist one of the West, the conversation moved on. But then something entirely unexpected happened, something that made me instantly forget about all my moral horrendousness for the moment. I was in the lounge of Safa's house, having just finished the dinner of rice and lamb—a true Palestinian meal, and delicious too, while Safa was describing her views on the role of women in the Arab world.

"This is the way I like it," she said, "I will cook for my husband, he will provide for me." Safa was engaged to be married in the following months and she'd sought her father's approval, not out of tradition, but because she wanted him to like the man. She *chose* tradition, not the other way around. Her father, a grand man who spoke German, English and a host of languages with colloquial fluency, was proud of her, and her of him. "I will give my husband a family and he will keep it safe." There was no shyness, no held emotions in Safa's house. Her father, in fact, had described the curfews quite openly: "The Israelis lock us up in our homes to kill one or two Palestinians, meanwhile what else is there for us to do but produce many more?" Safa and her mother had found this statement hilarious; being British, I'd felt awkward. But it was when Safa was describing the role of men and women in marriage and how this suited her down to the ground, that Yasmine had walked in.

"This is my sister," Safa said. Although she'd mentioned her sister before, I had not given it any thought. I nearly dropped my fork when I saw her though. "She is starting at An-Najah University this year."

"Hi," said Yasmine, with Safa's confidence and a soft lilt in her voice. "How is your time in Nablus?"

Almost subconsciously, I had tensed up, become more animated. Probably sucked my chest up, and yet she seemed oblivious, sitting on the couch with her knees tucked, relaxed, chatty. Even the lime-green pyjamas she was wearing looked good on her, and that's a statement I don't use lightly.

In my mind's eye, she made Kate Moss look like Elmur Fudd.

The evening had passed wonderfully, with the whole family giving me their thoughts on everything from clothing, food, housing;

misconceptions about life in Palestine, history, education. I did my best to keep up, hold my own, but my mind was focused on the next glance I could get of Yasmine. I'm sure she caught me, but when she did she just smiled. Later on, as the hospitality of her family flowed around me like a warm breeze, I decided that if I ever got dumped and somehow made it back to Palestine, I would find her and bloody well marry her, right there. Get a house in the hills and have millions of red-faced kids with lime green pyjamas.

I lay awake for hours that night, trying to preserve her smile. But by the time I awoke, I couldn't shake the mental image of Elmur Fudd.

The mind works in strange ways.

***

The following morning, I met Ala, the head of An-Najah University's PR department, and his deputy, Jalil. Safa had once worked as a student guide in Public Relations for Ala, showing foreign groups around the university and city, and had happily introduced us. Ala was a hard-working man, full of presence and charisma; tall and immaculately dressed. Clearly he was proud—proud of the city he lived in and proud of the people he shared it with. It was his mission to pass this pride on to those people, through art exhibitions, cultural displays, foreign exchanges, charities, whatever. Whatever he could think of to get people doing things, he'd organise it with the help and guidance of Jalil.

One afternoon, chatting over strong, sweet black Arabic coffee, in a restaurant perched on a hillside overlooking the city, Ala was telling me about the decline of the Palestinian sandal trade. He pointed to the ones on his feet and said, "These, my friend, are the best sandals in the world. And they are made here, in Palestine." To me, they looked like most sandals do, though they were humorously juxtaposed against the sharp grey suit he was wearing. "It is difficult to find places that will sell Palestinian sandals anymore, even here in Palestine."

"Where do all the sandals come from then?" I asked, not really knowing if I'd seen that many sandal-wearers in Nablus anyway.

"They are from China or Vietnam or wherever. People buy them because they are cheap, but it's ruining the economy of our country. Israelis have occupied our land, but China occupies our pockets."

"How so?" I asked, giving him the option to expand his point, which I suspected was what he wanted to do.

"Well, nearly everything in Palestine is imported. Clothes, shoes, movies. Even the shops are imported," he smiled.

"Shops?"

"Yes, I will take you to the malls later on, but more are being built and soon Nablus will look like everywhere else. These malls, you have them in Scotland too?"

"Um, well, I live in England these days, but yes, we have them."

"Exactly, they are imported. Imported shops. Imported like everything else." Ala leant back in the plastic chair, took another toke on the sweet-scented sheesha. We were looking out across the Nablus Valley, with the granite hills in the distance covered in tall grey clouds and the sun casting rays through them. A few buildings were under construction, exactly the same sand-coloured high-rise apartment blocks that already littered the foreground, and the echoes of cranes bashing and clunking were reverberating across to us, along with subtle notes of distant taxi horns.

"Our industry is stifled because of the occupation. Even the soap production here is failing because it is impossible to get the permits to tend the olive groves. The permit runs out, the olives die, the factories close. It's the same with everything; this is why we are so reliant upon aid, reliant upon the EU and Japan. Even America. Things are given to us but there cannot be any production here—it is like one big detention camp." Ala's face sunk into a disappointment that had obviously been accepted as a fact of life, something that hinted at a deep sadness, but it soon changed shape. "We are working, we are slowly bringing back the things the occupation has taken from us." He looked at me. "All we can do now is wait, but one day, we will have our solution."

Walking through an abandoned thistle-covered plot of land on our way to the parks later that afternoon, with the sweet smell of mint in the warm air and the stretched chant of the evening call to prayer in our ears, we chatted about the aspirations of the people in Nablus. The students, he told me, always left the West Bank if they could—there was simply nothing for an educated generation to do, except, perhaps, teach. Things were too difficult, the frustrations grew too strong, and the bright lights of Europe or America always shone through the incursions and checkpoints and blackouts of life in a West Bank city.

Those who couldn't get the permits or scholarships for America would head to Saudi or Jordan, where, he said, Palestinians were often treated as second-class citizens. "The Jordanian government will only accept Palestinians if they renounce their nationality and say that they are Jordanian. Almost seventy percent of people in Jordan are from Palestine originally and now the Jordanian rulers are sick of it, they don't want any more of us, so they treat us like dirt." But it was often better than facing a life of unemployment in Nablus and the end result was that Palestine had a brain-drain of epic proportions. An exodus of educated people that was doing almost as much harm to the Palestinian economy as the occupation itself.

There was a simple fact in this that I had not really understood from the news stories: the Palestinians were just like any other people. Not all the teenagers wore scarves around their faces and threw rocks and petrol bombs at Israeli tanks, and not all the old people were withering olive farmers or goatherds, scraping a living from the land left to them after settlers took the rest. Yes, people like that existed in Palestine, plenty of them, but so too did a huge population of *other* people—people who were just concerned with making the best of a bad situation.

"What is life like for those who stay?" I asked Ala, as he picked a few leaves of mint, crunched them up in his hand.

"Right now it is difficult. But during the intifada, things were very bad. The curfews lasted for weeks, with only a few hours to buy groceries every now and then. We were banned from seeing friends, from leaving our house. It kills your spirit. An entire generation, locked in one city without hope. It kills the spirit of the nation." He put his hand to his mouth and, breathing in the scent of the crushed leaves, Ala told me, "I am fortunate. I can emigrate anywhere, but I myself will prefer to die here, in Palestine. It is my country."

* * *

"I hate it here. This place is fucking shit." Tyseer was walking down the road into the city when I had asked him for directions and now we had started chatting. "You can't go anywhere, you can't do anything."

"So what do you do?" I asked.

"Nothing. I was studying—*am* studying, but I hate it."

"Why?"

"My father chose the course. Just like he will choose my wife, my job, my whole fucking life." In the dark, I could only just make out his face. "And because I hate my course, I am not doing very well at it. The only thing I am doing well at is English, but that alone is not enough."

"Can't you change?" I asked.

"No, or he will stop supporting me. I have no other way of getting education; there aren't any jobs so if I want to do well, I need to get a degree first and then I might get the permits to travel, but I don't think so."

"Why not?"

"Even the people here don't like people like us, and the Israelis—they *hate* us." He kicked a loose bit of broken pavement into the road. "I've never thrown a rock in my life, but they still assume I'm a terrorist just because of where I am from."

"Where's that?"

"Balata."

We walked in silence for a while, until I plucked up the courage. "Who?"

"Balata," he replied. "It's a refugee camp. My family are refugees."

"Oh. Right. So what does that mean?"

"It means we don't get any permits. Most Palestinians can go places. It takes time, hours maybe to travel a few miles, but they *can*. Because of my family, where we lived, I can't. I will be here all my life."

Tyseer, it emerged, was a few generations away from the Palestinian families who fled places like Jaffa and Tulkarm in the 1948 Arab-Israeli War. His family still lived in the same refugee camp—what was once a tent city but now housed 30,000 residents in just under one quarter of a kilometre square, all of whom were waiting patiently for the right to return to be ratified.

So far, they had been waiting for over half a century.

"I moved out, somewhere I could study from. Even now, after the intifada has ended, there are incursions into the camp every now and then, and the curfews keep people locked in their homes. A few months ago, my uncle was shot by a sniper as he sat on his balcony. It's still going on—I think there was a gunfight maybe one or two days ago; three people were killed."

"In Balata?"

"Yes, they were Al-Aqsa maybe, or Hamas."

"Could I go there?" I asked, feeling for the first time in a few days the rush of excitement that accompanies most stupid ideas I have.

"On your own, no. Israeli special forces came into the camp dressed as foreign journalists and killed a few people. Since then, the residents don't like outsiders."

"Could you show me around?"

"Um…yes, I guess so."

* * *

The brass case on the ground was 5.56 millimetre NATO, probably imported from the US and only recently used. I picked it up, dusted it off and the shine came back straight away. It was in a pothole in the middle of a narrow street, so it had probably rolled down from a firing position by the alley further uphill. Around the corner was a cemetery—conveniently enough, for that was where the most recent firefight had ended. Perhaps this was one last act of selflessness on behalf of the militants, ending their lives so close to the spot where they would be buried, to save the backs of the people having to carry them. Inside the cemetery, the last of the bodies was being put into a tomb by three men in black clothes. As I walked towards them, Tyseer had grabbed my arm and pulled me away. "They don't want to be disturbed," he said.

We walked further into the camp, passing alleys no wider than a man's shoulders that cut capillary lines between buildings several stories high. Tyseer had told me that in his family's house, you couldn't tell if it was day or night because the street was always so dark. Now I understood what he meant.

The place was bare, concrete. The only colour inside the camp seemed to be grey, varying in shade from light to near-black, and it was tall; every available inch had long been built upon, so the only way for buildings to go was up, which they did. A long way up.

There were more bullet holes than I'd ever seen in one place before—in windows, garage doors, walls, satellite dishes; not one piece of Balata had escaped the flying metal.

Across the main street hung a commemorative banner, with the pictures of three young militants, each holding Kalashnikov rifles of some description, and *shaheed* posters coated every available area of wall at street level. The majority of the so-called martyrs had been photographed with a snazzy-looking carbine with a nice big telescopic sight attached, and for a moment I wondered if they all had to go through exactly the same photo shoot when they joined the militias.

In the alleys, some kids were playing, kicking deflated balls around, chasing each other with sticks, smacking the occasional donkey, but there were very few young men anywhere. The only one we did see beckoned me over. "Look," he said, pointing at his phone. On the display was a picture of himself, holding an assault rifle with a purple band around his forehead, upon which was emblazoned the emblem of some Islamist faction or other. He then showed me another photo, this time of his brother. "Shaheed," he said, imitating a man holding a detonator. "Boom." Tyseer got noticeably agitated the more this young guy spoke. He showed me one more photo, this time a group one. "My friends. Shaheed, shaheed, shaheed…" he said, and uttered a few sentences in Arabic that I could not understand.

"Let's go, now," said Tyseer, firmly, steering me away. As we left, the young lad waved, grinned and drew a line across his throat with his finger. Then he laughed and patted his belt. When we were out of sight, Tyseer turned to me. "You know what shaheed means?"

"Martyr," I replied.

"Yeah. He says he wants to be next." Tyseer glanced back, then looked at me. "Some guys here, they will fuck with you, don't listen to them." Tyseer spoke with a slight accent, but his knowledge of English was impeccable. I was still amazed at just how educated everybody I had met in Nablus was. Then again, I guess there wasn't that much else to do, except fight.

"What does the writing on the posters say?" I asked, pointing at the red Arabic script that went across the centre of a picture of a young guy wearing a cap and holding the standard M4 Carbine as a photo prop.

"No peace without justice," replied Tyseer. "It's the motto of the resistance."

We made our way to the far end of the camp where we were welcomed into one of the houses by a small group of men. "It's safe, these are good guys. They would like to talk to you," said Tyseer, showing me a seat and positioning himself as a translator. Tea and a selection of biscuits were brought in and we started chatting.

It turned out that each of the them had spent considerable time in Israeli prisons and had belonged to the Al-Aqsa Martyr's Brigade—a Fatah militant group. They were the fighters, the ones who had survived to tell the tales, and they were older.

Sipping our steaming glasses of tea, the men described their lives in turn. And the more the men talked, trying to explain the mentality of the freedom fighter, the more I started to understand why Balata was so infamous. Hard living conditions create hard people, it seemed, and the residents of Balata were certainly that; they were fighters. Life in the camp pushed people into the militant wings of Hamas and Fatah. The lack of water, the spread of disease, the cramped conditions—all the things that made life tough had one cause as far as the refugees were concerned: Israel.

So, while it may not be in the interest of everyday Palestinians, fighting what they saw as the Israeli occupation of their land made perfect sense to these men. Their families suffered daily in the tough streets of Balata, the streets they described as an "open air prison", and for them, there was no other way to deal with their troubles. So, every few days, when the Israelis began their military operations, they would fight. Often, they would die, and their faces would then be printed on martyr posters alongside the slogan, "No peace without justice."

They told me this with no hint of pride or showmanship. Calm, patient, they answered my questions; the only glimmer of a smile came when I had asked how many people in Balata fought the incursions.

"Depends how much ammunition we have," they laughed.

The truth was, it was these guys that gave Israelis the excuse for the checkpoints, the curfews, the incursions. Hence, I'd guess, why the other Palestinians viewed them with such animosity. Places like Balata are a breeding ground for suicide bombers; so many disaffected youth with no hopes in life, the promise of a thousand virgins must seem damn good. It gave me all the more respect for people like Tyseer, who had done his best to escape Balata, albeit at his father's behest, rather than get bogged down in the conflict. But I could understand why others turned to violence. Especially after how I'd felt in Hebron.

When the tea was finished, I thanked the men and shook their hands. These men, men who Europe and America branded as terrorists, had given me their time and hospitality. They had shown me into their homes and talked freely, not to portray Israel as a monster, but simply to make me—a tourist, essentially—see where they were coming from. I left feeling honoured to have met them, these terrorists. Honoured to have shared their conversation.

The next day, I went back to Safa's English class. To the group, I asked, "How many of you have lost friends or family members to the war?"

Almost the entire class put their hands up.

SIXTEEN

I Don't Care Who You Are, Here's to Your Dream

At first glance, the West Bank can look like a set from Grease, the Musical: young men with slick black hair, wearing skinny jeans and tight sweaters, looking as cool as they do dangerous. There's one thing missing on this living stage though, and that's the lycra-clad hussy.

Before I left, Tyseer had asked me whether it was true, whether all women slept around in the West. It was a question I had been asked a lot on my travels, especially in the Middle East—whether we had more sex where I was from, whether relationships were easier to come by. Over a glass of Mecca Cola in his student flat, Tyseer had told me that he once had a secret girlfriend who he had kissed but never slept with. Even this was unusual, he said. His roommate agreed, saying that he'd never kissed anyone, that he wanted to save it for marriage.

"Have you ever had sex?" Tyseer asked me. To me, it almost seemed like a stupid question. I had been at university for nearly three years. I had a long-term girlfriend. But Tyseer was five years older than me and the question was serious.

"Yes," I replied, not knowing how to phrase it without confirming the view that all Westerners were sluts. "But not all people have."

His roommate's ears pricked up. "What is it like?"

"Um, what?"

"What is it like to lose your virginity?"

"Er…" I didn't really know where to start. Awkward? Amusing in hindsight? I settled for, "Yeah, it's okay." Fortunately, they seemed satisfied by this answer. I wasn't going to discuss the ins and outs with them, literally or figuratively, and I think they understood that. "But look, don't think of everybody as having sex with everybody else in the West. We just have a different outlook on things."

"So your wife, will she be a virgin?" Tyseer's roommate asked.

I could lie. Really, if I wanted them to think I was respectable, I should lie. But for some reason I didn't. Something stopped me. "No, probably not," I replied. Their faces dropped in mild disgust. "What matters is that I love her," I continued. "And that she loves me."

Eventually Tyseer said, "I couldn't marry someone who had sex with another man."

I suppose it made sense in a way that I had largely ignored—to know that your life's partner had been intimate with someone else in exactly the same way as they were with you *was* a tad weird. But the same would work in reverse really. So for the sake of not being a hypocrite, I'd have to ignore that. Which, to be honest, I didn't mind. That's just the way things were and I'd rather that than repeat those embarrassing fumblings I'd long since tried to forget.

But later, when I got back to Jerusalem, or 'uds as the Palestinians knew it,* I started to ponder this. Tyseer was a brilliant guy, he had shown me a huge amount of kindness and we got on well. I now considered him a friend, but I knew that this subject was where the cultural divide really lay. No matter how hard I tried to justify it, by their standards of absolute celibacy, all Westerners—the ones I knew at least—were loose with each other. Very few, if any, of my friends from university would be virgins by the time they left—even fewer through any choice of their own. It was just strange that the onus was placed on women to defend their sexuality in the Middle East so much more than the men. Surely both parties were as much to blame?

It took me a while to figure out why it always seemed like such a big topic when local guys talk to travelling Western men like me, and not just in the Middle East, but right across the more culturally conservative parts of the world. When it clicked, I wondered how I could have possibly been so naïve for so long.

---

* 'uds, being a shortened version of the Arabic name for Jerusalem, Al-Quds.

Here's what struck me: fundamentally, virtually all men are the same.

There are the overt types in the West—people who admit to chasing women and sex. And there are the repressed ones elsewhere, who are forced to dodge firewalls, both culturally and technologically, to find it. Yes, there may be more discipline in some areas, less drive, but it seemed clear to me that eventually, deep down, most men were prewired to seek it out. Only culture, expectation; discipline and inhibition prevented them from doing so.

You needed to look no further than the popularity of porn on the internet for evidence of this. Because the sad fact is, porn has crossed more borders and twisted the minds of more men than the most dangerous mutant virus could ever do. I'd seen it in internet cafés in Morocco, Jordan, Indonesia; I'd later see white girls being screwed on people's mobile phones across India, in the West Bank, even Nepal. I'd met young men, old men, outwardly religious men, Indonesian airline salesmen; but always the same clips, the same closeups, the same panting cries. I'd bet even the most hardline mujahid probably had a few megabytes stashed away somewhere to prepare for all those virgins he'd receive when he becomes *shaheed*.

The "veneer of human morality" I'd heard it called.

And what's worse about that is the effect it has on men who have more access to Western porn than they do to Western women: quite often, when they do see Western girls, they assume the best. I'd put a lot of rapes down to this disturbing fact.

But that was beside the point.

Tyseer's housemate had already admitted earlier in that conversation that he spent upwards of two hours on his hair per day; why do that? Why, when you're never going to pick up any fuzz anyway, go to all that effort? I guess it all came down to the off-chance, or the chase. Just like the way I had tensed up when Yasmine walked into the room back in Nablus, the effort I had made to be charming when I responded to her questions. Why do that, when I already had a girlfriend? And if I remembered correctly, I really liked my girlfriend. We'd had our ups and downs, but it was still going well; I didn't anticipate us separating any time soon.

It hadn't crossed my mind much since the evening I'd met Yasmine, probably because there were too many other things going on, but perhaps that was the first sign that the cracks had already appeared. I knew there was no way anything would come of my meeting with Yasmine, yet still, the openness with which I greeted her was possibly the first suggestion that the girl I was so convinced I was in love with back home was not going to be the one I would marry, and that truth made me feel more culturally alien to the people I had spent the last few weeks of my life with than anything else. Then again, the very fact I'd been like that meant that I was also inherently similar.

But all this thinking brought me to another truth, one just as fundamental, but perhaps less widespread. And in this truth lay the explanation of why I was here; at least, part of it.

I had gone back up to the Mount of Olives and I was alone, listening to an MP3 player, jotting a few notes down in my journal. Flashbacks of the last time I had been up here were still floating around in my head, but I had never quite figured out why I wasn't more upset by the way those two guys had got so shirty with me. I was genuinely scared that one of them would pull a knife, but there was something about it, about that situation, that I actually *enjoyed.* Just like when I'd heard those gunshots back in Nablus the year before, I'd felt giddy, like a kid on Christmas Eve. It was the same with the police in Papua, the sinking boat in the Philippines; any time I had been in a marginally risky situation, there had been the usual fear, stress, anxiety. But also this other feeling, creeping out from the more untoward recesses of my mind—some kind of glee. Like my subconscious was screaming at me from somewhere: *This is it! This is really happening!*

Each time something scary was going on, there was that excitement, followed by the sense of elation when whatever threat I faced was now over; I'd won, I'd conquered it.

Bring on the next one.

But this last trip to Nablus hadn't provided me with that. I'd achieved my conscious aim—I'd gained a valuable insight into the way of life for millions of people trapped by a brutal and persistent occupation, stuck in a life of violent tedium through no fault of their own; but another fix?

No.

I closed my journal and put it back in my bag. The fiery orange horizon, the clouds; the twinkling lights in the courtyard behind the Al-Aqsa Mosque. The medley of wailing muezzins. Medieval streets, swarming bazaars—these were the things I would leave behind. More than that though, I'd have to leave risk. That thing I apparently craved so much because there was relatively little of it on my plane of existence back in the UK. Risk, and the responsibility to look after myself, without endless fences and restrictions, rules and regulations. Because that was what it seemed to boil down to, this travel thing. That's what it was about, once you dug under the surface. Not just insight, not just global awareness, but freedom. Risk. Sure, I was interested in all that other stuff, very interested in fact. But to be honest, maybe it was just a happy coincidence. Maybe all the things that I saw as my reasons for travelling were the useful bi-products of something more innate, instinctive, perhaps even vain.

I'd started travelling because I felt there was a gap; something was missing from my life, and when I'd first encountered it, travel did more than just fill that gap—it took over it like a hermit crab to what undoubtably must have been a snail shell of existential inadequacy. Travel, that is, and the inherent risk it entailed.

But there was something untoward about this, and not just the hermit crab reference. As the nearest imam started trying to use his voice to impersonate a sixties electric guitar solo, I started to recognise that maybe I was addicted. Addicted to this risk, to challenge, to the uncertainty. Addicted to all those things that travel provided but home didn't. And the more I thought about it, the more I realised that it didn't matter whether travelling was a noble pastime or an abomination of the human condition. A gold-paved step on the stairway to enlightenment or a skin-deep yearning for social recognition. It didn't matter, because whatever it was, I had already gone too far to care. Just the thought of my routine back in Exeter had started to feel like watching a sports match after I'd already found out the score; it lacked excitement. It was predictable. From the top of the Mount of Olives that evening, home seemed like a place where I'd pass time until retirement or another trip, whichever came first.

And if that was the case, no matter how untoward the origins of this addiction were, I needed to make the most of it. I needed to focus on the good of it. What I could learn and solve and pass on. This was my affliction—dissatisfaction; the knowledge that home would never be enough—so rather than sulk about it, rather than mope across the world for years on end dressed as a circus performer like some backpackers seemed to do, surely I should follow Spiderman's lead and use it to fight evil?

Come to think of it, that would be a great idea—I could share all my investigations in the hope they'd offer a new perspective, show the other side of the debate, turn bad to good, ignorance to knowledge!

That's what I'd do. I'd be *Travelman.*

No, not Travelman, sounds too similar to salesman…*Backpack*man! Still a bit shit, but it'd have to do. And as *Backpackman*, I'd have to use my ailment for the benefit of the wider community; I'd save the world through travelling. I'd prove that Peter Parker hadn't died in vain!

Brilliant.

I looked out across the twinkling city, a renewed sense of purpose filling my eyes. And from the top of the Mount of Olives that evening, I felt invincible, indestructible. I felt like a true superhero.

Unfortunately, it wasn't to last.

* * *

For a while, travel plans were forgotten.

I had four weeks to write my thesis and revise for my finals, so I set about studying, collating all the notes from all my trips into one big pile. I'd seen a lot since I started the degree; I'd learnt a lot too. The gaps that my travels didn't fill, I felt as though my course research had. And now I needed to put it into some kind of Supertheory to go with my new comic-book hero persona.

So for the next few weeks I looked at all this stuff, this evidence, and put it all together into something I could understand. Something I could comprehend as a singular object. I looked back at my notes from Papua, from the Philippines. Borneo, Kuala Lumpur, Syria. I read and re-read my journal. And with the thoughts and emotions of the West Bank still weighing heavily on my mind, I tried to remember all those other times I had recently returned from somewhere, because that first month back was the only time I could view things with any kind of perspective. It was often the only time I felt I could gain any true relativity, see a different angle on my lifestyle, before I sank back into it.

So instead of reverting to old ways this time, I tried to immerse myself in the detachment. I built it up with all the memories and notes from the past, all the thoughts I'd suppressed and pushed aside, to feel them in their extremes. Not to hold back at all, but to embrace them. Recognise that although these thoughts were warped by experience and tales of injustice, if only for the sake of argument, they were worth airing.

In the weeks after I returned from Borneo, I recall how things had seemed tame, boring. After my glimpse at the life of the Krayan, I remember thinking how unconnected to nature it all was, learning stuff from books written by people who had spent their lives reading books, just so I could aspire to the fulfilment and sense of achievement that comes from a high-end career in advertising, finance, property or marketing. I'd recognised that if my trajectory continued, I'd soon be striving for executive status and gimmicky Italian-named coffee sizes; a life in which success would be defined by clothing, furniture, gadgetry; the cost of your car or the size of your house.

Back then I was still two years from being funnelled into a career in any number of graduate-level jobs and I recall wondering how far along that line I'd have to go before anything became *real*, how many words and pages and paragraphs I'd have to scrawl; how many sales targets, promotions, executive lounges I'd have to pass through. I remember wondering how many board meetings and productivity seminars I'd have to sit in before I came across anything that actually did something genuinely *productive*, like kill the animal that provided my family's dinner, knit the clothes they wore on their bodies, build the shelter that lay over their heads. Even construct the car that drove them to school and me to work, and my wife to the plastic surgery clinic that would allow her a few more years away from the fantastically lucid truth that we would *never* achieve all those things that decades of advertising would have us both convinced we would, and now I'd long since abandoned any nourishing contentment in favour of the more immediate satisfaction of ever-expanding wealth, only to realise that it was the basic things—sociability, companionship, family—that would make me feel ultimately satisfied.

After I got back from Borneo, deep down I saw the pure life of Long Layu as something humanity should be striving towards, aspiring to reach, not running away from. Not burying its head in technology and information, currency and commodity; all these things whose sole purpose was to bridge the distraction gap between the essence of living and the zeppelin of contrivances we'd somehow built it up to be. Even before I got to England, back when I was still fresh from the jungle, culture shocked and vomiting all over Kuala Lumpur, I'd seen it in a more global context. Tall buildings, glowing signs, business, commerce…all that stuff, when all people really needed was a rattan mat on the floor of a wooden longhouse. A forest with an endless supply of food, water, sustenance. Communities nearby from which to build a family, friendships and so on, *ad infinitum*. Later, I'd seen the same kind of thing in the Baliem Valley and among the fishermen of Palawan: the Simple Life.

It was a hard life too sometimes, what with disease, natural disasters and scary bastard spiders that looked like lobsters; and dangerous, compared to the cocooned world of Western suburbia—the world that apparently made young men enter fantasies of violence on games consoles and movies and TV; the world that seemed to rely on celebrity scandal, sex, intoxication. Yet those must have been the things that made this Civilised Life so appealing: the lack of hardship, the potential to live away from all the dangers, to raise a family where no children died from dysentery, food poisoning, animal attack. Life in a world where things were provided for you as long as you played your part, where people rarely starved to death, where fewer people hopped onto the purgatory wagon before it was their time. These were the dreams and in many places, they really were being realised.

So maybe I idolised the primitive way a little too much. To me, it hinted at the highest goods of them all: challenge and contentedness. And I liked that. It felt natural. Undisturbed. And I remember feeling that there should be at least *some* areas in the world that should stay like that, free from encroaching development. Free from palm oil and timber merchants, sales targets and profit. Then again, I was bound to think that. I'd loved all that woodland-living lark. So I was more than a little bit biased. I couldn't deny that for many, the city life really was a dream. All the possibilities in the world lay in pursuing it for a few years. Why seek out hardship anyway—to prove something?

Even at the time, I knew I was being cynical. It's just that as a dream for people to aspire to, I found it lacking.

It wasn't until I visited Papua, and later the Philippines, that I encountered the truth behind the fallacy of the developing world—that all countries will eventually become clean, all workers will eventually wear white collars and nobody will have to beg, steal, scratch a living from the rubbish tips or die in slumdog cholera epidemics. The theory that all countries will eventually be First World, given enough time and investment. Before Papua, I just thought the spread of Western ideals was pushing out people's option of whether they would choose to become "developed", or choose to remain "primitive". I just thought that our thirst for things, our hunger, our yearning for consumption, was eating into the last safe havens for those who didn't want that lifestyle. In fact, until Papua, I didn't know that this choice was often snatched away by desperate governments and greedy multinationals and the reward was not a sanitary life free from hardship and disease, but poverty and cultural erosion. And this was happening simply for the fact that an expanding First World needed an expanding Third World. "Symbiosis" wasn't the right word, I knew, but it was as good as I could come up with, because the alternative was "parasite". For a few to live in prosperity, many more needed to live in poverty; almost as though the entire global economy had been modelled on the premises of a Müller Lite advert—no pleasure without pain.

I remember looking at Papua and seeing how colonialism, oppression and what was left of tribalism and the Hindu caste system in Indonesia had made corruption rife throughout the province. But now, when I scanned all my notes and re-read all those journal entries, it occurred to me that there was very little difference in the amount of corruption between Papua and the West—in reality, the only discrepancy was in the way people went about it. Over here, corruption was systemic, embedded in the financial and economic institutions of our nations, institutions that allowed the rich to get richer at the expense of the rest. It had several names—the Free Market, Neoliberalism, Capitalism—and everyone who had the power to change it had already agreed that it was the only way we could continue to expand our living-standard bubble as we had been doing for so long. For a while, we were too far removed from the desperation of the losing side to even realise it existed, and that it was partly our fault, because without the Third World, there'd be no First World.

Even with our modern moralised outlook, very few seemed to recognise that this was the slavery of our time. The global apartheid. Feudal, racist and unfair. Which led me on to thinking that the only real difference between the First and Third World is that the people running the former were much more experienced, much better at global corruption than the latter.

After I visited Papua, I also started to recognise that there was an addiction cycle that was changing the world: those business leaders and financiers who were addicted to wealth, sponsored by the consumers like me who were addicted to new things, and the governments who were addicted to the votes that me and my fellow consumers would give them. And now, those governments were fighting wars against people who disagreed with that mentality, people who in true Newtonian fashion had gone so far in the opposite direction it was hard to tell who was more wrong. But after visiting the Middle East, I found the resentment uncomfortably understandable.

And that became my theory, my paradigm of the modern era: greed leads to exploitation, which leads to inequality, and inequality to resentment, hatred, and ultimately war.

Then again, I could barely talk, living the way I did, having the things I had. Using all the money I could get my hands on to indulge my obsession with risk and adventure. Using all this political craziness as an excuse to feed my very own addiction.

I'll be honest, when I was there, looking through all my notes, trying to put the pieces together, I felt as though I was some kind of revolutionary. I felt like a global volunteer, an ignorance-obliterating, poverty-smashing *International Relater*. I would tell people these things and the world would realise the error of its ways and spread the excesses out evenly, and I would be hailed as the King of Global Justice and everybody would be so happy because the world had never had such a good-looking king before. But, as I was yet to learn, things were never going to be quite that simple.

For all my ranting, I was clearly still naïve. Horrifically so. So when I was starting to sew badges onto my new anarchist's anorak, still under the impression that I was morally great and the rest of the world should be like me, I had no impression of just how difficult, how next-to-impossible it would be to stop myself from reverting to those ways I was apparently now scorning. What made it worse was that I soon came to accept that on my own, I was just as helpless as anybody else to stop it. And when push came to shove, this became as much of an excuse not to do anything as I needed. So after I'd passed my exams, done what I needed to do, I dropped the ridiculous alter-ego I'd adopted and set about forgetting everything I'd learnt over the past two years.

It was easier than I ever imagined.

SEVENTEEN

Out of Sight, Out of Mind

The sun was shining, the exams were over and Guy's van was now a palace. It had a bed, a compartment for his tools, his windsurf board, his sleeping bag. I'm fairly sure it even had a slot for his lovely girlfriend Charlotte.

Life was good.

I was back with my housemates, recounting tales of adventure and global injustice, spewing out theories worthy of the Che Guevara-wannabe herb-smoker I truly wasn't. What's more, I was happier than I had been for months.

For the first time in my life, time was my own. No essays, no exams, no lectures. No looming deadlines. From now on, I could become anything I wanted. I could be an anarchist, a priest, a diplomat, a stock broker. Unlikely as it was, I could even be a train driver, just like I'd wanted to when I was six. I cared not if all of these options weren't really suitable—that was irrelevant. The fact was that everything I did from now would be *my* choice. I'd churned out my theories, passed my course, and now the world was mine. My girlfriend had gone away for a few weeks to do some work experience and then some travel, and I was left to surf, play, drink the rest of my overdraft away. That didn't matter either—I'd soon pay it off, because *I* was a *graduate*. My notes went onto a pile, into a drawer somewhere; out of sight, out of mind. A formula which applied to most things in those hazy, crazy days of summer.

I figured I'd have a few months out before I got round to the business of saving the world. I'd enjoy things, reap what there was to reap from this system while I still wasn't a total hypocrite.

So I spent time with my housemates, going to pubs with Guy and Mark, listening to tales of debauchery from Kate, dancing and partying with Venetia and Amber. For the first time since Papua, I started truly enjoying Exeter again. I relished the carefree life of the student. Climbing around the ruins, jogging along the canals, bicycle-jousting up the high street at half one in the morning with traffic-cone lances. After a while, I got so caught up in the post-exam merriment that I forgot all about the days I had spent in Nablus and Jerusalem. Forgot all about the grand theory I'd devised that made the West out to be the scourge of the earth.

To be honest, life couldn't be better. Beer, barbecues, picnics. Fishing trips, surfing adventures, house parties. It was at one of these house parties that I met Emily, and a little while after that, things changed quite a lot.

In fact, it was Tim's birthday.

Tim, by now, *was* wearing a tweed jacket. And brogues too, probably. Lined up for a hotshot career in politics by virtue of his vote-winning hair, things were looking great for him, and he'd invited a load of friends over to his house in the Cotswolds to celebrate.

I arrived a few hours early to help set up and we got through a fair bit of booze before anyone else arrived. Tim had been surprisingly interested in my West Bank adventures, given what he thought they involved, and over a few girly drinks, I'd managed to explain my theory of the world. "You've just turned into a lefty pinko now haven't you?" he said when I'd finished.

"Cheers!" I had replied, and downed another glass.

Sometime later—it was all starting to get hazy—I was introduced to Emily. Slim and attractive, for a fair while we talked about this and that, odds and sods, and somehow I'd managed to remain fairly charming despite the surging blood-alcohol levels. Our conversation was eventually interrupted by a crazy Welsh man, as conversations often are, and we went our separate ways.

Until, a few hours later, I was at a table with a thumping beat behind me, a drinking game in front of me, Emily to my left, and her hand resting against my knee. Inadvertantly, perhaps. But possibly not.

At this point the story splits in two.

In the first instance, our lead character feels the temptation to let this hand stay where it is, with all the promise and connotation that entails, but he doesn't. He gently moves it away and explains to the lovely Emily that, gorgeous though she is, he isn't interested as he has a girlfriend whom he loves dearly. He then goes on to live a happy life as a graduate, satisfied with the amount of travel he's already done and reigned in by this girlfriend of his to getting a good job in the city like most of his mates. Occasionally, he saunters off on weekend breaks to Corfu and Marrakech, reliving the days of freedom and bliss until his wife comes running across the pool terrace to tell him that Wilfred's nappy needs changing again because, like his father, Wilfred had inherited an unusually relaxed approach to continence.

In the second, he doesn't.

* * *

"But I did too."

Now I'll admit, they weren't the words I was planning on using, but I guess they got the point across just as effectively. Initially I was relieved. But I couldn't walk and I still didn't quite understand what was going on. Nonetheless, it was one more thing off my chest, and that could only be good. Now life could move on. Now we could get over these minor glitches and rewire.

But as I was about to learn, things are never quite that simple…

Actually, maybe I've skipped a bit here, so let's take it back a couple of weeks.

It was the end of my stay in Exeter and now I needed to take myself off for a while. No surprises here. I booked a flight, to Sri Lanka this time. The war with the Tamil Tigers was coming to a brutal end, so that was enough of an excuse for me to show interest. At short notice, I asked Robin, one of my best mates from school, to keep me company.

We'd both set out with the ambition of finding out about the war, but really I just wanted to forget about England for a while, clear my head. I knew it wasn't productive, especially when I really should have been looking for work and moving myself on. But there was no reason to drop travel just yet, especially when I needed its distractive powers most.

So off we went.

At first it was good to be back in the real world. The heat, the smells. Small garage-front stores with walls covered in packet noodles and snacks. Little three-wheelers zipping about all over the place, dodging the choking roar of the oncoming buses. Skinny men, colourful women, dusty side streets and potholes. Vendors, everywhere.

At first glance, it looked just like Indonesia or Thailand.

There were more limbless here I noticed, hobbling the streets of Colombo, trying to get a few rupees; that's a product of the war though, I'd guessed. Still, as much as it reminded me of most other tropical places I'd been, there was a distinct colonial twist that remained very South Asian. Behind the cement and concrete façades—holding up the Sinhalese-English advertising billboards with the pictures of the chubby, now victorious President Rajapaksa—monuments to 19th Century British architecture were everywhere, in the form of rotting, semi-collapsed shells of grand buildings. The architectural equivalent of an octogenarian ex-supermodel—elegant, yet decrepit. Like many places, the capital of Sri Lanka had its gems. Tasty food halls, serving Colombo residents generous portions of chicken and rice at a low fare. Crumbling Georgian hotels with high ceilings and charming balconies. The waterfront, where the sun would descend into a golden haze every afternoon. As a tourist destination, it was brilliant. But like many places, I had an inkling that there was an undercurrent the locals were keen to hide.

From a visitor's perspective, Sri Lankans seemed like wonderful people; welcoming, warm, kind. And yet there had been a huge amount of tragedy in this tiny nation—a ferocious civil war had just come to a close and the damage from one of the deadliest natural disasters in history was still visible along much of the coastline. There were areas in Sri Lanka where people had been forced to suffer more than any other place I had yet been in the world, but at first glance, you'd have no idea. It wasn't until the third day in Colombo that I even had an admission from a local that the country was facing anything less than total normality.

At the time, British media was full of stories about the small island nation that sits in the Bay of Bengal like a teardrop from Tamil Nadu. These stories ranged from mass killings, systematic raping and indiscriminate shelling in the so-called "no fire zones" in the north, to tales of civilians being trapped as human shields between the desperate Tamil Tigers (LTTE) and the advancing Sri Lanka Army. In this tiny speck in the Indian Ocean, a full-blown battle of attrition had been raging for decades—possibly one of the most violent and cruel in modern times. One in which the separatist guerrilla faction had not only used suicide bombers and rifles, but at times, a navy and air force too.*

And despite my efforts, the most I could get out of anyone was this, whispered by the man I was sitting next to on a bus one afternoon: "We may be defeating the LTTE, but we are going to sacrifice our democracy for it."

So Rob and I went northeast to find out more, to see if we could meet anyone. We journeyed as far into the Tamil areas as we could without losing limbs from land mines and spent a few days there, playing with the local lads among the crashing waves in the beaches of Trincomalee, walking the streets as lightning flashed across the sky, trying to find out if anyone had even *heard* of the LTTE, let alone seen them.

For days, questions were redirected or met with stone-faced stares. Hard as we tried, we were getting nowhere—the Tamils of Trincomalee were eerily quiet.

Trincomalee; site of intense artillery bombardments a few years back, where now the only evidence we could find was the rubbish-filled crater that sat dead-centre of the rusting carcass of a playground near our guesthouse, between a creaking roundabout that could have been lifted straight out of Pripyat and some mangled swings that now served as a perch for the thousands of scavenging crows in the area. The coastline had largely been rebuilt by charities and volunteer projects, save for the occasional ruined wall and the remnants of tiled flooring and foundations—the only survivors of the tsunami when it had swept through. It was clear from a brief glance at the history of the area that Trinco's recent past was one of suffering, but for the first time in my experience, nobody would breath a word of it.

And when we'd eventually discovered that there was no way we'd be able to get anywhere near the conflict zones—thanks to the swarms of checkpoints and land mines and the Sri Lanka army troops who were fighting the war they'd waited decades to win—we

---

* For those who think it is just Muslim extremism that teaches youngsters to blow themselves up, it is worth noting that the Liberation Tigers of Tamil Eelam were predominantly Hindu, not Muslim.

abandoned the Northeast and headed back down to the tourist trail, confused and largely unaware of what had been happening just the other side of the checkpoints.

***

Cramped, clattering carriages took us through hills of rich green tea plantations, dotted with saris that floated like butterflies through rows of leaves, picking and tucking into baskets the tea that would end up in pots in the UK one day. They took us past elephants, through steaming rice paddies and cool woodlands; thick mists, blasting winds and magnificent sunsets; all the time tempting us with the lemon zest aroma of samosas, Lanka-style. Sitting in the open doorways of the rickety carriages, the landscape streaming past me, I'd had the time to mull things over.

Maybe this time I'd overestimated my thirst for conflict, because I wasn't that upset to be leaving the North. Yes, we'd failed in our mission, but I didn't really mind. I couldn't shake the feeling that there was something different about that place that I didn't really want to see. Even after Palestine and Papua, maybe I still wasn't ready for it yet.

Actually, when I thought about it, something about Trincomalee had been disturbing in a way I had never come across before. I couldn't place it; perhaps it was the way the crows all hung expectantly around the tsunami ruins. The way the Tamils had stayed silent—a minority population too afraid of what was to come to even whisper the name of the Tigers. Maybe I was imagining it, but the fear seemed to hang in the air, along with the souls of thousands of tsunami victims and civil war casualties. Trinco was not a ghost town, but for the effect it had on me, it may as well have been.

Contrasted against the rejoicing Sinhalese tourists who flocked to sample all the legendary beaches that had previously been off-limits, the Tamils were scared. Their people had fought hard for their independence, murdered the civilians of the enemy in suicide attacks without mercy, compassion, or discrimination—the very same civilians who were now swimming in their beaches—and now they had lost. Now, their enemy was taking it out in any way, on anyone, and they, the Tamil civilians, innocents who often had nothing to do with the LTTE, were going to feel the heat. So they were scared. Not angry, like the Palestinians. Not defiant, like the Papuans. But scared.

Terrified.

The truth was, even after Palestine, this was something else. A few days in Trincomalee had convinced me that as much as I thought I understood conflict and suffering from all those stories and experiences I had heard over the years—that glamorous disobedience of the resistance fighter, the humble rebellion of the peasant farmer; even the horrendous actions of the Indonesian army in the Baliem all those decades ago—I really had no idea of the dark truth of human cruelty and violence. The tainted, ugly reality that would no doubt change the way I saw things and I wasn't ready. There was fighting a war and there was waiting to be massacred; the despair and hopelessness of the latter must outweigh almost anything you could care to describe.

And in Trincomalee, I hadn't even *seen* anything.

I hadn't even *heard* a story.

For that, part of me was right to be relieved; as I would later learn, the worst of the rumours were true. Children, hospital workers, mothers, fathers, all killed in the worst ways imaginable. As many as forty-thousand civilians in the northern sector of Sri Lanka known as the Vanni had been rounded up, shelled, shot, raped and murdered, all in the months and weeks and days before we had arrived. Words cannot describe the horror these people went through in the no-fire zones, but all I had was just a feeling; I didn't, couldn't know how far things had gone. If I had somehow got further north to where the fighting had swept around to encircle the last of the Liberation Tigers of Tamil Eelam, I would probably be a very different person by now.

Amazing, really, that such a horrific event could be going on so close by and you'd have nothing more than an inkling that something wasn't quite right.

So instead of chasing conflict, this time Robin and I soaked up the mountain vistas of Kandy and Ella—towns that had been named after puppies for all I knew—and ate delicious curries in the sanguine comfort of the hills. Then we went to the beach where, along with half of the Israeli Defence Force, we rented boards and got into the process of ignoring anything that might have been happening in the area we had just left behind. Back into the world of petty dilemmas and insignificant worries. Out of sight, out of mind.

Just as Rajapaksa intended.

***

"So what are you going to do?" Robin panted.

"I don't know," I replied, trying to keep up with him. Tubby though he was, he was still fitter than me.

"Good answer. Keep it a surprise."

I let a few breaths pass with the beating of my feet on the sand, then said, "I haven't got a fucking clue."

To the left, waves were smashing, dumping their white horses on the shoreline like some kind of Irish stout advert; in front, the beach was stretched out under a towering column of pink and orange cumulonimbus. Black tar on the sand stuck to my feet, creating footprints in negative when I lifted them away to reveal the golden sand underneath, with flecks spraying out like the splatter of blood. All the time, the waves, the roar as they crashed like falling elephants. Crumbling and crumping with a dull boom.

"Are you gonna stay with her?" Robin called back.

I put on a quick burst, feeling the tightness in my chest rise with the burn in my legs. "I'll try."

I'd explained to Robin what had happened and he initially went to give me a high five, until he saw the expression on my face. Then he'd just laughed. Which was fair enough really.

But now he was starting to piss me off.

Somehow Robin, who used to be one of the most ego-boosting running partners on account of his belly, had managed to turn himself around and could not only outpace me, but had one of the hottest girlfriends out of any of my mates. To my mind, that made him a bit of a dick. Anyway, that wasn't what mattered right now. What mattered was the sand, the salty spray from the waves, the wind in our hair, the red sky above.

"Jim," said Robin, "I think all this comfort might have turned us into massive pansies."

"Yeah, I think it has," I shouted back.

Now don't get me wrong, I had nothing against oversized flowers and I enjoyed all this beautiful beachy stuff. But after a few weeks of fine dining and sharing wonderful rooms, this just wasn't what we had planned. Where was the challenge? Where was the adventure? Where were the beautiful girls we should be having this kind of holiday with?

The only surprising moment we'd had was when both Robin and I had nearly stepped on a cobra that was lying across a path near Ella, but even then, the snake seemed far too spaced out to pose any real kind of threat. It just slithered off into a bush, flicking its tongue out now and then, like snakes do. So we hadn't really had much to write home about. Hence, I suppose, why we'd taken to running up and down the beach in the evenings.

"Shall we do something cool?" Robin asked.

"Okay, race you to that fishing boat over there." I pointed a few hundred metres up the beach. "Last one there really is a pansy."

"No, I mean like…Jim? *JIM!*"

It was useless, I was already sprinting. So Robin upped his pace and came galloping past me like the Royal Marine he was about to become. With time to spare, he stood by the fishing boat and waited for me to arrive, flush and breathless, sweating like a cross between an asthmatic sumo wrestler and a red crayon.

"What I mean is, maybe we should do something more exciting," he said.

"What, more exciting than surf? There isn't anything," I panted, "we've already tried going north."

"We could explore some of the beaches south of here," Rob replied. "It's all ex-Tiger area—it all used to be punchy. There must be a few people who'd tell us about the war. At the very least we could find some better surf spots."

"How would we get down there?"

"Bike?"

"Yeah okay." I caught my breath for a moment and another wave slammed with oceanic force onto the heavily sloping beach. "Where from?"

"In town. The guys from the café have a few and they said we could use them." Robin took his hands from his hips. "Just as long as your bike skills are better than your surfing skills."

With that, he started jogging back towards the village we had come from. Where the beach levelled out and the curve of the sands went with the swell, you ended up with one of the world's finest point breaks. Further around the headland where we'd decided to run, it was all dump and crash. When the warm winds picked up, this sent sea spray straight to our skin and the whole combination—running barefoot on the beach at dusk—couldn't fail to turn a man.

Rob was right. We needed the thrill of a motorbike. Just to bring us closer to the adventurers we once were. I panted after him, looking for the areas of sand where the water had washed over and hardened the surface.

***

The first thing I noticed was how quiet everything was.

Then how hot.

We'd been going for a while, all morning and most of the afternoon probably. I had relished the feeling of zipping along the dirt tracks, passing through wicker-fence villages and areas of open scrubland until we hit the coast. Hunting for crocodiles in the dried swamps nearby, trying to suss out whether the break in the surface of the water was a submerged log or a pair of waiting eyes.

Before we set off, we were told to watch out for the herds of elephant and other more rare game, such as leopard, that occasionally strayed near the tracks when you got south of the confusingly named village of Panama, but we hadn't seen a thing. So we zipped along what was left of the road—now more of a rutted sandy track—taking in the sensation of being completely alone in one of Sri Lanka's least populated corners, with the breeze blowing the sweat from our backs.

We were nearing Yala East National Park, one of the last pockets of LTTE violence outside the Vanni, where as many as a hundred cadres were once holed up, causing havoc through raids, land mines and massacres against the local population and the nearby Sri Lanka Army camps. Now, in the middle of the dry season, there was little more than scrub, bush and fauna; in fact, it was more akin to the Australian outback than any jungle I'd seen before.

For quite a while, Robin had been ahead of me. He was a much better rider—more confident, more aware of the mechanics of motorbiking—and was using the challenging stretch of track to see how fast he could go. I, on the other hand, was pottering along quite happily, watching the scenery pass by at a pace that let me concentrate on other things. Then came a length of straight road, so I decided to test the throttle.

Revving the bike and shooting up the gears, I was just starting to feel the thrill of speed and the sensation of rushing wind, when I saw the rock. It wasn't huge, and if I had been going slower, wouldn't have posed much of a problem. Last I checked, the dial was hovering around sixty, but I didn't have time to check again. I loosed off the throttle and went to cross the rut in the middle of the track, feeling the vibrations shudder through the wheels. The back of the bike bounced slightly, jumped, and I did my best to hold on.

The rest I remember in an extended blur.

I could feel the catch in the wheels as they crossed through the rut, but the back tire slipped as it left, pushing the bike back into the soft sand in the middle of the track. At first, there was only a slight trembling, but then it grew quickly until the front handlebars started wobbling violently, wrenching themselves from my grasp. I grabbed harder, using the full force of my arms as my body was lurched from side to side and then, suddenly, it was all dusty and I was noticing how quiet it was.

And how hot.

My first impulse was to swear, so I did that a few times, just to get it out of my system. Why not—nobody was around to hear me anyway. Apart from a few elephants perhaps, but they probably wouldn't remember.

Once I'd done that, I looked about, trying to suss out where I was. It was just as deserted as everywhere else—a single track crossing through a huge dried-up riverbed, with scrub either side. This was more than likely a roaring torrent in the wet season, but without the air blowing by on the back of the bike and with the sun beating down relentlessly on the cracked earth, it felt like the driest place in the world. The still air was stifling.

I noticed that everything was covered in dust, but I seemed to be okay. The skin on my foot looked a little strange, but it didn't hurt so I stood up. Then it did hurt, so I sat back down and watched as the white, ruptured surface turned bright red, pouring down to the sand in seconds. It wasn't too bad; I could put my weight on it, but the blood kept pooling, soaking through my flip flops, making them sticky.

That'll teach me, I thought, finding the lesson slightly amusing in a how-could-I-have-been-so-stupid way. Flip flops on a motorbike?

Great idea.

On the plus side, they had survived the crash and were obviously very sturdy, so I made a mental note to tell the managing director of O'Neill how good his products were.

Fortunately my first aid kit was still attached to my belt so I pulled a few antiseptic wipes out and started clearing the dust from the wounds. They stung and the blood kept pouring, but I could tell the cuts, deep though they were, were just superficial. Prodding a few tender areas around my feet, I didn't seem to have anything broken, which was good news. I'd used up three or four wipes though and there was no point in wasting any more. The wounds were still too fresh, so wiping the blood off was like trying to block a river by kneeling in it.

The bike was thirty or so feet away and I couldn't quite tell if it was sunburn that I hadn't noticed when the wind was blowing, but my whole body had started to sting. My ankle felt tender when I rolled it, so I rose to my feet more slowly this time, testing each of my joints in turn.

That was lucky, I thought, as I hobbled past the cracked helmet visor towards the scratched and dusty motorbike. I noticed a few more cuts and grazes on my legs and knees as I went, but not much else. Just blood trickling down and the foot, which dust kept clinging to as I hobbled along.

How the hell had I got away with that?

The engine was off, but the keys were still in the ignition. I picked up the bike, feeling a slight twinge in my arm, and propped it onto its stand. Then, a sudden weakness spread through my body and my forehead started sweating. More than sweating, gushing, and not through heat, not this time, because my hands had started to shake. I slumped on the dirt in time for the faint feeling of nausea to start, my peripheral vision to close down into a fuzzy black and then I passed out.

It must have only been a few seconds, maybe a minute or two, but when I came around, there was a silver car stopped right next to the bike and a lady walking from the passenger side with a look of horror on her face.

"Hi," I said, trying to sound upbeat, but struggling to sit forward. "Think I might have had a little motorbike crash." *Morbiash,* I thought, before quickly realising that now was not the time for poor attempts at word combining (wombining). More interesting things were going on.

"Goodness gracious," said the lady. She was well-dressed and the car looked expensive. "Are you okay? Do you need help?"

"No, it's fine," I said. I tried to stand, but the blood went from my head and I slumped back down. "I will be fine," I said, "just in shock a little I think."

I looked at the dirt around me. Somehow, there was a lot more blood than before, but I didn't know where from. My foot didn't look that bad and my shoulder was stiff and stung but there wasn't any red on my hand when I checked it.

"You need to go to a hospital," said the lady, as a man and a teenage girl got out of the car and walked across to me.

"I'm okay. Look, do you have any water I can use to clean with please? I can pay you. My friend is coming back so I will be fine in a minute."

"He needs to go to a hospital," the lady said, but not to me, obviously. The man nodded. They looked Sri Lankan, this couple. But they spoke with a vague British accent.

"Really, I'm fine. Just a bit shocked."

"I don't think so. Look at your arm," he said, and I did.

So that explained the growing pool in the sand. I couldn't really see it, but it was deep. Deep enough that it made my skin split apart like a miniature canyon. The man grabbed a bottle of water from the car and passed it to me. Piercing the bottom with my pocket knife, I squeezed the bottle and a jet of water squirted into the wound, momentarily clearing it of blood.

"I can see the bone," said the lady, by way of reassurance.

The sound of an engine spluttering from a distance hinted at Robin's imminent arrival; when he turned up, he said, "Jim, you need a hospital—I can see your arm bone."

"Bollocks," I think I replied, but by that stage I was starting to feel faint again.

There was some discussion going on behind me and after a few moments, the man came across and said, "There is an army post nearby, we'll take you there. They have a medic, but you need to go to hospital soon." I was helped into the car and we drove off down the road, leaving the bike where it was. I later learnt that this camp also happened to be the Sri Lanka Army post that was overrun two years previously by the LTTE, so they were used to dealing with wounds.

From the car, I hobbled to the medical post with Robin, thanking the family for their help. In hindsight, I wish I had found out their names, because if it hadn't been for them, things would have been a lot more difficult. They waved and drove back down the road in a cloud of dust and I never saw them again.

For the next few hours, a Sri Lanka army medic expertly dealt with each cut individually, using peroxide to sterilise the area and tweezers to remove the fragments of rock and dirt that had become lodged in my arms, feet and legs. Meanwhile, a crowd of about ten soldiers had gathered around to see the silly tourist who'd fallen off his bike. I, being the silly tourist, tried to see the humorous side and when the peroxide fizzed and bubbled inside my arm, I tried to grin and laugh as opposed to grimace and cry. It would be misleading if I said it worked.

Still, the leftover adrenaline was suppressing the pain so I wasn't too fussed. Once the wounds were dealt with, I was given a few temporary bandages and taken to a nearby doctor's surgery for stitching.

Lying on a table, still without having been able to see the full extent of the damage to my arm, a nurse had begun preparing the cut. Under the cool blowing wind of the fan, she gently wiped the area, but she was sweating. As she prepared the syringe for the anaesthetic injection, she started shaking. I turned to face her and asked, "Are you okay?"

The nurse nodded slightly, then put the syringe down. She walked over to where Robin was standing, said a few words.

"Rob," I called over. "What's going on?"

"They're going to dress it, but you've got to go to the hospital."

"Why?" I asked, still not yet feeling the damage properly.

"Jim, it's pretty bad."

* * *

It had taken the rest of the day to get us and the bikes back to Aragum Bay. The military post was fantastic, helping us in any way possible. We thanked them profusely, but they just shrugged it off with a humble tilt of the head.

I was damaged and yet things could have been a lot worse. Thanks to the kindness I had been shown and the quality of care I'd received that day, most chances of infection had been staved off. Which was fortunate really, because the hospital in Pottuvil was more of a malaria incubator than a medical centre. The waiting room was packed with pregnant women, some in chairs, some on the floor, who stared, silent, as I walked in. To them, I must have looked ridiculous. A lone tourist, covered in bandages, with blood pouring from his arm. What's more, when I get nervous, I either talk incessantly or grin moronically.

So there I was, standing in the dark foyer, bleeding, with a beaming smile on my silly red face while a hundred pregnant ladies eyed me up. Within a few minutes though, I was whisked off into a side room, much lighter and airier than the dank waiting room I'd been standing in before. Then I was shown a plastic-covered bed by a nurse, who left just as a guy in a brown tunic and the smell of whiskey entered.

Maybe that's the disinfectant they use, I thought, quite optimistically.

His eyes were bloodshot and he walked with a slight stagger.

Maybe he's just had a heavy underwater swimming session in a highly chlorinated pool and he forgot to wear goggles and has now got sore eyes and is physically exhausted, I thought, very optimistically.

He grabbed my arm, twisted it around his way, and the pain started. Without gloves, the man gripped the skin together and started pushing a needle through, tugging hard to tie up the loose ends. I was clearly overawed, because I should have worked out by now that he probably didn't have red eyes from all the pool chlorine. In fact, I doubt he'd even been swimming at all that day, and the smell probably wasn't disinfectant. What was most likely to be happening was that an alcoholic had staggered in and was now trying to sew my arm back together with a clothes thread.

At the moment when it all became clear, another, more presentable man walked into the room, shouting something at what I had presumed to be the male nurse, who instantly let go of the needle and stood up. After pushing the first guy out, the smartly dressed man introduced himself. "Sorry I took so long, I was with another patient. I'm the doctor."

"Right," I said. "So who was that guy?"

"He's a cleaner. Has he done anything?"

I showed the doctor my arm. "I see," he said. "No anaesthetic?"

"No."

"Good. We'll have to take these out."

He called the real nurse back in—a portly lady with a nurse's uniform on, funnily enough—and told her to prepare the anaesthetic. At least, I presumed he did, because she started to prepare the anaesthetic.

The needle went in and after a slight burning sensation, the area went numb. Only problem was, it was the wrong area. In some ways this was good, because that part of my arm also had some painful cuts, but I could feel every stitch being pulled out, then the new ones going back in; I could feel every tug to tie it off and every little poke the doctor used to hold the skin together.

When the job was done, he said, "It is contaminated now so you should take the stitches out if you get any fever."

Brilliant.

"Thanks for your help," I said, leaving some money to cover the cost of my treatment, but on my way out I was stopped by the cleaner who'd tried to sew me up earlier.

"Piss off," I said, quite diplomatically.

Clearly he didn't understand English that well, because his response was, "Donation."

"What?"

"Donation, give."

"What are you on about?"

"Donation. Rupee." He touched his hand to his mouth.

"No way, dickhead." What planet was this guy on? He's just caused me a whole load of gratuitous pain and now he's asking for money? I would have punched him right in the head if I had the strength. Knocked his pissed little body off its chubby legs.

I hobbled out of the hospital onto the main street, all the time with the alcoholic cleaner following me, asking for money. Eventually he gave up, but not before asking for cigarettes and booze too.

That afternoon, Rob reminded me why we'd been friends for so long—he helped me change my flight and arranged a minibus to take me back to Colombo, to make sure I was back home before any infection took its toll. A few days later, I was on a flight back to the UK, with the obligatory stopover in Dubai—the airport equivalent of purgatory. Then I was home, remembering that something needed to be done.

EIGHTEEN

Ramble On

"I'm so sorry, but I met someone else."

"What?"

"A few weeks ago."

"What?"

"We got on really well and…God, this is difficult. Look, I'm so sorry."

"I don't understand."

"Please don't be like this. I'm…I feel so horrible right now. I can't believe this is happening."

"I don't understand, what?"

"Please stop saying that. I feel terrible, please don't make this any worse."

"But I did too." Like I said, not the words I was planning on using, but they got the point across.

"What?"

"I did the same."

"I don't understand. *You* met another guy?"

Initially I had felt relieved. Gutted, but relieved. For the first time in weeks, I wasn't peppered with guilt. She'd done the same, hadn't she? She'd met somebody else, just like me.

Met someone else…

Wait, this wasn't quite the same. Actually, this wasn't the same at all. "Are you…Am I being replaced?"

"No, what we had could never be replaced."

Had. Past-tense.

"What do you mean? We can move on, right? We can get over this?"

"I really don't think we can, Jamie."

The realisation struck me. Even before this conversation had begun, it was over. Probably even before I met Emily, it was over. And now, here I was, wondering how I'd managed to mess up quite so royally, before I had even managed to royally mess up. She hadn't even done anything wrong. She had met someone else and decided he was better for her than me. That was it: she wasn't admitting guilt to doing anything, she was just dumping me.

I had just been dumped.

In the duration of that conversation, I went from extreme guilt, through mild relief, to disappointment, and then misery. And the worst thing about misery is that it breeds, it self-replicates; it is not just an emotion, it's an emotional virus. As the days and weeks tick by, it finds more excuses for the grasp it has on you, more reasons for you to be miserable. It also blocks out truth. It makes you think that whatever happened to you had nothing to do with your own actions. Nothing to do with your own choices.

And from that moment on, I was miserable. So miserable, I could no longer see what had been right under my nose for months. Possibly longer.

***

The weeks dragged by, like faceless customers at a shop counter. I saw a few friends, met a few girls, but like the weeks, they just dragged by. Like nights behind a bar.

The first few days had been the worst. With no money and unable to walk properly, I wallowed. There was nothing more I could do until my injuries healed and I could get a job. When that happened, I had visited Emily once, where, overcompensating for my post-breakup depression, I let my terrible sense of humour run riot. It was nice to see her again, but a few days later, I got a message saying that, hilarious as I was, it just wasn't going to work out. So I spoke to Chris and he got me his old job in a sports bar, living upstairs and working downstairs, while he went off travelling again. It was a young crowd, and entertaining. Nightly lock-ins and access to alcohol helped distract me from things for a while and I went through a string of semi-relationships with different girls. They were lovely, all of them, but I was not.

My nightly drinking and the deep-fried pub food was only tempered by the impulse to run, to exercise. Some days I'd finish a shift at half-one in the morning, put on my shorts and pound pavements for an hour or two. In those weeks and months, it was the only thing I really, truly, enjoyed.

The occasional afternoons I'd get off, I would emerge from the dank, stale smell of dried beer, the gloomy pub lighting, the noise of dance and rock going full-blast, into a world of cool, fresh air. Sometimes even bright light and sunshine. And for the next forty minutes, I wouldn't have a care in the world. All there would be was the breath in my lungs and the ground beneath my feet. Then I'd get back in, past the sickly smell of the bottle skips, and head up to my barren, rotting room that cost me around twenty quid a week. Within seconds, my world would close down, descend back into that little box, where I slept on a bare, suspiciously stained mattress and all my clothes remained in the bag I'd had when I first arrived.

The irony didn't escape me. Here I was, clever and motivated and curious, with a wealth of experience behind me, a good degree, and I was working for minimum wage in a cheap bar. Living in a shitty room, getting drunk on free booze every night and sulking my way through an empty, tedious existence. Of all the things I thought I'd end up doing after I graduated, this wasn't one of them.

Until one afternoon, perhaps not so coincidentally the day of my pay check, I realised that nothing I was doing right now would ever get me anywhere. After my sweaty shift behind the bar that night, I sat alone in the dank room, harbouring dreams of mountains, space and purity. A lifestyle, free from the distractions of girls and alcohol, where I could start to understand what I would do with my future. So, between the stark walls of that mouldy room, the idea for the trek was born.

For the next few weeks and months, I spent all my free time researching routes and options. I was searching for a place that was developed enough that I wouldn't need a guide and I could resupply en route, but was still able to get well out of the way if I wanted.

In simple terms, I was after air, open space and freedom. After doing some research, I realised that Nepal would provide all three.

So I narrowed it down.

My mountaineer experience was minimal and I wanted to go it alone. Just as in Jordan, I wanted to give myself the time to get things back into perspective. But where I had gone wrong in the desert had been the fact that other than stroll around, I'd had no real aim. This time would be different, this time I'd go with a goal. A route, a distance.

A challenge.

It would be just me, my bag, and the hills. Of course, going it alone, this meant I had to take Chris. Who, when I asked him, replied, "Yeah, all right dude."

So that was that.

***

Over the next few months, the feeling dulled, but it never really left. I left the sports bar and worked a number of different jobs, a few waiter positions, and each time I served another drink, I was one drink closer to the Himalaya. Each time I delivered another plate of food, it was one plate closer to the Khumbu. After a while, it was all I could think about; it consumed me.

So I filled my free time with extra shifts, gave up on a social life. For weeks, my routine became one of sleep and work, nothing else. Sunlight became a phenomena that existed for fifteen minutes on the morning walk in, if that. On the occasional day I had off, I would plan, jotting down to the tiniest detail the kit I would need and the route I would take. I memorised the peaks—legends in the mountaineering world. Celebrities. I learnt their names: Cho Oyu, Amphu Lapcha, Lhotse, Cholatse, Nuptse, Ama Dablam…Everest. Names that would develop into personalities the more I watched winds sweep their ice-capped horizons, but that wasn't yet. For now, they were points on a map, little triangles surrounded by orange lines to show their impossibly, unimaginably steep sides. Black squiggles to denote scree slopes with boulders the size of double-decker buses, blue ones for ice cliffs four-stories high; black dotted paths that would be our lifeline for four weeks.

Four weeks, and all I would know would be these mountains. All I would see would be their peaks and the rocky moonscape in between. I tried, I almost convinced myself that I could imagine it, what it would be like. Walking at five and a half thousand metres above sea level, waking to the sight of one of the world's most challenging climbs. Standing within arms' reach of the crowns of Earth. But I couldn't. Not from behind a bar, popping the cap on another beer. Searching metal trays for the tips that would finally allow me to discover this dream.

My head was in the clouds, but they never parted to reveal the truth about that place. I tried as hard as I could, but nothing in that closed, restricted lifestyle even hinted at the space I would explore, and I was excited.

* * *

I shut the window cover and pulled the journal out of the chair in front of me. The post-recession, pre-retirement flight attendant passed out the dinner trays and I fell back into my seat, opened my journal on the last pages, where I was ranting about the injustices of Hebron and the improvements Nablus had made, and tried to cover the last months in a few words: dark, unsatisfying.

Depraved.

And the more I wrote, the more it became obvious that travel had affected my life quite drastically. It had changed nearly everything about me; my personality, my interests, my social life, what I did with my free time. Even the relationship I'd been kicked out of—it was clear to me now that it had been doomed long before I met Emily. Long before I had even started becoming introverted. Its destiny was scratched in stone for both of us when I had first stepped off the plane in Istanbul, got a bus down to Aleppo. The first time I sat in the desert, watching the sun fade behind the rocks, I was sacrificing everything my home life stood for. My friends, who wanted to go out partying with me, who wanted me to share their fun. My girlfriend, who wanted me to spend more time with her, get to know her friends too. Even the degree I told myself I was researching for.

Papua, the Philippines, they were just the decisive blows. Even Borneo; that was what started the ball rolling initially. From then on, I may as well have been a single guy with an unhealthy compulsion and an empty wallet.

The thing about travel addiction is that, for all the world experience and knowledge it dishes out, each trip is like a drug high: fun while it lasts, but the reality will always hit when it's over. And I was running out of lives, surely. I'd stepped on stonefish, I'd fallen from a motorbike, I'd had countless bouts of food poisoning and other ailments. I'd nearly been swept down rivers, nearly stepped on a cobra, nearly had the shit stabbed out of me by some lunatics in Palestine. I'd even *nearly* shagged a pair of Canadian twins. On a roof in Malaysia. With sexy disco lighting.

The fact was, I'd been more places and had more narrow escapes than most, and I had barely reached legal drinking age in America. And now I was on my way to the place where many of the pioneering hippies left their drug-fuelled hitchhiking legacies behind. Where they finished their flowery trails to return to mundane lifestyles, fed on the memories and tales of an exciting youth. What if that was more than simple coincidence? Could it be a sign? A divine revelation perhaps? Could this be the forces of the universe coming together to tell me something momentous?

Fuck no. Only minorities believe in that sort of shit these days.

Still, as the flight attendant cleared the remains of my dinner, it was with an unusual sense of nostalgia that I put my journal down. And with the in-flight entertainment beckoning, I made a pact with myself. This trip was where I'd embrace the spirit of travelling. I wouldn't go searching for conflicts, I wouldn't go looking for danger. I wasn't going to find a tribe or a rebel group or anything like that. I was just going to go where the mood took me. Go wherever I felt like and appreciate it for what it was. See what I'd see, soak it up, then move on.

Right now I wanted to see the mountains. I wanted to see them all, and Chris was going to join me. But after that? I had no idea.

Wherever my mood took me.

NINETEEN

Splurge!

"Hashish?"

"No thanks buddy."

"Hey man, dope?"

"No mate."

"Hello friend, trekking? You need a guide?"

"No."

"Want smoke?"

"Piss off."

The air was cool enough for me to be wearing a thin fleece, but the locals were wearing thick down-fill jackets; North Face, Mountain Hardware, Lowe Alpine. Or in the case of some, North Fake, Mountain Software, Lower Alpine.

"Hey, hey man…Nepali girls?"

Even the ones offering me hash.

"Sexy Nepal chicks? Hey, man. You want sexy time? Sexy sex sex?"

"No man, try him." I pointed across the road to a guy with dreadlocks and flappy clown trousers, which I assumed meant that he would show more interest in that kind of thing than me, purely out of necessity. "He hasn't got any other option," I said.

The tout shook his head. "Watch."

A beautiful girl in similarly fluttery clothing strolled out of a clothes shop and kissed the man. Confused, I carried on walking.

The street was lined with mountaineering shops, crammed to overflow with knockoff trekking equipment and boots that would explode into dust after exactly three miles. A few arts shops selling knives and a whole load of local knickknacks and Nepalese handicrafts that were probably handmade by machines in China. More signs hanging overhead than anybody could read in a lifetime, advertising bungee jumps, tour agencies, restaurants. High rise guesthouses with rooftop gardens, caught in the stranglehold of a spiderweb of power cables and wires.

And touts. Hundreds of bloody touts.

"Hey, how are you?"

"Yeah, fine." Another one and I was barely three metres from the last. These guys were nearly as persistent as the prostitutes in Manila.

"Which country are you from?"

"England," I responded. No need to be mean just yet.

"Capital is London," he said.

"Yes, it is." I kept on walking, past the cycle rickshaws, the taxis. Bookshops, restaurants, more arts and crafts stalls.

"I can name the capital of any country in the world."

"Good times."

"Aks me." He was a little guy, young-looking. Maybe fifteen at most. "Aks me three."

"Um, okay." At least he was keeping me from the pimps and dealers for the time being; this wasn't too bad. I remembered the boy in Manila who I'd made best friends with after I picked him up, how he'd repelled all kinds of unwanted offers. What did this guy want anyway? A sweetie? Some milk? *Sometimes it's good to have allies,* I thought. So I decided I'd humour him.

"What's the catch?" I asked.

"If I get them right, you buy me milk."

Ah.

Well, it's an interesting proposition. Might as well try him on it. "Okay then, what is the capital of Pakistan?"

"Islamabad," he replied.

One out of three. Not bad. Time to try something further afield.

"Australia?"

"Canberra."

Shit. Two out of three. Time to see how good this kid really was. "How about Eritrea?"

"What?"

"Eritrea?"

"It's not country," he protested.

"Yes it is, it's next to Ethiopia and Somalia."

"It's not count."

"It does. What is the capital?" I asked, my competitive side rearing its ugly face.

"I don't know." He looked lost, dazed, confused by the intellectual onslaught.

I shrugged. "No milk for you then. Sorry."

"Please, I am a student," he tapped my arm. "I need food."

"What are you studying?" I asked.

"I study at a monastery," he replied, largely ignoring my question.

"Don't they feed you at the monastery?"

"I need milk." My arm was tugged again. "Please."

"Well you should have found out what the capital of Eritrea was then shouldn't you?" I replied, smugly. "How about a biscuit instead? A sort of consolation prize?"

"Give me milk!" he shouted, which largely settled my mind to the contrary. If it was up to me, I'd have chosen biscuits over milk any day. What kind of lunatic would turn down a biscuit? It didn't make any sense.

I carried on walking. Past the arts and crafts stalls, restaurants, bookshops.

"Sexy Nepal chicks? Sexy sex?"

Oh, for God's sake. "Don't you recognise me?" I asked.

The tout paused, thinking. Then he smiled, "Ah, you make *boom-boom* last night?"

"No, mate. I literally walked past you three minutes ago."

"Oh. I remember." Another pause. "Hashish?"

There was nothing for it, I had to get off the street.

A small alleyway to my right promised the sublime beats and moody surroundings of a global institution: the reggae bar. I took it, walking up a single stairway to a terraced open-air haven of wicker chairs and small circles of Westerners chatting over large bottles of Everest Beer. The terrace was lit by candle flames perched on mountains of solidified wax dribble. By the bar was what looked like a magician, with a huge clot of dreadlocked hair wrapped in a grey beanie the size of a spaceship, and on each of the green, cream and burgundy walls, around the Bob Marley posters, were a million messages, scrawled in marker pen by hordes of travellers over the years.

The crude, wise, mundane musings of an eclectic gathering.

Dreams are what I am made of; reality is what I am.

Peace Corps was here.

Here was the perfect refuge from the street touts and the camera-pointing gore-tex brigade. Bamboos decorating the walls, good music and enough wisdom to never need a drinking partner.

Pronoia: the sneaking suspicion that everybody is out to help you.

I sat down by an empty table on the terrace and looked around.

The sky was dark now, still faintly blue, but the mountains and smog had long since crowded the sun out, leaving the winding streets of Thamel lit by headlights and the occasional lamppost. Honking and bicycle bells carried over the sound of mellow dub-reggae on the stereo, but the mood up here was different. Around me, the few remaining unlit candles were being sparked up and the night's conversation was just starting.

"Hey man, what do you want?" The waiter had the build, hairstyle and tattoos that would have made him look at home on the streets of Los Angeles.

"Um, Tuborg please. A big one."

"Sure."

Chris would be arriving at some point today, so I sent a message to his phone, telling him where I was staying and where to go if he got here in time for a beer.

If at first the idea is not absurd, there is no hope for it.

Can you fart with confidence? (Then you haven't been in Nepal long enough).

My beer arrived and I took a few sips.

This wasn't Kathmandu, I knew; it was Thamel. Just like Khao San isn't Bangkok. Jalan Jaksa isn't Jakarta. Chinatown is nothing like the rest of KL. But just like all of those places, Thamel was a convenient meeting point. A base for nights out when the rest of the city would be closed down. Beer or weed; live music or soundsystems; prostitutes or supermarkets: choose your sin.

Housing trekkers, backpackers, package-tourists and hippies, the conveniences on offer were quite astounding. Especially for Nepal—a forbidden kingdom that only opened its doors to outsiders in the 1950s.

I wish you bluebirds in the Spring,
To give your heart a song to sing;

And then a kiss, but more than this I wish you love.

So this must all be a result of the money that came with having the world's most impressive mountain range in your country. Yet this concentrated patch of swanky, Western-priced shops and eateries was clearly not destined for the same backpacker market as the fried noodle stools of Chinatown or Jalan Jaksa. This could only be aimed at the upmarket holiday trekker. And still the young, bedraggled, scruffy traveller was ubiquitous. The stingy backpacker who normally sought out only the cheapest restaurants and places to stay, the best drinks offers, the funkiest bars and the most potent weed. Only, they now had enough money to fill the chairs of a high-end pizza restaurant too, after spending a few hours browsing the web alongside mountaineers and package tourists in an expensive internet café.

I had to admit, I didn't understand Kathmandu at first. Earlier on that day, I was walking around the area of a historic Durbar Square, just a few hundred metres south of Thamel, and I'd eaten a small meal on a panoramic rooftop café nearby. Just south of me was Jochhen Tole, known in tourist-speak as Freak Street—a living museum to the heyday of hippie culture, popular back when soaking up the local atmosphere in a place was as important as seeing its sights. It was an older, more traditional backpacker hangout, now as much of a dot on the Kathmandu sightseeing round-robin as Durbar Square itself, but the tide had long since swept away from that kind of travel.

Happiness is a journey, not a destination.

Marc and Ewan, Everest Base Camp. June 2009.

As I waited for my meal, I pondered the notion that the fun-loving, free-roaming days of backpacking had been overshadowed by the guidebook-hopping adventurers of my very own generation, the insatiable generation, who in true Western spirit wanted to cram it all in with as little discomfort, time or effort as possible. I'd heard the idea being floated by many old hands at that stage, and the rampant commercialism of Thamel fitted the story all too well.

If those golden oldies were to be believed, travel nowadays was more a case of joining the dots between points of interest, having a few days to catch up on the all-essential comforts of home that didn't exist elsewhere, then head back into the fray. In Thamel, it seemed, that was exactly what everybody was there for—home comforts. Kathmandu: the Himalayan cauldron of Hindu and Buddhist culture; the valley-city whose intricately designed, hand carved temples of wood and tile and gold plate served exotic Gods and fascinating traditions; whose winding streets, bustling chowks and icy rivers were nestled in amongst the most impressive mountains in the world; now it was just a place to get one last fix before moving on.

I had your mum.

Who is Frank J. Stevens?

And there I was, staring at the attractions, waiting to hit the mountains myself. Seemingly indifferent towards the true culture of the Nepali capital.

Then another idea occurred to me: perhaps this change wasn't just to do with the way people travelled nowadays. Perhaps it had happened because Kathmandu wasn't *that* pleasant anymore.

From my rooftop café I had been lucky enough to glimpse the clouds swirling around the distant mountains of the Langtang for a few brief atmospheric moments, but the polluted haze that belched and spewed out of the mob of trucks, cars, motorbikes and power plants in the Kathmandu Valley soon pulled the grey back in.

And it wasn't just the fact that you couldn't see mountains. The main streets of the city were dusty exhaust-traps, the rivers black with filth and toxicity; everywhere, dogs and children were picking at the litter that flowed lava-like through the waterways. Only in the narrow, cramped side roads did you discover the traditional city—through ornate wooden doors, metal workers hammering away at glowing embers; in the squares, kids playing games and chasing each other. Butchers chopping at goats, skinning them, hanging the carcasses out for sale. Trade, commerce, industry, in the most old-fashioned sense. Stop for a second to watch though and you'd be run down by a shiny new imported Indian scooter with two or three people riding pillion. Take another turn and you're back on the main street, along with the Tata trucks and windowless buses, white taxis and cycle rickshaws. All around, smog and pollution and exhaust and honking.

And in Thamel, touts, taxis and pimps.

That intoxicating blend of old and new that travel magazines always bang on about, the lovely clichéd story that's worded like a conspiracy to get history-starved Americans to travel more—the fascinating mix of ancient versus modern, the shitty and dull and crumbling juxtaposed with the shiny and concrete and bright—that blend truly is Kathmandu. But it's not a good thing. Not here.

I liked the city. Probably in the same way some people liked terrible films or Cliff Richard; there was something in the utter awfulness that I found endearing, unique. But when the crisp air of the Himalaya was what you're after, it was no wonder the city had become little more than a staging post on the route to amazement. A place to splurge, to binge, then get on with whatever you set out to do initially.

So this explained the backpackers sitting in the restaurants, eating their ten-dollar meals. For them, on their tight long-term budgets, this was a *splurge*. An exception. And now here I was, sitting with my beer and my newly opened mind, totally happy to be going with the flow. So in an effort to embrace the spirit of the new Kathmandu, I decided to splurge. And then I splurged again. Soon enough, I was so splurged that I started to find all the people on the neighbouring tables very interesting and so I began splurging with them too. The bar was filling up by the minute; the other two wicker chairs on my table were taken by a friendly Australian girl and her volunteer buddy from Essex.

I stayed up all night wondering about the sun…then in the morning it dawned on me.

Together, we splurged until a whole lot of beer and cheap mixers swirled in the pits of our stomachs. Over the road, a live band started up, wailing along to loose variations of Jimi Hendrix, AC/DC, The Eagles, and we chatted and laughed as more people joined the growing crowd, pulling tables together for more space. A trekker from Germany, a pair of girls from Holland. More volunteers and finally, a group of Danish people.

Sex is like bridge: if you don't have a good partner, you'd better have a good hand.

Splurge followed splurge followed bar followed club; beers, cocktails, mixers, good bands, terrible bands. Great songs; Oasis, Starsailor, The Verve, Turin Brakes…some played well, others ripped apart like a beautiful maiden trapped in a pit of werewolves, and the Danish group's two girls, Sofie and Kira, one of whom kept glancing in my direction every now and then, and with laughter and chatting, drinking and singing, slowly, the night descended into the smoggy haze of Nepal's polluting capital.

* * *

I was woken the next morning by a loud bang.

Thinking quickly, I grabbed the blanket and threw it over the bed, but the door was wrenched open from the outside and I was left, stark naked, standing by the entrance.

"Dude, you stink!"

"Thanks buddy!" The first thing I noticed was that Chris had a beard. A shit one. It looked like someone covered his chin in glue and threw a handful of pubic hair at it. The sporadic patches of fur made me laugh until my head was smashed apart by the Hangover Hammer of Thor. "What happened to you?" I asked, pointing at the facial fuzz.

"I went to Cuba," Chris replied.

"Fair enough," I said, giving him a handshake and a firm pat on the back, just to show that although I was naked, the gesture was still manly. The bed started to move and a confused face popped out. "Oh, this is…um, Sofie, isn't it? Sofie, Chris. Chris, Sofie."

"Hi," said Chris, "very pleased to meet you."

"Hey," replied Sofie in a croaky voice, sitting up with the blanket held around her chest.

"Well, looks like I'd better leave you guys to it. Typical," he muttered, "I've only just got into Kathmandu and I already feel like a spare part."

"Don't you mean a tool?"

"Whatever. Call me later dude. We have some mountains to discuss."

After a wink and a wave, Chris closed the door behind him.

"Who was that?" Sofie asked, letting the blanket slide back down.

"It doesn't matter my little pastry, we have much more important things to think about," I replied.

In fairness, I *was* going to the mountains for a month.

***

"We fly in here, walk up here, go across here, over that bit, then walk up to this point, which is-"

"EBC."

"Exactly."

"But we don't stay there long?"

"No, we just go past it to get to the other valley."

"Right. Where we find Cho Oyu, then?"

"We go past Cho Oyu, climb that bit and walk down there, do the next pass, then we're back in Namche. From there it's a few hours back into Lukla and away."

Chris scratched his head. "So how long is that going to take?"

"Well, including all the side trips and day climbs…around twenty-eight days."

"Okay." He paused for a moment. "So we've got a flight, food."

"Tent, sleeping bag, cooking stuff?"

"Yeah, I brought all that."

"Coat? It's going to get cold."

"Yeah, sort of. I've got a jumper. It's a big woolly one though, *and* it has a reindeer on the front."

"Guess that'll have to do."

"I've also got a blow-up duck called Judy."

"Right." Leaning forward, I picked up the map and folded it into my pocket. Thanks to the daily power cuts, we were reading it by candlelight and couldn't see much of the detail anyway. "Sorted."

Seven blasts from a car horn interrupted the conversation for a moment, followed by some shouting.

"It will be good to get out of here," said Chris. "This place is a dump."

"Thamel?"

"Yeah. It's got all the character of the Wetherspoons in Eastleigh."

I leant back. "Yup."

Just below my balcony, I could see the street kids harassing tourists for food, bumping into them and tapping their arms. A few were following foreigners around, presumably asking for milk. "You know why they do that?" Chris asked after a few seconds of silence.

"Because they're hungry?"

"No dude. They get you to buy it at a high price and when you leave, they sell it back to the shop."

"Really?"

"Yeah, I read it somewhere. Or someone told me, I can't remember." Chris leant forward on his chair, peered over the metal railings towards the street. "Then they give the money to gangs who pay them in glue."

"What, for fixing things?"

Chris ignored me. "Go up that road and you'll see where they all sleep." He pointed west, towards the diplomatic quarter. "The soup kitchens keep them alive, so the money just feeds the gangs. You could probably use that as a great little case study to prove how money corrupts a place if you wanted?"

"Yeah, thanks mate."

"I was taking the piss."

"Oh."

I'd been along there a few times and pleasant enough as it was during the day, after dark the street corners repopulated with overweight prostitutes and glue-sniffing street kids, holding one of their grubby hands out for change while the other clutched onto a plastic bag of some sort, filled with solvent. Proof, in some shape, of the more desperate side of Nepal.

"Some guy asked me for milk yesterday," I said, watching the cyclic scene play out below. "Think it was some kind of con."

Chris looked up for a moment, his rubbish beard glowing as the power came back on. "It's probably the same scam. Buy the milk and sell it again. Did he ask you about capital cities?"

"Yeah."

He stroked his furry face, wisely. "Apparently the guys who do that are run by gangs too, it's all a way to get money from tourists. Name the capital, get rupees. Simple."

It made sense in some warped, tourist-conning way. But I couldn't imagine it was very successful, unless the tourist happened to be fairly naïve. "This kid was pretty good," I said. "He knew Canberra was the capital of Australia. Nobody knows that, not even Australians." I peeked over the ledge, down towards a group of wretched-looking street urchins who were scrapping over something, pushing each other around, trying to get this thing. A bottle of coke, it looked like. "He also turned down the offer of free biscuits."

"Really?"

"Yeah! The one thing all people across the world can appreciate and he didn't want any!"

"What a nutter. Did he get the questions all right?"

"Did he bollocks," I laughed. "Caught him out on Eritrea."

"What's that?"

"It's a country on the Horn of Africa. It used to be part of Ethiopia until it broke away in a protracted civil war that left over two hundred thousand dead, ending with a referendum in 1993 in which the Eritrean people voted almost unanimously in favour of independence."

"Oh I see," Chris nodded. "So what *is* the capital?"

"Fuck knows."

We sat for a while, listening to the car horns belting down the street and some white guy with a shaved head singing Hare Krishna and banging his drum, until Chris spoke again. "It's the hippies too. Got caught chatting to two earlier. They wouldn't shut up about *learning how to breath, man*," Chris said, in his best hippy voice. "What a massive pair of tits. Speaking of which, I bumped into that Danish of yours too."

"Oh right, where?"

"In the bakery, funnily enough. Asked if we were around tonight."

"Sweet." I blew out the candle and stood up. "Could do with a Danish. Shall we?"

"We're in Thamel. What else is there to do?"

Only losers find themselves.

TWENTY

Dances with Yetis

I stopped for a moment to catch my breath.

Ahead, a scrub path led up the side of a hill, up to where it crested between a few large boulders and continued out of sight. Behind and below, the semicircle of blue and green roofs had edged further away, the sun reflecting brilliant white on the peaks above them. My lungs were already straining to suck in enough oxygen and my head was starting to pound, but I couldn't quite tell if it was through dehydration or altitude. Still, this would be my first glimpse of the mountains we were to spend the next month living amongst, and I was not ready to turn back.

The air was cool, clear, free from pollution and traffic noise. Just eagles, snow, rock; and sunlight—hard, fierce sunlight.

To think that two nights ago I had been in Thamel, dancing in a thumping club that reeked of cigarettes and feet, dodging pimps and kids, druggies and late-night fights to have a few more hours with Sofie. That evening, I had immersed myself in exactly the things I was in Nepal to escape—alcohol, ungratifying hedonism—perhaps to remember what it was that I was leaving behind. It had been enjoyable at the time, partly as I'm of the era who believe that white men *can* dance (just look at Michael Jackson) and partly because of the ample opportunity for hilarious Danish-based bakery jokes with Chris. But it wasn't intentional; I didn't feel like I'd earned it.

I remembered the flight out the next morning. I'd left Sofie, just as Chris had left Kira, Sofie's friend, and it was early—early enough to see the orange glow of sunrise glinting against the morning dew that had collected on the fuselage of our small twin-engine Dornier 228 as we boarded, bleary-eyed, feeling weak from the night before, and took our seats either side of the narrow aisle. The propellors had spluttered into life, pushing the aircraft past a few ruined military helicopters, before building in pitch to a constant drone and lifting us into the air.

After we left the smog of Kathmandu, a corrugated landscape of rice paddies, hill villages, gushing rivers and forests thick with pine floated beneath us, undulating dramatically until we reached the high foothills of the southern Solokhumbu. Out of the window, I could see the land rising, building up, and within minutes we were drawing parallel with peaks that towered far abovc us. Eventually, the ground rose to meet the aircraft at Lukla and we were out, walking through the mass of porters and would-be guides that waited for flights of trekkers to arrive that day. We had marched past the Irish bar, the trekking shops, the commerce of Lukla and headed straight for the trail, following a roaring torrent of milky-grey water through the chilly villages and pine forests of the Dudh Khoshi River Valley. Past long metal-wire bridges, over diamond-clear streams and around Buddhist monuments. Several times, we walked alongside dusty trails of yak, who snorted and hoofed their way up the rocky paths with surprising agility under the weighty loads of mountaineering gear and fuel, the gentle *dong* sound of cowbells following them.

Over the Bridge of Eternal Peril, up a hill and we were in Namche Bazaar. At first glance a quintessential Nepali mountain village, tucked into a sheltered cove in the hillside, Namche had evolved into a teahouse trekker's paradise. Like everywhere on the tourist trail in Nepal, it seemed, the locals had managed to make the impossible possible, building coffee houses that sold Starbucks and pizza, bars full of Carlsberg and Everest lager, places stocked to overflow with trekking gear and crampons and a library of international books. The real miracle was that with no roads from Lukla, nearly everything had been carried in on foot. By and large, that was the task of a steady stream of porters, who had transformed the place into one last chance to pick up goods—trekking poles, fluffy hats, snickers. A high-altitude, friendly version of Thamel, where trekkers could acclimatise to the thinning air in a comfortable setting.

Our route in had been obscured by hanging mists that dropped sleet sporadically on us and the yak train we were following. Sleet turned into a light dusting of snow by the time we reached Namche, and we collapsed through the doors of a cosy, almost Bavarian-style lodge with one loud simultaneous thump. We went to bed early that night, before it got dark.

One day's sleep later and the sky had cleared enough to catch a view of the route we would be taking for the next few weeks. So I kept plodding with the sun beating down and the thin air tearing holes in my lungs.

After the crest, the dusty track opened up, leading through bushes, over grass, up to the top of one final hill and there it was: the Khumbu Valley. The names I had memorised months before—Cholatse, Taboche, the pointed peak of Ama Dablam; dwarfs at under 7,000 metres. In the far distance, over the gullies and ridges of the lower Khumbu, the white curtain of rock and ice that is Lhotse, Nuptse and Nuptse Shar—the knife-edge ridge that shields the southern side of the highest mountain in the world—standing tall above the path we would be walking in a few days' time, with a slither of Everest visible behind.

Before me, the Gods of the mountaineering universe: mounds of rock and ice that made anything I had seen before look like ripples in comparison. A landscape that would probably make Bear Grylls want to slide around, squeeze water out of yeti shit and do all manner of other elaborate attention-seeking things, and it was all mine. True solitude at last.

I looked over my shoulder to see a Korean tour group, completely covered in gore-tex—hoods up, face masks on, snapping away frantically, taking pictures of everything and anything that wasn't the mountains, like the sign to the nearest teahouse or a rock or a clump of grass. Intrigued, I watched for a while, as these high-altitude spooks angled themselves for the perfect shot of a tiny piece of yak dung, totally oblivious to the magnificent surroundings. Then one of the group pointed in the direction of Ama Dablam and suddenly the shutters of a hundred DSLRs were bouncing up and down, trying to capture every little detail of the mountain. After that, the same with Nuptse, Cholatse, Everest. Captured and stored in megabytes for later consumption. The digitisation of the Khumbu.

Soon enough though, on they went to the next viewpoint, leaving me in peace. I stayed for a while to appreciate the scenery, but the mist was closing in and once it had all but disappeared behind cute fluffy clouds, I hopped and jumped down the hill, leaping in a few short bounds the distance it had taken forty minutes to walk up, and I was in a good mood.

A bit of trekking, a bit of eating, a lot of sleeping—all in scenery like *that*. This month couldn't fail but be glorious.

***

"Dude, I think we're lost." Chris had taken his rucksack off with an awkward lurch and was now standing, holding the map, with a humungous stain stretched dark brown across the back of his T-shirt. Around its edges, concentric white circles of sweat had formed, like the rings of a tree but instead of years, each stain represented a day's walking.

"Bollocks mate, the path leads up there." I pointed to where the gully narrowed into a V-shaped channel between the high scree wall on the left and the steep side of a hill on the right. There was little evidence of a path, but there rarely was when you got away from the main trails now anyway. What we had followed—a sandy track up a sharply inclined slope—had opened up to a child's fantasy sandpit of about sixty metres in width and over a hundred in length. The amount of yak poo hinted that the lack of grass was not a natural feature and that we had mistaken the correct route for a herder's grazing spot. But if walking downhill meant having to walk back uphill unnecessarily, it was to be avoided at almost any cost.

"You'll see, up that little rivet there, see how it leads up the side of the scree? We'll be across in no time."

"Er-"

"It doesn't look *that* big," I said, peeking over his shoulder. "See how thin it is there?" I pointed at the grey tongue on the creased map. "Even if this isn't the crossing point, we'll probably be able to find a route."

We were sheltered; fortunate, because the sun was shining with such force, it was easy to forget how cold the air really was when you weren't being blasted by it.

"Okay dude," Chris said as he threw his rucksack back on, momentarily struggling with the weight of so much food and equipment. We were still climbing, as we had been for days now, and the altitude gain made it necessary to take a few deep breaths after the effort of hoisting straps back on. Sometimes, I would lie down where I left my bag, put the straps on first, then crawl over onto my front and stand from there, but the more we marched on, the lighter our bags became and the stronger and fitter we got.

"Are you sure about this? It flows down from Nuptse; that's a big mountain."

"Yeah it is. There's only one way to find out though."

We clambered up the rocks that filled the channel, up towards where the hillside met the scree wall. When we got there, I stopped and looked about for stacks of pebbles that acted as markers. They were placed along prominent points on most paths in the Khumbu and, sometimes, were the only way to find out if you were going the right way. Spotting them could be a relief of epic proportions, as we would later discover, but there were none that I could see. The bottom of the gully had levelled out and on either side it was a steep climb. Nothing hinting at footsteps, not even dirt left behind on rocks from the occasional paths of Sherpas and their yak herds.

"See anything?" Chris looked up at me as an incredible creaking sound—like a monster waking from a deep sleep—reverberated through the hills and reached a crescendo of crashing and crumbling, before settling down to nothing.

"Fuck, that was a big one."

Behind us, framed in the V, Ama Dablam rose high across the far side of the valley. To its left, although we couldn't see it from where we were, an incredible snow pass bridged the gap between the great Ama Dablam pinnacle and Amphu Lapcha peak, curving around until it met the towering white wall of Lhostse and Nuptse, where it fell away, creating what looked like a gigantic china bowl with a wedge missing. That wedge was where we had entered a few days ago and in the centre lay Island Peak, sitting like a truffle coated in icing sugar—tiny, dwarfed by the magnificently jagged walls of ice surrounding it, despite being higher than any mountain in Europe.

After leaving Namche just under a week earlier, we had spent a few days exploring the area, climbing the glaciers and scree mounds to look out over tremendous frozen lakes, sandy basins and some of the most unbelievable scenery I had seen in my life.

In places, it just looked plain unrealistic. Ice—pure, brilliant and white—rising vertically from sand and rubble to pinnacles kilometres above. Mountains, caught by the light in such a way that they looked like they had been covered in aluminium foil by a devious yeti. Tucked here and there along the paths were small memorials to climbers who had died trying to reach those pinnacles—brave men, whose foolishness was made entirely justifiable by the possibility of such an achievement.

More rumbling, quieter this time, but closer. "I can't see anything in here," I said. "Let me just take a look up this scree, see if I can find the path from there."

Chris, whose bag was heavier than mine largely thanks to his choice of wooly jumpers and inflatable rubber ducks over technical down jackets, was resting with his hands on his knees, trying to relieve the ever-present ache where shoulder straps hung against neck muscles.

"Okay," he panted.

For the sake of not wasting Chris's energy unnecessarily, I scaled the scree alone. It continued much further than I expected, a rising mound of smashed rock and gravel that crumbled as I pushed my hands and boots into it. After a few breathless minutes, I crawled my way up to the crest and looked over. Butterflies instantly started raging in my stomach as a rock I had just displaced fell down the far side, bouncing and shattering with each impact, before exploding well below me.

"Christopher," I shouted, "think we might have to turn back." A small landslide confirmed my advice as it flowed down the slope, bringing football-sized rocks tumbling along with it. They had splintered into deadly fragments by the time they reached the maze of jutting ice and moraine that was the Nuptse Glacier.

I stared at it with a face of mild surprise mixed with total discontent; icy ponds that would crack with our weight and drop us into hypothermia, wedged between huge boulders and blocks of frozen scree the size of houses. Like the map had shown, it was only a few hundred metres wide, but what the map didn't illustrate was quite what a few hundred metres that would be.

"No way dude!" Chris yelled up at me. "I'm not going back down."

I was reluctant too; we had already made some tough progress to get this far. The thought of having to do it all again just to reach the same spot was fairly unpalatable.

But this, surely, was *suicide*.

I tried to look for a possible trail, even a route from the rubble ledge that lined the glacier, that wasn't just plain silly. From the scree wall, *if* we made it down without anything falling on our heads, we would still need a relatively clear path to get us and our packs through without ending up in an ice bath or trapped under a boulder. Not to mention the danger of unseen crevasses.

Then I saw it: there was a spot where the scree ledge widened, the slope down was not so steep and though we'd have to traverse some fairly hectic terrain, it didn't look impassable. "Chris!" I yelled, not taking my eyes from the route for one moment. "I think I've seen a crossing point!"

"Where?" he replied, standing right next to me.

"Oh, sorry, I thought you were down there still."

"No dude, you've been standing up here for half an hour."

"Oh…well, what do you think?"

"Bit dicey, but we could."

I considered it for a minute. For what was essentially lazy unwillingness to walk back down to where we had started, we were preparing to cross the Nuptse Glacier without knowing a safe route, without crampons, ropes, any of that stuff; should an accident happen, we would have a drama on our hands. In honesty, it was pure, mindless, stupidity. Any fool could tell that this was a terrible idea.

"Okay, let's do it."

We made our way along the scree ridge, clambering over the boulders and rubble until we found the right spot. Setting a compass bearing for the most friendly looking area on the far side, we sat and pushed our way down, going fairly slowly but still creating a miniature landslide.

Then we were standing on Nuptse glacier.

We looked up to a sound like a building being demolished and watched as a large chunk of the scree wall on the far side of the glacier crumbled and disappeared into a cloud of dust. With the constant groaning of the ice, the rock falls and the occasional landslip, it soon became clear that the whole thing was alive, slithering like a tectonic snake towards the deep valley we had just climbed up from. I'd heard stories of these glaciers, of climbers who had been missing for decades emerging at the bottom of the frozen masses of ice, fully preserved. I had to admit, thinking of those stories didn't help my mental state much.

We edged our way slowly across the rocks, stepping carefully to make sure our footing was stable. The larger the rock, the more likely it was to be a secure foothold, but the greater the danger if it wasn't. Slowly, we contoured through the glacier.

We had made it halfway when I fell.

It was an innocent enough looking rock—roughly the size and shape of a settee cushion—but when I put my boot on it, it rolled. My ankle twisted and I lurched over, landing on my back with a thud. Luckily, the impact was broken by my rucksack, but the much bigger boulder I'd fallen against started to move too, opening a dark chasm beneath me, a chasm I could not see the bottom of. As quickly as I could, I leapt off it, grabbing Chris by the arm as it clunked heavily back into place.

"Shit!" I shouted, hobbling my way up Chris's more secure perch. "Didn't think a boulder like that would go anywhere!"

"Nah, me neither dude."

I was grinning, but behind the shiny white teeth, I was scared shitless. The boulder was as large as my kitchen at home.

We clambered on, over the stones, past the rocks, as far from the frozen ponds as we could, wobbling, listening to the creaking of the very landscape we were standing on. The sense of trepidation only eased when we had reached the far crest, breathless, grinning, amazed that we had managed it.

* * *

The boulder field that covered the ice of the Nuptse glacier took nearly two hours to cross, even though it was less than a kilometre wide. At some points, the rocks seemed to fill deep crevasses; when the stones we dislodged fell between the larger boulders, they would take a while to hit anything. We couldn't see how far they went down, but for our peace of mind we didn't want to either. Still, save for the odd fall, we were somehow unscathed and the sense of elation at our success was only matched by the disappointment of having to skirt around another scree-covered slope before we met any real paths again.

Eventually we dropped down into the valley leading towards the Kongma La—the mountain pass that was our next objective.

Timings had slipped; the afternoon clouds had already started to form around the higher peaks and were slowly tumbling down to our level. We walked up to the next hill, but the swirling mists cloaked our route now. Without the sun, the temperature would quickly fall well below freezing.

For a while we searched for an area of flat land, traipsing around a crusted moonscape of dark icy fog, with the visibility dropping to around fifteen metres. Then, in gusting winds, we erected our tents and stretched the guy ropes far from the groundsheets for stability.

Getting inside was something wonderful; escaping the fierce weather to crawl into a warm sleeping bag and light the stove in the shelter of the small tent porch. In many respects it was my favourite part of the day. Funny, how the minor comfort of being warm and dry can seem like such a big thing given the right context.

After a meal of freeze-dried lasagne and a quick snooze, I opened the flap of my tent a few inches and a smile settled on my rosy, now slightly bearded face. The mists had parted to reveal the beautifully triangular north face of Ama Dablam, bathed in glorious sunlight across the far side of the valley. The snowy afro on the pinnacle was dazzling—pure white, with a deep blue glow in the shadows. "If that mountain was a woman," I shouted in the direction of Chris's tent, "I would take her out for a nice seafood din-"

"Hang on!" The sound of a tent door unzipping and the scruffy image of Chris's face, with its even more hideous beard. "What?"

The moment was lost.

"Nothing."

Chris shot me a confused look, then the mountain caught his eye. "Oh bloody hell! That has to be the sexiest thing I've ever seen."

It was true—Ama was by far the most picturesque mountain in the whole area. So picturesque, in fact, that we had started using her first name.

The wind had calmed down now and the sun shone sporadic beams through what was left of the thinning cloud. I pulled my thick down jacket on and sat in the entrance of my tent, trying to make eyes across the valley at Ms. Dablam, the saucy minx that she was. After a few minutes the cloud dispersed entirely, floating down into the valley that lead back across to Namche, no doubt bathing the poor occupants of that village in the icy gloom of a Himalayan afternoon.

It was one thing that always came to amaze me about the Himalaya: no matter how horrendous, how dark, how violent the cloud seemed when you were inside it, as soon as it passed you'd be in blazing sunlight again, looking back on a large, happy bundle of cotton wool that seemed to have been stolen from the land of the Teletubbies.

Of course, the same was also true in reverse—see the innocent white fluff creeping up the valley or down the hillside towards you and have fear, because at this altitude any warmth you may be feeling is just a malicious deception created by the sun. Block out that warmth and suddenly the iciness in your bloodstream returns and life becomes a lot less enjoyable.

It was this fact that stopped our attempt at the pass that day; while there was plenty of light left, the weather systems in spring often brought clouds down from the highest peaks as early as midday, and they could take as little as a few minutes to form. To be caught out by these weather systems not only meant poor visibility—which on the dicy routes up to some of the passes could be dangerous in itself—but also the risk of frostbite or hypothermia if adequate precautions were not taken.

I stood up, walked down to the icy lake we had now found ourselves camping next to, and started pumping water through the filter into our plastic bottles. To occupy my mind while I pushed little squirts of purified liquid into the cold containers, I thought again of the life I'd been leading for the last few months, and how I'd given it up and come to Kathmandu, revelled once again in the substance abuse that made my head spin, my body wretch and crawl, my brain throb. Only in Kathmandu, it was fun because it was special. I knew I was in Nepal on a mission to break that cycle; I'd had all the experience to know how pathetic I was being, and how I didn't want it. But the opportunity was going to end soon and something about that made me rediscover how much fun it could be.

Binge—just in moderation.

Now all that was over and I was here, in the Himalaya.

I was *here*.

Here, where the days were challenging, progressive enough to keep me interested. Where I was continuously doing enough not to fill them with regrets and pitiful distractions. Just like the Philippines and Jordan, living the simple existence once more. And unlike Jordan I was happy, because as much as I tried to fill my head up with reasons to be miserable, I couldn't possibly be. I had company. Today had been demanding, exhilarating, rewarding—all the things I wanted this trip to be about. Tomorrow would be the same. I just had to accept that I was a postmodern romantic, who, instead of self-mutilating and painting rubbish pictures to get over lost loves, got drunk a lot and went travelling. And in the beautiful, slender glamour of Ama Dablam, I had found my perfect rebound.

"Someday I'll climb that mountain," I told Chris as I walked back up the slope towards our tents, the plastic of the water bottles creaking in my arms. "Someday…" I gazed into the distance for a while, to illustrate the sincerity of my ambition.

"Yeah dude, you can do it with me."

"I don't think I'm quite ready for that yet."

"Climb the mountain."

"Oh, right. Okay."

* * *

I awoke as the first piece of ice splattered against my cheek. The sun was on the tent already and time was running out. As gently as possible, I pulled my sleeping bag down, my trousers up and my down jacket over my shoulders, then unzipped the tent. More chunks dropped onto the sleeping bag as I did so, and I crawled out of the trap slowly, slipping my cold boots on in the process.

Pleased with the delicacy with which I had extracted myself this time, I failed to notice a guy rope had caught on my laces and as I stepped away, it released itself with a twang and a sheet of ice fell from the inner roof of the tent onto the floor.

It was an irritating ritual I had to follow at dawn every day; from the first drips, I normally had about fifteen minutes to get myself out before all the frozen condensation from the night fell on me. Much as I needed a wash, the tent's tendency to give me a freezing shower each morning was unnecessary, in my eyes. Still, it got me up early and in the glorious morning light, I laid my ice-encrusted sleeping bag out and aired my clothes while I waited for the water in our bottles to melt and for Chris to stop snorting and get his fat arse out of bed.

After the torments of the Nuptse Glacier, the Kongma La was surprisingly friendly; certainly the most demanding of all the passes we crossed in the area, physically speaking, but we were boosted by the comparatively easy crossing of the Khumbu Glacier and the gentle trek to Gorek Shep afterwards. Stopping off at Everest Base Camp for the obligatory nude photo (which the Korean photographer expedition loved) and a climb of Kala Pattar—a hill with magnificent panoramic views of Nuptse, Lhotse, Cholatse, Ama and of course, the rather bland-looking Everest*—we spent a few nights in the popular teahouses of the Khumbu Valley, soaking up civilisation before moving on.

Teahouse trekking is a fairly unique concept; only in Nepal can you walk for weeks among the highest mountains in the world and stay in such comfortable accommodation. I didn't know what made Nepal so suited to it, but for many years before tourism, I knew that the trails and valleys of the Solokhumbu region were populated by the Sherpa, a mountain people now known for their strength and incredible fitness. With pink cheeks and a cheery disposition, I felt I had much in common with these rugged snowy types, who used their yak herds and traditional Nepali head-slung baskets called dokus to help establish trade routes with China and Tibet. But things had changed significantly since those not so distant days.

Now with the influx of tourism, small villages that once served as summer grazing for the yak herds had been transformed into oases of comfort for the hordes of trekkers who visited the Khumbu each year. Such was the wealth that this process generated, the local economy suffered from huge inflation. Prices soared, which was fine for the comparatively well-off tourists—but for locals not involved in tourism, things became harder. This, in turn, pushed more people into the arms of the industry, making the Khumbu one of the most expensive areas in Nepal, if not all of South Asia.

Word soon reached the impoverished alleys of Kathmandu and from those alleys, Nepalis with little hope of otherwise escaping a life of destitution left to find their fortunes in the gold-paved trails of the highest trekking region in the world. In Gorek Shep, the last village before Everest Base Camp, I stayed in a dormitory with a few of the porters who were waiting for their tourists to finish looking around Base Camp and Kala Pattar. One evening, they explained the pay structure and life of a porter.

The going rate for a load carrying porter, they told me, was roughly one hundred rupees per day,* per twenty kilograms. Not bad

* In Nepali, Mount Everest is known as Sagarmatha, which translates as "Forehead in the Sky." In Tibet, it is known as Chomolungma, which means, "Goddess Mother of the World." Clearly the snow is whiter on the other side.

* At the time, the exchange rate was roughly one hundred rupees to the pound.

for this part of the world, but a dormitory cost them around fifty rupees. Food at the lower altitudes was around one hundred rupees for daal baht,* the Nepali staple, but up here could be as much as four hundred. The locals, they said, often treated porters the same as tourists in terms of pricing, because as they saw it, a porter from Kathmandu was just as much an outsider as a trekker from Europe. Concessions would be made if they brought supplies or encouraged tourists to a village, but no discounts were given otherwise.

When a porter arrived fresh-faced and eager in Lukla, he would be greeted with the reality that unless he took on backbreaking loads, he would not be able to make a living from the job. In some cases, the younger men carried over a hundred kilograms, just so they could make the effort worthwhile. For the first few years, the porter would compete with yak herds to offer value for money to the business-minded teahouse owners. Occasionally, through some lucky break, the porter might move on to working with tourists. This was better paid, at the time being around seven hundred rupees a day for less weight, but after meals it only worked out at one or two hundred rupees profit—barely enough to keep him going when he was not being employed.

Most porters, these men said, mixed it up. Taking supplies to the villages and working for tourists where possible was the best way to earn a living, but the real money was in guiding. Often, understandably, it was the local Sherpa who had the more lucrative jobs—mountain guides, tour leaders, teahouse owners—and most non-Sherpa porters became disillusioned when they realised their true prospects for reaching this kind of work. Things were fairer now than before and the life of the porter was getting better. But for the amount of money in the area, it struck me that portering sounded like a surprisingly bad deal, compared to the relatively affluent lifestyles of the owners of more popular teahouses. On the trails around Namche Bazaar, I had seen these porters walking with such big loads in their dokus that they looked like gigantic baskets with legs, which was amusing to watch but probably not so much fun to be.

But I couldn't see an easy solution. If tourists didn't use porters, these guys would either starve or be forced back to Kathmandu. Pay them more, and the local economy would become even more inflated and yet more wannabe porters would be attracted to the region. So

* Rice and lentil curry.

maybe, unfair as it was, this was just the way things were. The way they had to be. But then again, perhaps this was just another one of those little lies we tell ourselves to make it all feel okay.

A day or two later, after another quick saunter up Kala Pattar, Chris and I were sitting out in the large sandy area in front of the village of Gorek Shep, where Chris had pitched his tent. While he was fiddling around with his stove, I had passed on what the porters told me.

"Doesn't it bug you?" I asked him.

"What?"

"Well, all that."

"You mean the economic thing?"

"Yeah. Everywhere it's the same. Same as Papua and the Philippines."

"People have shit lives at home too dude."

"How shit? Hauling a hundred kilograms of hairdryers and Carlsberg for two quid, shit?"

"Well, yeah. It's different though isn't it." He pulled a face, probably intended as wise, but with his silly facial hair it looked like he was doing an impression of a goat.

"In what way?" I asked.

"Different standards. What would you rather—sit in an office or do this?"

"Well…I don't know." I leant back into the sand, soaking up the high altitude rays for a moment. "That's a silly question because I'm a bit weird," I said, squinting. "And anyway, I don't think I could do this for the rest of my life. I mean, at some point I've got to settle, get a job and that."

"Why?"

"Well, that's what everyone does. How else will I ever start a family?"

"You see—it *is* different. What if all your friends and family were in Nepal? If you came from here, you'd see it differently."

"But everyone seems to want to get out. Everyone seems to want to live in the West."

"I see…and no Westerners want to come here. You think, deep down, these guys would rather the nine to five? Living in an office, placing orders for packets of viagra or whatever all day? Trying to sell phones to people who've already got them? You think they'd prefer that?"

"Yes," I replied. "Probably."

Chris looked stumped. "Yeah I suppose they would. But the grass is always greener." We both sat quiet for a few moments, as the wind whipped up the tent, making the entrance flap about before settling down again. Then he said, "Just look at us. We've got fuck all cash, we're hauling a load of stuff up passes even the porters don't cross, we're sleeping outside or in dormitories or the occasional tiny room. Against your criteria, our lives are worse right now than they were before we came here. Especially compared to that restaurant job you keep whinging about."

"It wasn't a bad job, it was just such a rip-off place."

"Yeah but look at us now. Back then you had a roof over your head, you had central heating, you had a bed, plenty of food, and you have chosen to give that up to come here and live like you've got nothing."

"So have you."

"Yes dude, exactly! And I actually quite like it here."

Although we both knew he was arguing the toss just for the fun of it, Chris had a point. Especially on the money front; he had brought around the same as a porter would make—just less than two pounds per day—and he was getting by okay. His wooly jumper was probably colder than most of the hand-me-down jackets the porters wore and instead of a roll mat to sleep on, he'd found some kind of blanket thing that a kind Tibetan lady had bestowed on him out of pity back in Namche. I had more money by virtue of being an incredibly charming young waiter when I'd handed out all those Italian dishes in the preceding months, but there was a certain level of discomfort we both shared, and it was enjoyable discomfort at that. It was discomfort we welcomed. We were carrying less than half of the weight that the majority of the porters we'd met were, so it wasn't really that comparable to them, but it was on the same tracks at least.

"But it's the choice thing that gets me," I said after a few moments of quiet. "We have the choice to be here; we can get out whenever we want. We can go home and carry on living our lives. Most people in the world would kill for that choice."

"Dude, choice isn't all it's cracked up to be. Think about it. Remember those guys from the Philippines? I'd give my right nut to live there and have their lives, be part of that culture, have family and friends and all that there, just like they've got, and they weren't empowered with our choice. Choice is bullshit dude, it's an illusion."

A trail of yaks crossed our path, their bells donging and clanking away, followed by a trickle of tourists heading for Everest Base Camp.

"Choice is why we have to fill our time with shit like this, rather than just getting on with life."

"I thought you said you liked it here?" I said, shivering from a gust of icy wind that blew around the shelter of his tent.

"I do, but that's not the point." I could tell Chris was starting to enjoy this now, even if he was just talking for the sake of it. Being a physicist, you'd expect him to have a more straightforward approach to conversation, but that simply wasn't the case. "Look at us. Choice has turned our society into the kind of place where people get so lost they need to *find themselves* in countries like this." Chris pointed towards Everest direction, where the last of the trekkers were disappearing behind a hill. "If we want to escape, we have to walk for a week. I like that. I like that we can't have everything we want up here. Choice is hugely overrated if you ask me."

"So you're saying that you'd rather not have the choice and have to haul backbreaking loads for the rest of your life—and that's better than what we've got right now?"

"No, dude. I'm just saying that it isn't all fluffy kittens and honey. You get used to what's around you. You can't compare peoples' lives against some dodgy universal ethic. It just doesn't exist. That's like saying it's unfair that the cavemen had to live in caves. 'Oh, poor cavemen, that's so horrible for them!' It's like saying it's unfair I get more women than you, just because I am far better looking."

"You don't."

"But I could."

I almost said something, but then I held back. "Whatever. So we should give up our choice and that would be the best thing."

"Exactly, screw democracy. Screw freedom. Make choice so rare that when you finally do get a whiff of it, you appreciate it like you should, and then you'd make the right decision. And you can't keep telling me these people deserve our pity. Sympathy is just another form of arrogance. My theory is it's all about the firm grip. People need to be given a role in life, have things prescribed. *You* will be a carpenter. *You* will be a mechanic. *You* will sweep the streets, entertain the children, farm the land," he said, pointing at each of his imaginary audience in turn. "Learned helplessness is far better for people's mental wellbeing than choice."

"You'll make a wonderful husband one day."

"Damn right. Society needs to be run like a household. Democracy can piss off with its personal liberty and moral superiority. Benevolent dictatorship, that's what it's all about. Just like parenting. Let us not be ruled by selfishness. Let us be ruled by, I don't know, a guy with a big hat who knows what's best for everybody. Someone like Gandalf the Great."

"Gandalf the Grey?"

"Yeah."

"Or Ray Mears," I said.

"Exactly, Ray Mears. He's a good egg. We should take the power away from the people and give it all to someone like him, someone who knows how to bring true benefit to the whole community. Someone who serves a higher purpose. Only then will the community work together in harmony."

"Then we can all divide things out equally?" I asked.

"Yes," he stated, with a proud look on his face, having apparently devised a new system of governance off the cuff.

"That beard has changed you," I muttered.

"What do you mean? What's wrong with my beard?"

"Nothing," I replied, finding some interesting cloud shapes in the sky to observe. "It's just, you know…"

"I know *what?* What's wrong with it?"

"Nothing is *wrong* with it exactly…it's just, well, it's just a bit rubbish. You look like a shit version of Abraham Lincoln who's been dipped in bleach and caught in a flash fire."

"I look like what?"

I paused for a moment, trying to imagine other, less outlandish things that resembled Chris's new beard. "Um, a badly trimmed hedge? A seventies porn clip?"

"Well you're hardly one to talk!" he interrupted. "If people are what they eat, you've clearly been eating a lot of beetroot lately."

"What? That's so obscure I don't know what to say." I pulled my coat up so it covered my face a bit more. "Speak the plain English. Stop talking mambo jimbo."

"Eating too many tomatoes?" Chris suggested. "Red peppers? Strawberries?"

"Nope, still not getting it."

"Watermelon?"

"No idea what you're talking about."

Chris's eyebrows raised hopefully, "Red felt pens? Red paint? Other red things that are red?"

I could just about see what he was trying to say here, but I decided to hide this fact. "I don't understand, Che. What are you trying to tell me?"

"What I'm trying to say is, I can shave any time I want but you'll always be stuck with that ridiculous red face of yours."

"Sounds like it's not the only thing that's red around here, Cuba boy."

"You're one to talk, Jamie 'Ooh-let's-all-pretend-to-be-moral' Alexander. You know who you remind me of?"

"Ghandi?" I suggested.

"Nope."

"Jesus?"

"No dude." Chris looked up. "You remind me of those fucking annoying hippies I met in Kathmandu."

"So not Jesus then?"

"No."

Pause.

"Sure?"

"Yes."

Another pause.

"You know he only started doing cool stuff when he was thirty don't you? And I'm only twenty-one."

Chris sighed. "You'll never be Jesus. You're just a spoilt tit with too many ideas. If you love the porters so much why don't you just go home and get a good job and give them all your excess money?"

"Why don't you just shut up?"

"Because I'm right."

"Oh so you are Right? Really? I get it. So now you're the new Hitler are you? Get rid of democracy, give the people what they need, not what they want. Con them into thinking that you're a liberal, then *Bam!* Get all jingoistic on their arses and execute all the hippies. Teach them a bloody lesson in humility. Great idea. Why not just go ahead and exterminate some other minorities while we're at it. Bayonete some gypsies. Cremate a few short people. Benevolent dictatorship, my arse. You're just another bloody tyrant wannabe. And there I go thinking you were idolising Castro. Cuba's turned you into a fascist, hasn't it?"

"I meant right, as in correct. Not right-wing. Do you fancy some noodles by the way? I think I made a few too many."

"Yes please."

Chris dished out some noodles. We both took a few slurps, before he asked, "What were we talking about?"

"Uh, Jesus. Wasn't it?"

"Oh yeah, that guy. See, *he* had a beard like this…"

And so the conversation continued. We both knew it was a fairly ridiculous discussion, but Chris had raised a valid point in his consistent disagreement: maybe choice *wasn't* all it was cracked up to be. I mean, in some cases it was, of course. Where it stopped terror, torture, repression; where it prevented people like Pol Pot, Idi Amin and Stalin from massacring millions, choice was great. I'd still maintain that for the porters, it would be nice to have the choice to not live in such challenging poverty, especially when there was so much money in the area. But when it came to other things, less pressing things, surely there was only so much choice a person could have before they became spoiled? That's what liberalism was all about: choice, freedom. The ability to make decisions on things, have control. But what if people with too much choice consistently chose the wrong things? Things that, in the long run, they might look back on with regret? What if people needed guidance, help; the ability to make an informed decision?

What if the Official UK Top 40 Singles Chart was evidence of this?

With all this recession malarky about to start taking its toll, maybe the problem was less to do with people facing an incredibly tough future and more to do with the fact that we'd all had far too much choice for far too long, and now that reality was hitting us back to where we should be, we were finding it difficult to cope. I knew that at some stage, I'd have to face this recession too. It would be my generation who would apparently be hit the hardest. And it was not entirely through choice that I had ended up working fifteen-hour shifts in jobs that would have been unthinkable for a graduate two decades ago, but that was not all to do with the recession—it was also thanks to Blair's qualification inflation policies that graduation wasn't all it was made out to be. But now, because I had done that, because I had worked those hours and been relatively frugal with it, I could afford to come here.

So I still had that choice. And for a short while, I'd felt like I'd earned that choice. Although, in comparison to the porters, I hadn't really earned it, had I?

TWENTY-ONE

Botmas Manche

It was getting chilly and Chris was looking back the way we had come.

"I told you we should have set off earlier," I said, being rather petty. "Now our last glimpse of Ama has been ruined by your morning poo."

"Looks cool though doesn't it," Chris replied, and it did: in the foreground, cairns stood menacingly at the edge of the small plateau and after that, the scree and rubble dropped a thousand feet towards Dzongla, the village we had walked from that morning. On either side loomed tall white mountains with their heads poking towards a dark, swirling vortex of grey. Less than twenty minutes before, I had been pulling a hood over my peeling ears to protect them from the sun as we climbed, but there wasn't much need for that now.

"Let's get a wiggle on mate," I said. "This is going to float down soon."

For the last few days, the weather pattern had broken, giving us mostly clear afternoons for our stay around Gorek Shep. Now, it seemed, things were settling back into their old routine. But that was fine; we were acclimatised, we knew what to do in the cold and compared to the Kongma La, this pass was fairly easy. Saying that, there was a glacier to cross and we were still well above five thousand metres, so we couldn't let our scraggly hair down too much.

I followed Chris as he trudged through the trodden ice of the Cho La glacier, snapping a few pictures of the imposing walls either side of us as I did. Suddenly, the crust under my foot cracked and I lost my leg in the snow. The weight of the bag was clearly not helping—I couldn't wait to get rid of the thing, just walk normally. Climbing Kala Pattar had been wonderful, we'd virtually skipped up without the weight of our camping equipment and food, past the painfully slow groups of trekkers who walked like they were on the moon, but now we were reunited with the rucksacks and the sores were beginning to form again. So I undid the waist strap and let it slide from my back, hoisted my leg out from the hole. I'd not really been looking where the path was leading, so I made a mental note to not stray too much.

Picking up my bag, I took one last picture of Chris—a dark silhouette before the sloping trajectory of snow—and carried on. The cloud was just about touching the peaks either side of the Cho La now, but we still had enough time to get across the glacier and that was the important thing.

Eventually, we found the cairns that marked the pass itself. They were wrapped in Buddhist prayer flags, intended to spread goodwill as the wind blew over their scripted mantra. Clearly the weather was not taking any notice of their compassionate message today, for they whipped and cracked in the wind angrily.

"Dude, it's fucking cold." Chris hunkered himself down into some rocks, his reindeer jumper making another appearance under a thin black raincoat.

"I know," I shouted. "Can you see where we go from here?"

We were at the top of the Cho La now, about to descend into the next valley along from the Khumbu, but the visibility was low and dropping.

Chris peeked out from his hiding place, taking a chomp on one of the chocolate bars we'd each reserved for the tougher parts of the trek. "There's a path, but I can't really see where it goes. I think if we head to the left of that hill, we'll be all right." He pointed out to the only hill we could see, but it wasn't very far away. In fact, it was at most a bump in the steep slope back down.

"Okay man." I set my compass nonetheless, making sure we had something to go on, and took out a Bounty bar. The tropical wonders nearly cracked my teeth when I bit into them. "Mate, my Bounty's frozen!" I shouted.

Chris responded, but the howling gale meant that I couldn't really tell what he was saying anymore, so I crawled up to him. All my warm layers were on, everything I could find, and I was still shivering. "What?" I yelled.

Chris ignored me, looking down from the pass. "For fuck's sake," he said, "why does this always happen when we're on top of things?"

I looked over the rock, down towards the hill. It wasn't there anymore. "Oh. Got a bit cloudy down there hasn't it?" I yelled.

"That's not just cloud," he shouted back. I was only two feet away from him, but it was all I could do to hear him. "That's a blizzard."

"Bollocks," I said.

"What?"

"BOLLOCKS!"

Chris looked at his watch. "Half-past one," he yelled back.

I moved closer. "Let's get down there before the cairns disappear." I stuffed my Bounty back into the top flap of my bag and pulled my hood up again to stop the stinging in my ears, then set off, with Chris close behind.

The first flakes started hitting us, but instead of falling, they were being swept up from below, caught by the wind and thrown into the sky like a swarm of icy locusts. I drew my hood in tight, dragged a neck warmer over my nose so that only a small slit was open in front of my eyes, and started down the hill. More flakes whacked against the waterproof layers of my jacket and we started jogging, leaping from rock to rock like mountain goats, trying to escape the incoming weather. I'd look up, find the next pile of stones and virtually sprint there, now almost completely ignoring the weight of the rucksack and the steep incline. Then at the next stack, repeat. Join the dots, leaping, bounding down the scree before it all became too slippery. Before the blizzard enveloped us completely.

Down we leapt, further and further, until we realised we had descended the steepest part of the Cho La crossing in under fifteen minutes. We were lucky; while the flurries were flowing uphill, nothing was settling, but the top flap of my rucksack had iced over already.

Breathless, grinning, I turned to Chris. "Shit me, that was fun."

"You'll enjoy the next bit then," he replied.

Ahead, a wall of white was surging towards us, billowing, swirling, coating everything it touched, and within seconds, the visibility was under ten metres.

Lips cracked, I shouted at Chris, "Where's the next cairn?"

"Under that snow!" he called back.

Chris led the way, climbing through boulders and rocks with hands and knees, slipping as the snow piled up thick. We reached a few more stone markers, but soon they ran out, along with any evidence of a path. "Trail's gone cold dude," Chris grinned.

"Oh that's funny," I replied. "Really funny."

We carried on, following the rough bearing I had set on my compass even though we were probably well past the hill by now. Rock after rock, covered in several inches of white, and Chris and I slipping around all over them; the sweat started melting into the back of my jacket with the effort. We passed through inlets, over sheets of ice that collapsed when we put weight on them, sending us thigh-deep, twisting joints awkwardly and making us fall. With everything covered in a christmas cake icing of fresh snow, we could have no idea how the ground would hold out.

Up steep slopes we were sure weren't on the map, over ridges we knew the trail didn't cross, but we kept on walking, slipping, sliding down the hills and ending up in crumpled piles at the bottom.

Slowly, we were making progress.

Ice shelves creaked and groaned, threatening to snap and drop us into the freezing rivers below—rivers we could hear gurgling invisibly underneath our feet—and we followed the compass blindly; sky white, ground white, ourselves turning whiter.

Eventually, after a few hours, the visibility increased and a ridge loomed high above us. It was the only significant feature on the map we had, torn and tatty as it now was, so we climbed it and descended the valley on the far side where Chris pointed to the first snow-caked cairn we had seen since the blizzard began. My spirits lifted; at last, we knew where we were going.

As we walked through the valley, the wind died down and the snow stopped falling. Soon, a glow in the white sky hinted at the imminent arrival of sunlight and by the time the next village was in view, the whole landscape was a fairytale wonderland, sparkling and shimmering, icicles dripping and glinting. Yet again, the Himalayan weather had changed its mind.

I galloped happily down towards the Ngazomba glacier with the sound of George Michael's "Faith" inexplicably running loops in my head.

It had been a good day.

***

Our time in the mountains was coming to an end and we spent what we had left in the high Himalaya by the Cho Oyu base camp, in an area surrounded by glaciers, sawtooth ridges and high, snowy pinnacles—the perfect spot to soak it all up before we rejoined the lowlands.

For the best part of a week, we moved no more than a couple of hours each day, soaking up the sun, the cold, crisp air, and the pink reflections of sunset on the tips of the highest peaks in the evening. More than anything else, it was the space, the magnitude of the place that we absorbed. My routine was now more than perfected; I awoke before dawn and climbed out of the tent to watch sunrise. Shortly after, I'd open everything up to air—tent, sleeping bag, unwashed clothing—in the bright morning rays. Breakfast would be whatever freeze-dried meal I fancied, with water pumped from the nearby lakes and streams the day before (breaking the ice to get at the liquid). Then, I would go for a short walk to conduct my morning necessaries and re-break the ice to get more water, all the while thawing my toothpaste by holding it in my armpit.

With no time limit, the routine was relaxed, allowing us the chance to expand into our surroundings, clear our heads of whatever it was that had filled them. Leaving the tents up in the deserted sandy plains, we barely saw a soul in days. Our company was the groaning, creaking glaciers with their crumbling moraines, and the mountains with the roaring avalanches that often marked sunrise—avalanches that shook the ground like earthquakes. By the time the noise reached us, all we'd see would be a dusty white cloud where an ice shelf or scree wall used to be. A floating reminder of what was part of the landscape a few seconds before.

Mornings in the high mountains were always perfect, but for the first time, I started to appreciate the evenings too. Me in my thick down jacket and Chris in his woolies, we'd sit out as our evening meals boiled in the stoves, hunkered behind rocks to stay out of the sharp winds, talking of yetis and other strange creatures of the night. With his ragged facial hair and unruly eyes, Chris had actually started looking like a yeti by now, which explained why the few trekkers who did venture up this far often ran away very soon afterwards.

Sitting, hunched up in the icy plains those evenings, we'd had the time to gather our thoughts, as our minds as well as our bodies wandered the jagged wilderness around us. Very little of what they came up with was of much use. If anything, the grandness of the scenery around us seemed to be inversely linked to our collective intellectual capacity.

I remember the conversation we'd had on our last night in the area. Perched behind rocks, the wind pressed ice blocks to whichever side was facing it. Faint stars like distant LEDs were glowing through the wide, deepening sky. Chris was leaning over to check his stove was still alight. It wasn't, so he swore, pulled some matches out of his pocket and tried to get the thing going again. "Bastard," he said. "Never trust a multi-fuel." With a pop, the flames burst up the side of his jumper and singed a few of the reindeer's facial hairs, and he settled back down.

My stove was fine, simply because it wasn't a stove—it was hexamine. Solid fuel blocks that rarely blew out once they had ignited. The only trouble I had was igniting them, so I'd had to use Chris's stove for that.

"I can't wait to be warm again." I cupped my hands around a freshly boiled food packet. It was for no real reason though, because I was still wearing gloves. "As in properly warm, not just wearing this humungous coat. As in, hot-warm."

"Hot-in-a-thong warm," Chris nodded, knowingly.

"Yeah, exactly. Hot-in-a-thong warm. Whatever we do up here, something's always numb. It's my left bum cheek right now."

"I can't feel my entire head."

We both started eating, with the sky darkening and a blustery wind threatening to blow Chris's box of matches and my cooking equipment away. Ice had already started forming in the water bottles. I picked mine up and rattled it. "How do people live up here?"

"Apparently the Sherpa hate climbing mountains. Much higher than five thousand and there's no point."

"What are we at now? Five one? Five two?"

"Yeah, something like that. Seventeen-thousand feet or so." Chris gulped down a few mouthfuls of pasta. "Can't wait to be able to breath properly."

"Yup, true that. And eat chicken."

"Oh, God yeah. Chicken. What I'd do to eat a chicken right now… Hey, Look at that, dude." Chris pointed to the tip of Hungchhi, a pointy mountain to the east, over towards Everest. The last of the day's sun was glinting red against the snowy pinnacle, making it glow like ET's finger. "I am really going to miss this place," he said solemnly.

"Me too."

We both watched in awe while clouds like pink flame clung to the higher peaks. The wind whistling and whipping against our hair and our cracked, dry, dusty faces, Chris looked down at his meal, deep in thought for a few moments. Then he said, "I wonder if anyone's invented freeze-dried yaks yet. You know, add water and it suddenly comes to life and carries all your stuff for you."

"What, like those grow-in-the-bath dinosaur things?"

"Yeah."

"I don't know, probably."

Chris nodded his approval. His eyebrows then furrowed. "Also, I was wondering, what *is* the point in Goths?"

Perhaps we had been alone in the hills for too long.

But it didn't matter. Two days later, after three weeks above the altitude of Mont Blanc, and a month in the mountains, we crossed the stunning Renjo La and then we were back in the lowlands.* Back in the world of living things, where the evenings were comfortable and golden, the rhododendrons pink and the air thick with pollen and oxygen. Walking through the Thame Valley back to Namche, it felt like someone had just switched us from black and white to full colour. We trotted and skipped the trail, jogged through the glowing, warm villages and sweet pine of the Dudh Koshi River Valley, dusty with the pre-monsoon weather. I barely noticed the weight on my back anymore, and the hills were impossibly shallow. Gurgling brooks, flowing rivers and prayer flags by the million.

Everything was pleasant.

Everything was easy.

Everything was sweet.

Not only had we got through some relatively hairy moments largely unscathed, but I felt stronger, fitter and happier than I'd ever been in my life. Things were perfect. Which, I suppose, would be fate's excuse for what happened next.

* * *

---

* Lowlands, of course, is a relative term in Nepal. We were still between three and four thousand meters above sea level, as high as the High Atlas, which is pretty high.

Until Phakding, the only time we'd genuinely suffered in the mountains was the day we'd realised sun cream didn't work retrospectively. But that was a few weeks ago now and things had been going smoothly for a while.

I remember the walk in fairly well—herds of dzo, yak-cow hybrids, bred to carry the same weight for half the cost of a thoroughbred, plodding over the metal-wire suspension bridge, and then a dusty track lined with stone-walled lodges. Lodge City, I'd heard it called. Row after row of teahouses, each with little courtyards of colourfully dressed trekkers eating plates of buffalo fried rice or egg noodles, a few with the same large bottles of Carlsberg and Tuborg we'd last had over a month before. A far cry from the solitude of the upper Ngazomba, or even the Thame Valley.

As we walked in, I remember feeling like a completely different person from those first few days, when I was weighed down by too many petty things. Ex-girlfriend whoever, restlessness from a few months' tedium in whatever job. Now, I thought, I had completely left all that behind. Unlike Jordan, I had actually achieved it. My mind was as floaty as a dzo's eyes.

Calm.

Peaceful.

Detached.

"You know what dude," Chris had turned to me, "I feel fucking Zen right now."

"Same," I'd replied.

Look at them: all those trekkers with their gossip and excitement, apprehension about the trail ahead, and us—been there, done that, plus a bit. Glances came our way from the tables; in our minds they were looks of amazement at the mountain veterans, with our blister-scarred noses and our straggly hair. They were looks from people who were wondering how on earth we had become so damn *cool.* Either that, or Chris still looked like a yeti.

But neither of us were that concerned. We only had a few more hours' walking to go and then we'd be back in the mountain mall of Lukla. We were in no rush to get there.

"You know what, this place looks pretty chilled, shall we stay here?" It was the last of a string of teahouses on the right hand side, one of the southernmost lodges with an unbroken vista of the river valley and pastures behind it.

"Yeah sure," Chris said, and we walked in, got a small twin room with a good view. The lodge owner, a short guy wearing an orange-lined black zip coat over a green sweater, asked what we'd like to eat. I had egg noodles and a pancake, Chris had shared my pancake. But then, how was he to know?

Now I'd spent nearly fifty hours with my face over a bucket and my arse on a toilet seat, proving that men could multitask after all. Sure, I'd had bouts of food poisoning here and there, but *this* was different. This was epic, destructive. Knives twisting in the gut, wrenching my insides into spasm.

Five days on and I was still choking bile.

That night, we'd gone to bed and I was feeling fine, but something had told me that would change. I mentioned it to Chris.

"I'm going to be sick before tomorrow morning," I'd said.

"Why? You all right dude?"

"I'm fine now, but I've just got a feeling."

And that was it, we both fell asleep.

Then it was the middle of the night and I'd woken up in a cold sweat. My stomach was spinning, my throat churning, and the nausea was rising. Lying still, like a water balloon on a bed of drawing pins, I said, "Chris."

"Chris," I said.

"Chris mate, get me a bucket, quick."

Chris groaned.

"Chris." I lay still, still as I could, trying to delay it as the inevitable rose up. Then it did. "Oh shit," I mumbled, prophetically.

"What's up?" Chris said.

Three.

Two.

One.

I sprinted down the corridor, smacked open the door, and roared the multicolour opera into the toilet. Seconds later, the other end decided to join in for a bodily-function duet, culminating in what was probably the best impersonation I've ever done of a US Republican presidential candidate. And there I stayed, retching, roaring with everything I had in me, liquid-screaming to get it out.

Two more hours and Chris was doing the same.

* * *

For the next few days, we were *Les Misérables*, incarcerated in the teahouse by our own bowels, while the owner grew increasingly frustrated with our presence. He himself had failed to convince us that it was not his food that had caused our problems, so he sent his son, his wife and a small boy to tell us that it really was our fault. No help, no water, just blame. "You eat something bad," they said. "You eat cheap food! Where did you get this?"

"Here," I told them.

We ate here.

Tell the truth, I didn't care what they thought, I just wanted the diarrhoea to stop, the vomiting and the spinning to go away, the stabbing cramps to disappear. I didn't care whose fault it was. That was irrelevant. I just longed for it to end.

Yet, for whatever reason, they *did* care.

On day two, the owner came in with his son in some sort of show of force and said, "You do not use toilet."

"What?" Chris replied, both of us lying on our beds in foetal positions.

"You make it bad for other guests."

"What?"

"You eat dirty food, this is what happen!" he shouted, pointing at me. I rubbed my eyes, hoping this wasn't happening. His son, staring at us, he had this look of hostility in his eyes, like he was just waiting for the opportunity.

"This is what happen," he repeated.

"The only thing we ate was here. The only food we had all day was here. It was *your* food," Chris snapped. "You gave us food poisoning, understand? You. Food poisoning. Kana kharab."

"Shut up!" the man hissed. "DO NOT," he yelled, "USE TOILET!" And then he slammed the door and we heard his footsteps in sync with his son's stomping down the corridor.

"Use *the* toilet," Chris muttered.

I was in a daze, I could barely walk. Even the loo was too far from the room for me to get to sometimes, so I'd had to stay on it when the bouts got bad. Maybe that's why he was so angry, because the other guests had seen me half-naked, decrepit, waiting for the lurgy to hit again and been put off. I looked at my waist, naked under the sleeping bag, hips jutting out from a shrink-wrapped skeleton. And then the vomiting started again, but I didn't have time to make it to the toilet I wasn't allowed to use, so this time I opened the window.

"That's going to really piss him off," Chris had said with a wry smile. "Fuck the bill, let's just get out of here."

We timed our departure well—a large tour party had just arrived and the family were busy catering for them in the lodge's dining room. Chris, faring better than me for having eaten less of the contaminated meal, carried his own rucksack and helped me with mine as I held up my trousers with my spare hand and walked down the stairs, out of the door, past the small courtyard and towards the teahouse across the road.

After explaining that we were very ill, the new teahouse's staff kindly helped us to a room directly next to a flush toilet, the first we'd seen in the Khumbu. For a day we had stayed there anonymously. Out of the window I could see the wife of the owner of the original teahouse looking up and down the street, storming around, the irritation obvious behind her narrow eyes.

I didn't really want to admit it, but the angrier she got, the happier I became. I'd never had anything this bad, nor had I come across any lodge owner who'd shout at their guests after making them ill. Give me sinusitis, bike crashes, stonefish. Give me anything, but not this.

And it was *them* who caused it. It was *her*. Her with her malevolent face; in my sunken eyes, she was evil. There she was: ranting, marching up and down the street, and I was giggling from the bedroom window and she looked up, saw me. "You come back!" she screamed.

I knew I should have kept my mouth closed, but I replied anyway. "Why?" I shouted. "So you can poison me again?"

I'd timed it perfectly, just as another tour group was strolling into her courtyard. She exploded into a fury, yelling in Nepali for a few minutes while the tour shuffled awkwardly on to the next teahouse, evidently wondering what the hell had happened. I closed the window and lay back down. I didn't really see myself as the spiteful type, but it was the best thing that had happened to me in days. I thought it was brilliant.

Chris walked back into the room and I told him what happened. He agreed with me.

"That's brilliant," he said.

The glee was short-lived. By now, I had lost over a stone and a half from an already slim body. I was dangerously underweight and completely incontinent. While the vomiting had just about stopped, I still couldn't hold anything in for more than a few minutes. With the rising tensions across the road and given my condition, we needed to get out of the village, and fast.

Two days later, when I was just about able to walk, we made our break.

* * *

It was just after lunch; the village had been relatively quiet. There had been no trekking parties come through just yet, but we went anyway. We thanked our lodge staff profusely for their kindness.

Leaving as much of a tip as we could, we sneaked out through the back door, away from the main road. Still weak from illness, I struggled after Chris. Trying to stay out of sight, we climbed up a hill to a garden above the teahouse, using a tree to get over a wall to the yard of the next stone building along. Chris went first, helping me with my rucksack, but then he stopped. "Dude, I think they've got lookouts," he said.

I hopped down from the wall awkwardly. Seeing a boy perched by the main track just around the corner of the building, I turned to Chris. "Let's go back and try again later then. I can't be bothered to deal with these fuckers yet."

When I looked back, the kid was gone.

Shouts reverberated from behind the building, from the direction of the first teahouse, and suddenly the short lodge owner with his orange-lined black coat was sprinting around the corner from the track, past the building, climbing the ladder up to the garden we were in.

"You stupid!" he screamed, storming towards us. He got to Chris first and I watched as Chris held his arm up in a block, but the stick smacked into his head and he cowered under the blow. I walked forward with my hands in the air. "You stupid!" the guy screamed and the stick struck my arms and head, but in my state I couldn't do much about it. More people were coming up, and he was still shouting "Stupid!" at us—the only offensive English word he knew apparently. Cute, in a way. But not when he had that stick raised up above his head.

"Botmas manche," I replied—the only offensive thing I knew in Nepali.

Naughty people.

No surprise, he didn't back down. More guys were up in the garden now, grabbing Chris, pulling him down to the ladder. Chris outmatched and me useless, we had no hope.

Chris pushed them away. "Alright," he shouted, climbing down. Then there was a wailing from the alley next to the building. The owner's wife ran around the corner and I got a lump in my throat because she had a large knife and she started lunging at Chris, swiping at him with the ten-inch kukri blade. Chris shouted, and he was clearly slightly scared, because he didn't normally react to much like that. Still, I was getting pulled and tugged, shoved down the ladder and I could barely hold my bag and now there was a renewed urgency, because in my excitement I had accidentally unclenched. I dropped my bag over the wall and slid down to Chris, where he was using his rucksack as a shield, but there was a load more men of all ages down here, pulling the woman back, grabbing at Chris and me, shouting.

"This was a rubbish idea," I said to Chris, over the melee.

He was now just being pushed, knocked about, but there was no knife slicing inches from his face so he looked calmer again. "Have you got any money left dude?"

"Yeah, don't worry mate," I replied, and a stick smashed into my head again. "Botmas manche!" I yelled, raising my fist to the crowd. Chris pushed his way through—most of the village had turned out to watch this now, along with one or two gormless trekkers—and nobody, *nobody* looked friendly. To this day, I don't know why, but we took our bags off and Chris sat on his, right in the middle of this throng. "So what do you want?" he asked, calmly.

The lodge owner thrust a piece of paper in front of us. "900," scrawled in scruffy writing, and Chris said, "We're not paying."

"You pay, you stupid!" the owner shouted, raising the stick again, but he was held back by his son, the son with the aggressive look, the look of distain in his eyes. The look we'd mistaken as intentional.

"You gave us food poisoning, you stopped us using the toilet, you made us leave your teahouse. And now you've just smacked us with a fucking *stick!*" Apart from the last few words, Chris said this in an even tone. "So we aren't paying."

"That's not very good customer service," I agreed, quickly realising that it was a fairly stupid thing to say in the circumstances. Then again, excuses can be made for people in my condition. *Speaking of which…*

"Mate, I've got to run."

"Now?" Chris looked up at me in astonishment. "Right now?"

"Yup, sorry. You'll be fine—they're a friendly bunch. And I think that woman likes you."

"Fine, fuck it, on you go."

I walked through the crowd who parted with confused looks, straight into the next teahouse along, found the nearest toilet and cleaned myself up.

When I re-emerged, I truly was Zen. Thirty people had just seen me shit myself, we had just been beaten up by an angry mob for the cost of two meals, Chris had nearly been dismembered, and I had knives tearing holes in my intestines from a parasite that would significantly alter the next two years of my life.

What's not to be calm about?

Chris agreed, and when I walked back to him, was politely suggesting that we wouldn't pay in a mixture of English and Nepali, although I was sure there were some old Norse words mixed in there too. Four-letter Norse words you wouldn't use around your grandparents.

"Fuck it. Have the money," I said, throwing a twenty pound note at the owner. "Happy? Botmas wanker." I picked up my bag and told Chris, "Let's get the fuck out of here mate."

"Okay dude."

Slowly, the throng stepped aside, allowing us our exit.

When we were about a hundred metres away, the son ran up to us with a note. It was a thousand rupees, roughly ten pounds.

Our change.

"I'm sorry," he said as he handed it to me. The sinister look was still there, but he seemed genuinely upset. "My father thought you were Israeli."

I was stumped. I didn't know what to say. *Israeli?* Where the hell did he get that from?

The son walked back to the village and we watched the crowd dissipate. I looked at Chris. "I should have known. Bad things happen to me when people think I'm Israeli."

TWENTY-TWO

The Real India

Sumrubish Guesthouse, Calcutta. 29 April.

A sense of adventure, a desire for the unknown; a drive to see unusual things in beautiful places, meet different cultures; hedonism, escapism—these are the things that make people travel. But for me, it is something more. It must be.

I sweat the days away on a crowded oven-on-wheels just to spend the night playing Bedbug Roulette in the seediest part of an impoverished exhaust pipe of a city; hedonism, this isn't. I pour all my money, time and effort into going somewhere that will riddle me with illnesses, places where I never really know what is going on and who to trust; a sense of adventure just doesn't quite cut it. Sure there are strange things happening, but the scenery around me right now, if you called it beautiful, you wouldn't be using the word conventionally. As for escapism—take me home and I'd be more relaxed, safe and healthy than I have been for months now. Everything I need is back home: good food, comfortable house, great friends.

I used to know why I travelled. There was *a reason for it, and a pretty good one at that. I thought it would educate me, teach me about the ways of the world. If I'm being honest, I think I saw it as an opportunity for self-improvement. But where I am right now, that's difficult to believe. The education is all there, but I do nothing about it. And I can hardly call the loss of this much bodyweight to dysentery the next step towards perfection. There must be something; something abstract, not immediately obvious—to me at least—that draws me back time after time, journey after journey, back to the drudge of living out of a backpack, to the uncertainty of not knowing how things will pan out day by day.*

Whatever that reason is, for now, the best I can do is to equate it to an addiction. Before the wheels squeak against the damp tarmac on a Heathrow runway, I'm already thinking about where I'll get my next fix. Which jungle, city, desert, mountain range or archipelago to poke my sweaty red face into next. By the time I've lifted my rucksack from the carousel, the decision has been made; the rest amounts to covering the necessities before the cold turkey gets too bad.

Find some money.

Book the flights.

Pack a bag.

Go.

Truth be told, maybe travel is *a kind of drug. Maybe it's my version of the brown sugar, the Big H, liquefying on the teaspoon. Strange and daunting at first, but after a while you always look forward to it, because this isn't some chicken-shit habit. After a while, this is the only thing that makes you feel normal. Now I'm sure there are differences; the trips last longer and highs are not guaranteed. But when you're there, dodging semi-male prostitutes in the steamy armpit of a dilapidating city, scrambling up the sulphurous scree of a recently active volcano; when you're being woken by monkeys howling through a jungle clearing, life seems amplified. It puts the jump back in the flatline, reacquaints you with the extremes.*

Under the stimulant effect of Travel, it's almost as though someone grabs the TV remote and turns the mute off: suddenly everything becomes tangible. Step out of the bubble, and it all feels so much more real.

At least, it should.

So now I've just got to ask myself: is it worth it?

* * *

With the rumble of traffic overhead and the sweat dripping from my nose, I looked at the journal in front of me for the third or forth time, started flicking through the pages of jumbled, scruffy handwriting again. For a brief moment, I watched in horror as my bus nearly tipped into a ravine, and I saw myself trying to ignore the throbbing pain in my foot and the blood streaming out of my nose as I hobbled through the streets of Bangkok. More pages went by, and a moth the size of Jupiter attempted to decapitate me, then a pisshead in a cleaner's uniform clutched my skin together over the bone and pushed a needle through my arm. Skip forward to only a few months ago, and I was being beaten for the sake of two meals and one parasite. And the pages turned to the last journal entry I'd written.

With my feet in the water and the chatter behind, I read through that last entry once more, and my eyes settled on the final sentence.

So now I've just got to ask myself: is it worth it?

It was from a little over a month ago, after Chris flew out of Kathmandu, off to Amman or Oman or somewhere, man, and I decided to go to a hot place after all those mountains. India—someone once told me to go India. I was pretty sure it was hot there *and* it was in the middle of a heatwave. It had some cool islands off its coast too, so why not? I spent the next twenty-four hours on a bus, a train and, to keep the theme going, a boat. Then, for another twenty-four hours, I got on a different train to Calcutta, to the rooftop conversation I could barely recall.

I'd taken the bus from Kathmandu to the border with India and then on to Gorakhpur. But from there, I had no idea how to get to Calcutta, to the launch point for all those cool islands. Out of impulse, knowing it was heading roughly the right way, I got on the next train to Varanasi. I recall, after plodding around Varanasi for a while and then finally completing the last leg of my journey to Calcutta, sitting on the rooftop of the guesthouse. More specifically, I recall the hallucinations. I remember feeling slightly worried about them.

What was it that was happening?

Ah, yes. People's heads were exploding. Bursting like lemmings in a blender. Yet, what was so worrying about them was not what I saw, nor was it how I felt. Rather, it was what I didn't feel.

At the time, I had been awake for long enough for hallucinations to be near-enough inevitable. Given what I'd seen the previous day, it wasn't surprising what those hallucinations were. And yet, the only thing that was telling me that there was something not quite normal going on, was a faint memory from a distant past; an echo, which kept hinting that the images running through my mind were not the kind that sane minds had all that often, and if a sane person did somehow end up having this kind of vision, they should be horrified. But I wasn't. And that girl, with the cardigan and the dreadlocks. When she said what she said, I'd almost laughed out loud.

If my mind got any broader, it would fucking explode…

That was what worried me.

The night I'd had those hallucinations, I had opened my journal and written about travel as a drug. I'd implied that if it was, I was addicted. But I'd known that for a while, so there must have been a better reason I had written about my hobby in such a way that night. There must have been something else to it.

Another waft of incense, this time mixed with hashish, floated by, collecting under the overhanging leaves and branches above me. A few petals drifted past from the ghats upstream.

Now don't get me wrong, the message was great. Even if it resembled the effect of giving a toddler a seismograph and telling them to write their name by jumping next to it. This too was understandable; I was so sleep deprived I could barely see, let alone write properly. So the next day, I'd rewritten that entry, and I had tried to remember the feeling I had that night, my mind still fresh from the crowds and bustle and the visceral stench of rotting human flesh. When everything was stained with the dreamlike quality of extreme fatigue. But I couldn't. So in my efforts to recapture it all, I had missed out the most important question it raised. Not the obvious query—is travel worth it—but the more subtle, more pressing, when does travel stop being worth it?

With the cramps in my stomach and the chatter behind, I could remember that question now. It was a while ago, but I was back in Calcutta again and for a few reasons, the same question was on my mind. Along with another that was perhaps more in line with the simile I was going for at the time: If travel is like a drug, how do you know when you've overdosed?

I remembered the woman I'd briefly met back in that dark, Reggae-infused offshoot of a steamy Bangkok night all those years before. I remember her telling me that India was still travelling. What I think she meant by that was that it was a place that challenged your perceptions. Broadened your mind. A country that took a needle to your Western comfort bubble and burst it like a firecracker. What I think this woman meant, in her warped, semi-belligerent way, was that it wasn't a theme park. Not somewhere to gawp and laugh and snap pictures and question, but to absorb until it all somehow made sense. The travel equivalent of a 3D stereogram puzzle, where if you looked long enough, a clear picture emerged from apparent chaos.

Now I was back in Calcutta for the second time and a tiny part of me couldn't help agreeing with her: as an outsider, sometimes India didn't just confront your preconceptions, it actively smashed them apart. At least, it should. So was the drug really wearing so thin that I just couldn't care about anything anymore?

Yesterday evening, I had been sitting in a restaurant, picking at the leftovers of the last meal I'd eat before I got a taxi to catch an overnight train towards Mumbai. Last night, I was back in the peeling room of some rubbish guesthouse, wondering when it's too late to refund a ticket for a train I'd missed on purpose.

This morning, I was reading that the wreckage of that train is still in West Bengal somewhere; that they still hadn't recovered the bodies of thirty people because the carriages were too mangled. This morning, I was reading that nearly a hundred and fifty people had been found dead, many more injured. I was reading that it's one of the deadliest Maoist attacks in years.

Now, under one of the largest cantilever bridges in the world, watching petals float past me and incense rise up through the foliage of the banyan tree, I was wondering if it was fate, luck, or just brute fact. And behind me, Amy was finishing the rice and curry we'd been given, and Amy was talking to the sadhu and his trainee. And behind me, Amy was the probably the reason I was not in a field in West Midnapore right now, along with a hundred and fifty other people who weren't dead yesterday. Behind me, Amy—a temporary travel companion I'd met barely a week before—was oblivious to the fact that she might be the only reason I'm still alive.

So she didn't care, but that's normal. What wasn't that normal, I don't think, was that neither did I. I didn't feel any more alive for the fact that I could have been dead, and I was still waiting for it to sink in. I was still waiting for the information to *mean* something. But I wasn't sure it ever would. Just like with the hallucinations, or even the sights that had prompted them; when it had all been going on, I couldn't *feel* anything. I tried, but nothing happened. In all honesty, it was as though I was attempting to squeeze significance out of the fact that I'd once eaten natural yoghurt.

Some say travel opens your mind; maybe mine was already open so far that anything could slip in and I'd hardly notice. This was a real possibility, because I was now a lot more accepting than I had once been. Now, I could eat tofu without feeling bisexual. I could listen to dance music without convulsing. I could watch a Julia Roberts movie without nausea.

So maybe it was that. I doubted it though.

Sitting under the bridge that day, I remembered something that had occurred to me after I returned from Papua: everything is relative. Take one step in the wrong direction when you're standing by red traffic lights back home and you're running a higher risk. It's just a numbers game.

So I was sitting here, listening to Amy talk religion with the sadhu. I was sitting with a thousand people walking over my head and thousands more driving over it. And on this side, the east side of the Hooghly River, under the eastern end of the Howrah Bridge, I was sitting between crumbling edifices and dark overhangs in a claustrophobic Hindu hash den that jutted straight into the brown flow like some kind of holy junkie's city retreat. I was sitting with the water lapping against tiny concrete steps, with my legs dangling in the warm murk and the aromatic smoke floating through the leaves of the banyan above me, wondering if I'd feel like this if the same thing were to happen in Britain.

No, probably not.

But then in Britain, the chances are I'd never find out anyway. And now I was sitting here feeling guilty for not feeling any real remorse, wondering if I was just like this in India because there was too much else going on to care about that kind of thing, and maybe that was affecting my own emotions in a sort of crowd-mentality way. As I said, everything is relative.

But even *I* wasn't totally convinced by that.

So maybe the drug *was* wearing thin. I remember when I'd first arrived in Calcutta, listening in on the conversation on the rooftop while the hallucinations did their thing, the guy who'd said if you travelled long enough, you'd see so much that nothing would seem so new anymore. The thought had occurred to me then that perhaps that's when you'd know it was time to take a break from travelling. When nothing seemed to surprise me, when nothing seemed so exciting—the spell; when that magic was lost, perhaps it was time to do something else with my life for a while. Now, in this darkened pocket of drug-fuelled spiritualism, I couldn't help but feel that time had come.

I took one last dip in the water and crouched back into the dingy hash den we'd inadvertently stumbled on, where I told Amy I'd had enough and perhaps it was time to go home.

"Good idea," she said, conspiratorially. "They've started asking me how much my camera costs."

"No, I mean…" I paused. "It doesn't matter. Yeah, let's go."

We made our excuses and walked past the shrines, back through the garlands and hordes of the flower market, past the worshippers making their way to the holy water of the ghats; we walked back up to the road, back to where we could catch a rickety blue and yellow bus towards Sudder Street. And we got off early, wandered through the meat markets and the slaughter houses, where bleating goats were being decapitated to start a short journey that ended with a spoonful of delicious curry. The thick wafts of blood drifted up our noses and in the heat, the stench was almost unbearable, so we left the meat market and went along a different alley, past sweet shops and air conditioned malls, ending up at a Bollywood cinema, where we watched a film about Indians going to America and living the life of diamonds and Ferraris just like all the Westerners do, and came out, wondering how warped stereotypes could work in reverse too. And then we watched the sun set from a rooftop bar over a beer and met a guy who truly understood travel because he'd been in India a few months already.

This guy was telling me all about Varanasi and he didn't know I'd been because he hadn't asked. He showed us a picture on his digital camera display of an Indian woman with her face all rotten through her sun-bleached sari, the bare teeth grinning away, and said, "It's crazy there."

Death porn. The Western equivalent of the video of the blonde girl gyrating on the mobile phones of young local men. Funny, how people crave what their home environment doesn't give them enough of.

We chatted a while longer, mostly about how he'd gone to stay in a village for a month where nobody could speak English, how cool it was, and when I asked him if he knew any Hindi or Bengali, he said, "Nah, man. Anyway, language is just a barrier for true communication," and I started to realise what Chris meant when he described the hippies he'd met back in Kathmandu.

"Hey, if you want to know the real India, you guys should head to the countryside, do the ten-day silent meditation course," he suggested, and in my head, something clicked.

I didn't really want to argue the toss. I didn't want to ask him how an outsider could ever understand what the real India was, especially if they didn't speak the language. I didn't want to ask him whether he knew what the villagers had thought about some rich white guy turning up on some kind of spiritual journey that had nothing to do with religion, sitting there for a whole month without even bothering to learn how to talk to them. I didn't want to ask how they reacted to him treating their home like a zoo, spending all his time staring and fiddling with his chakra, when all he had to offer them was his money. I didn't want to ask him any of these things, because I was a *nice* guy. So instead, I asked Amy if she fancied a chicken curry somewhere.

"Hey, I wouldn't eat meat here man, none of the locals do."

Take a deep breath in and *relax*...

"Just remember what I said about the ashram, it'll help you understand everything so much more," he called as I turned away. "You got to let go of your Western outlook."

I knew then that I never wanted to be like this. I didn't want to sit on my high horse and tell people what they were doing wrong. I also didn't want to travel simply to *understand;* I needed more than that. What's the use in having a broadened mind if you never actually did anything with it? So sod it. If only for the sake of Chris, I had to say something.

"Look mate, I'm sure ashrams are great if you're a weed-smoking, flappy-clown-trouser-wearing hippie, but I'm not and if it hasn't felt pain in dying it's not what I'd call a meal, so why don't you take your self-help bullshit spirituality and your wannabe-Eastern circus clothes and fuck off?"

His face dropped. Chris would have been proud.

"Well," I said to Amy. "Looks like my work here is done."

"I hope you feel better now," she replied. "Curry time?"

As we left the table, Amy turned to me. "You should think about doing that course," she said. "It would definitely sort you out." Then she started giggling.

We walked back through the alleys, past the mobile phone vendors, past the beggars and open urinals and glue-sniffers and junkies and climbed the stairs to the rooftop courtyard, just as the clouds broke and the first of the monsoon rains pummelled the concrete with machine-gun pellets of water, and the storm flashed neon blue across the darkened city sky.

Amy went downstairs to change and I was left standing on the roof, the very same roof I'd been just over a month before, and I thought of the journal entry I had been reading down by the Hooghly. The last journal entry I would write while travelling in India.

* * *

It felt like a lifetime since we left the mountains, sick, anorexia-thin, when Chris flew off to continue his world tour and I finally escaped the rampant tourist-vice village of Thamel and started to explore the other Kathmandu; acoustic evenings with Nepalese pop stars, fantastic tandoori restaurants and cheap daal bhat hovels; beautiful gardens and acid club nights with aid workers in embassy compounds. Wonderful architecture, beautiful people, astonishingly bad wine…

And now it was just over a month since I had first arrived in India, weak, pained by cramps and lack of sleep, gripped by heat I wasn't used to and plunged headfirst into a culture and society I had no familiarity with. Just over a month since the hallucinations in the midnight heat, the river, the train-carriage blur of my arrival in Calcutta.

It had been thirty days since I left the city and got a diesel-fume ferry to a beautiful tropical island in the turquoise lagoons and teeming coral reefs of the Andamans, where the monsoon rains were just about to smash the place apart. Thirty days since I started to wonder if there was more to these cramps than plain old food poisoning.

Now it was barely a week since the palm trees, hammocks, drinking and phosphorescent crocodile-dodging in the Andaman Sea; three days since I arrived back in the junkie's piss-stench alley, and now I was back, I wasn't sure what I enjoyed the most. Now I was back, standing on the roof of what must have been a top contender for Crowded Planet's *Grubbiest Hostel of the Year Award* and the monsoon had just started up and lightning was flashing around me like the biggest, most impressive New Year firework display ever, and the miles-thick waterfall people called rain was punching puddles through ceilings and the power grid was failing and even the junkies had run away from the flash flooding that turned the entire city into a Venice-style extension of the Ganges, but men were still out there, pulling their handcart rickshaws like the lunatics they were, through the waterways and canals that used to be streets and roads, yanking their passengers above the floods, doing a job that would reduce their life expectancy to a third of what it should have been; and now I was back here and all this was happening, I wasn't sure what I enjoyed the most, because this was damn cool too.

In the last twenty-four hours, I'd opened my diary amongst the hash and Hinduism of the Hooghly. Read the entry from the month before. Realised what I should have realised long before I directed my little outburst at the unsuspecting guy on the rooftop bar. And now I was content at last, because I was finally beginning to understand what my travels had been trying all these years to teach me.

With the electrical storm bursting, splashing blue everywhere, I thought back to the society I'd been brought up in; the virtual life, where nothing seemed to have any value beyond its ability to entertain and make profit, where every need was taken care of, where there were no real consequences.

The sky roaring, booming, tearing, I recalled how a craving for life experience had taken me to Borneo, and how Borneo prompted the investigation, the attempt to satisfy my curiosity by understanding more about the way this society was really influencing the planet. And on returning home from the Philippines, the quest to discover whether I really could be virtuous, and the realisation that when it came to it, morality was simply a case of where you chose to draw the line of responsibility—that every act in this globalised world was an exercise in Capitalist Chaos Theory: like conventional decision-making, but with a stark neocolonial economic twist.

The rain thudding into my forehead, my arms, my shoulders, I remembered how this knowledge had worried me, made me seek something else. Anything else, to fill the void that remained after my sense of purpose had left. And now, with the monsoon pounding my face, soaking my hair, withering my skin, I could see how this had cemented an addiction, turned me into a global pinball. Seeking risk in the Middle East, escape in Sri Lanka, deliverance in Nepal, and not truly achieving any of these things in the end. But now I knew what it all amounted to. I knew the grand total of these trips, journeys, adventures. And that grand total could be distilled into a very simple statement. A liberating statement. A statement that would change everything from now on. Because that statement was brutal in its simplicity:

Nothing I'd done had made any real difference to anyone but me.

EPILOGUE

Why is it we travel? Is it to see new cultures, ways of life, perspectives? Or is it to prove something? Gain life experience? Feed an addiction?

These were the questions I asked myself in the weeks and months after I returned from India. I often believed what I was doing was good—good for me, and good for the people I came into contact with. But as I came to realise that my society had a lot to answer for, rather than face up to that problem, address it, find a way to change things, I used travel as an escape. I am certain that I was not alone. Everywhere I went, I saw people with habits that defined them—habits that often had damaging ramifications. I often asked myself why these habits went unchecked, and the best answer that I came up with is that maybe the people who had them were simply unable or unwilling to recognise and assume responsibility for the consequences. In other words, people like me.

I am from a society that outsourced life experience to places like India and South America decades ago, to places that put people back into contact with extremes. Poverty, suffering. Hardship. But perhaps most importantly, consequence. And now, to my mind, the concept of travel has been so manipulated by this idea of life experience, and the expectations that places on young people, that it has turned travel into something much less valuable than it could be. It has turned travel into a stepping stone, a stage. An unwritten yet essential element of the middle class life plan. Get born, get an education, gain some life experience, and then you can go and find yourself a good job. It's a way of seeming more well-rounded, a better person in the eyes of a peer or prospective employer. It's a large part of the reason I started travelling initially.

So what is life experience? For many, it is the process of undergoing some kind of hardship and learning to look after yourself in an environment where your choices have real consequences. But perhaps the issue here is that travel has become one of the only ways of achieving this for many young people in industrialised countries. When all the restrictions designed to protect people are combined with the ease of living a virtual life, for many there are few other ways of making that fundamental link between choice, action and outcome. As a result, addictions are all too easy to develop, and consequences all too easy to ignore.

Unfortunately, so long as travel is used as a way of gaining life experience in this sense—that is, of reconnecting with consequence—it will only ever be an extension of the society that it seeks to escape. It will become yet another addiction. Because, truth be told, even travel itself can have unseen consequences that slowly destroy cultures and peoples in the same way that consumerism does.

But does this mean that travel is doomed? Far from it.

I can still remember the sense of adventure, the excitement, the thrill, that accompanied my first trip to Borneo. I gained an insight into a different world, and that affected my judgement in what can only be a positive way. Because what that trip to Borneo gave me was a sense that the people I met—people whose lifestyles were at risk of being destroyed by commercial enterprises that benefitted industrialised regions like Europe, North America and East Asia—were fundamentally the same as the people I'd grown up with as a kid.

The truth I realised after spending time in Kalimantan was that those people who lived in a rainforest thousands of miles away from my home country could have become my best friends if I'd spent longer with them. And that truth has been reaffirmed by every journey I've been on since. There was no "us" and "them", like the more reckless elements of the media would have many people believe; there was only an "us". And as my understanding of the world around me grew, so too did my discomfort that people like me in Borneo, Papua and the Philippines were being threatened by people like me in Britain, Europe; China and the USA, and that the war-mongering that had focused around the Middle East for all these years was nothing if not a complete misunderstanding about the true differences between people.

If there is one vital lesson that travel teaches, it is that no matter who we are and what our background is, the world is full of people like us, and the only differences between us come from the circumstances and societies we've grown up in, the problems we've faced, the values we've learnt to adopt as our own. Some of us have different talents, some live with different challenges. Some live in what is most commonly described as the Third World, the part of this globe that has apparently not done so well at developing as the part of the world I come from. But again—and this is another lesson that travel teaches well—there is more than one way to live a good life, and it is arrogant and racist in the extreme to think that a certain people are inferior simply because they have not followed the same path.

All of these things, I would not have learnt—indeed, I would not still be learning—without travel. And this is why travel should be something we can cherish, promote even. Not because it makes us more employable, or helps us grow up. Not because it makes us wiser than everybody else, or more worldly—and certainly not to feed an addiction—but because nothing else makes a person confront their prejudices and correct their preconceptions as much as living among people with a completely different set of values and ideas.

And that is why travel is, and always will be, worth it.

(And for the record, I didn't stop travelling. Hopefully, I never will.)

AUTHOR'S NOTE

I wrote this book for two main reasons. The first is because I had the time. I wish it wasn't. The parasite I caught in Nepal stayed with me long enough to prevent me from doing very much for quite a while, and I had to put my focus into something. The second is that I feel it is a story that needs telling. The world is quickly changing. Many of these changes are negative, and the people who instigate them are sometimes too sheltered from the effects to ever realise what is happening until it is too late. These people, the ones who are driving this change, are people like me. People who have grown up with excess, who know no other way to live. So this book is as much a description of this phenomenon as it is a story of my travels. If the world is to survive the next century intact, people like me need to recognise our limitations and act before our addictions drive us into the dust. It is not simply enough to know, to understand. At some point we must do. Hence, in my case, this book.

It is worth noting that names have been changed to protect the identities of those who are at risk of political repercussions and in those instances where permission could not be sought. Every effort has been made to maintain the authenticity of the story; where notes and transcripts weren't available, conversations and events have been reconstructed to the best of my (rather stupendous) ability.

If you have enjoyed reading this book, I urge you to recommend it to every person you meet from now on. Stop strangers in the street if you need to. Yell through open car windows in traffic jams. Scream it at the top of your lungs in town centres.

If on the other hand you haven't enjoyed this book, tell absolutely nobody. Apart from me.

To see photographs of the adventures written about in this book, please visit www.jamiealexander.org and click on the photography link. Feedback is very welcome; see the contacts page of the website for how to get in touch.

And finally, thank you very much for taking the time to read this book.

10665610R00173

Printed in Great Britain
by Amazon.co.uk, Ltd.,
Marston Gate.